LOST SOUL?

Daniel J. O'Leary

Lost Soul?

THE CATHOLIC CHURCH TODAY

the columba press

First published in 1999 by
the columba press
55A Spruce Avenue, Stillorgan Industrial Park, Blackrock, Co Dublin

Cover by Bill Bolger
Origination by The Columba Press
Printed in Ireland by Colour Books Ltd, Dublin

ISBN 1 85607 262 2

Acknowledgements

To Margaret Siberry for invaluable encouragement with *Lost Soul?* when doubts were high, and for immense practical support when energy ran low: also for writing *The Sacrament of Humanity, Leadership from Within* and *The Primacy of Green*. Mary Gardner and Theresa Laverick wrote *Ministry of Women* while David Jackson wrote *A Church with No Walls*. Without the co-operation of parishioners such as these, together with Doreen Mills, Pat Unwin, John Grady, Sr Monica O'Sullivan and Gill Davis who proof-read the text and offered valuable suggestions, this book would have remained a lonely article on a floppy disc. The members of St Benedict's parish, whom I came to serve eight years ago, have enabled me to believe in the vision of a church renewed. They are the living proof that such a vision of transformation is not only possible and necessary, but exciting and rewarding in its gradual realisation.

Copyright Acknowledgements are listed on page 251.

Contents

Introduction

This is such a special time. The possibilities for change and growth are endless. The opportunities are most exciting where the threats and anxieties are strongest. Even the hard-nosed realists across the world are moving with this sense of transformation. The challenges are especially obvious where the beleagured mainstream Christian churches are concerned. This book is written out of hope. But for hope to be authentic, it needs a sure foundation. That is why some hard questions about our Catholic Church are asked within these pages.

At the risk of being labelled disloyal, alarmist or misguided, the author and contributors to this book suggest that the Catholic Church has lost its way, if not its soul, in departing from the vision of Jesus as it pursues its own self-preservation. In the face of fear, insecurity and suspicion that often arise from a flawed understanding of the doctrine of original sin, many of those who govern the Catholic Church today are asked to believe, also, in the goodness of all creation. They are urged to take new risks in trusting the integrity of humankind like Jesus did, and to see themselves as privileged servants of God's people in whom the Holy Spirit primarily dwells.

As with almost all attempts at renewal, what is first offered by those who are deeply concerned must, by definition, be very tentative, unfinished and open to radical revision. So it is with this offering. We hope it will evoke supportive critiquing rather than negative criticism. Either way, the Holy Spirit will have her day.

This book will be dismissed by some, ridiculed by others. Many readers will feel angry because they are threatened by it. But it is written to affirm those who have open hearts and open minds; for those who are anxious about what is currently happening to our church, but who still carry the faith of our fathers

7

and mothers in divine providence. While the book is critical and challenging, it is written out of love for the Catholic Church. As one born and bred in the Irish church of the forties and fifties, how else could I feel about the whole, often-nurturing, spiritual context in which I grew up? I myself am now the fruits of the seeds of those times.

And while the book acknowledges the possible end of the institutional church as we know it, it is a book of hope. It traces the manner in which the church lost touch with its creation-centred tradition but also suggests how it can regain it. In a culture of secular power and in a climate of fear, a deadly dualism set in and the radical but gentle vision of Jesus was lost. With the help of the Holy Spirit, this vision, too, can be brought centre-stage again. What happened down the centuries was that the spirituality of creation in general and of humanity in particular, could not survive the fixed mindset of a church that saw the incarnation mainly in terms of sin and redemption. Unfortunately, this is still the way it is.

Is the church paying too much attention to itself, its hierarchy, its laws, its exclusions and its suspicion of other denominations, of other religions and even of the world itself that it exists to serve? In its myopia, is it peering only through the lens of its Roman, Western history, largely blind, for instance, to the culture, experiences and needs of millions of Christians in the southern hemisphere? Has it lost its soul, its vision of the outgoing, self-forgetful, trusting, self-emptying humility of the human, sacred heart of Jesus? 'Why,' asked young Michelle, at a recent Diocesan Pastoral Council meeting here, 'does love seem to be forgotten?'

There are two main transformations called for on the part of the church institution, if the hoped-for Jubilee Springtime is to happen. At the root of the current malaise within the Catholic Church is its unbalanced focus on the sinfulness of the world, its fear of matter, its distrust of humanity. It is only when the current leadership recovers its mystical heart, its divine belief in the goodness of creation, that it can transcend its suspicion of the world. It will then present its human face to all and begin to trust its people, empowering their leadership qualities, their imagination and their creative gifts.

This grace-filled shift cannot happen unless the original, dynamic and fearless passion of Jesus for the equality of *all* of his

Father's creation will once again flood the hearts of his fright-ened, faithful followers. It is the unclouded vision and radical compassion of Jesus that needs to be recovered and reclaimed. Only love will shift the minds and hearts of those who see the current laws and decisions of the church as totally justifiable and non-negotiable.

These two transformations will make all the difference. And these two holy insights are really one – the revelation of the meaning of creation in the light of the incarnation of the man Jesus. The imbalance will then be adjusted. A new dynamic will happen. The greening and resurgence of our ailing church will be recognised in the new Advent of Christianity. And the slow, stumbling, faithful pilgrimage will continue with fresh hope.

> What we now see is the poor church of sinners, the tent of the pilgrim people of God, pitched in the desert and shaken by all the storms of history, the church laboriously seeking its way into the future, groping and suffering many internal af-flictions, striving over and over again to make sure of its faith; we are aware of a church of internal tensions and con-flicts, we feel burdened in the church both by the reactionary callousness of the institutional factor and by the reckless modernism that threatens to squander the sacred heritage of faith and to destroy the memory of its historical experience.[1]

In general terms, the missing dimensions of our church have to do with issues of spirituality, ecumenism, feminism, authority, ritual and ecology. The struggle to reclaim some of these lost values and find a new balance may not be a lesson in harmony. Such a reclamation is rarely a pretty sight. We can only pray that the often bitter and superficial conflicts, the angry exchanges, the blaming, labelling and wild accusing that are currently draining the life-blood of the Body away, will be replaced by a more charitable, knowledgeable and trusting search for a new birth. There are enough intelligent people of integrity and faith around to facilitate this beginning.

The church of tomorrow has to face the challenge of division, suspicion and mistrust in the world, and within its own ranks, through taking the risks demanded by a love which transcends the limits set by society or nation. It can do this only when there is a renewed commitment to the person of Jesus rather than to any one institution, and an experience of Christ at work in the world and through his people. Karl Rahner's vision for the fu-

ture (above) can be achieved only by letting go of the human desire for a manageable and predictable God, and allowing the
true God of wonder and mystery to rekindle the faith which inspired the early Christians to take risks in the hope of a redemption through love.[2]

Not all of our leaders have their heads in the sand. To revitalise the 'drifting dioceses in a drifting society' one bishop is celebrating the millennium with a proactive, enthusiastic strategy,
collaboratively ministered, to regain the courageous, missionary, outward-looking and Christ-centred model of church.
These are times of decision, important moments of discernment.
As another of our bishops put it recently, 'We are in a critical
time of waiting at the foot of the cross of another death, believing that a Holy Saturday of immense change will prepare us for
a new and unimaginable Easter.'

For all of us a miracle of grace is needed to bring about an internal change of heart for institution and for individuals, an
inner passion for justice and peace, for freedom and equality,
that can only spread outwards when it first catches fire. 'This pilgrimage takes place in the heart of each person, extends to the
believing community, and then reaches to the whole of humanity.'
These beautiful sentiments of John Paul II in his Jubilee Letter,
Tertio Millennio Adveniente,[3] echo those of the mystic: 'Where to
begin?' asked Meister Eckhart, 'Begin with the heart.'

PART ONE

Lost Soul?

Who set the Compass?

The other side of 'crisis', the wise ones tell us, is 'opportunity'. A desperate situation often leads to a clarifying and creative new focus. The sorry state of our Catholic Church today may well provide the impetus for some life-giving spring-cleaning and purification of its self-understanding. For a start it would be extremely foolish to deny the urgency of the situation. While number-crunching is only one symptom of an ailing, despondent church, it is at least, a measurable one.

Many attempts are being made to find common reasons for this truly alarming drift away from communal weekend worship. Among those most frequently mentioned are lack of spiritual nourishment, irrelevance to the experiences of daily life, and absence of affirmation and support at testing times. According to a recent research project, people stop going to church because of the gap between personal values and those of the church establishment, failure of the church to accompany people into an adult, questioning faith, and a lack of guidance and encouragement when someone is undergoing a major life-change, such as leaving home or getting divorced.

The survey recommends a number of steps for churches which aim to hold on to their members. They should 'avoid blowing out any embers of faith', respect people 'where they are' culturally and spiritually, help people grow in faith through meetings and courses, attempt to display gospel values in their own lives, and offer people a sense of true community.[1]

This book is offered as the beginning of a conversation about such matters. The conversation is about the role of the Catholic Church in the world today. How does the Catholic Church see itself *vis-à-vis* other denominations, other religions and the world itself? Is there a deep dualism in the church's self-understanding – a dualism that characterises the tone and texture of many official church documents and common preaching? Is this reflected in the lack of urgency regarding ecumenism, in our deep-seated attitudes to our own humanity, in our understanding of mysteries such as grace and nature, in our perceived meaning of the sacraments, in the various policies of admission to these sacraments, in the conditions laid down for church membership, in the church's understanding of salvation, evangelisation and mission?

A God too Small
There is ample reason for initiating a conversation that courageously faces these questions. There is, in every institution, a danger of losing the clarity of the original vision of the founder, of slipping into exclusivist mode, of adopting ghetto-characteristics, of not seeing the wood for the trees, of mistaking the pointing finger for the moon.

Is there evidence of this in the way the Roman Catholic Church conducts its affairs? Are we too suspicious of the world around us? Are we too protective of our own interests, too mistrustful of the holiness within the 'outsiders', too dualistic in our understanding of the human and the divine unity in all life? Is our fear too great and our God too small? During the nineties especially, there are many anxious and sincere voices calling attention to some basic Christian principles. This book seeks to encourage an authentic soul-searching in response to these voices.

I have tried to keep the outlines of this conversation fairly simple, even though the issues are profound and even radical. The conversation calls for a readiness to re-examine our first foundations of two thousand years ago, and for a positive and objective look at our current pastoral practices. Some of the questions that need exploring have to do with the various interpretations of incarnation, with the many meanings of salvation, with balancing a theology of creation with one based on redemption, and with the notion of Jesus Christ as the centre and sacrament of all creation.

How accurate, for instance, is the manner in which the church embodies the first vision of Jesus, and in which it incarnates, for all time, the central themes of revelation such as the unconditional compassion of God for all creatures, the equality of all God's children, the immortal dimension of all nature and the love and meaning at the heart of creation?

The nature of this embodiment is found in the preaching, teaching and pastoral practices of the church. Does the embodiment measure up to the role-model of its cornerstone? Does an institutional embodiment tend, eventually, to be exclusive rather than inclusive? What values, for example, are being held up by the manner of our sacramental catechesis, especially in the case of baptism and first eucharist? What is the foundation for our policies (haphazard though they may be from parish to parish) regarding acceptance and welcome into the celebration of these sacraments? How far removed from the attitude and approach of Jesus to the 'others' in his lifetime, is our current teaching on questions such as intercommunion and the position of those Catholics denied access to the eucharist, for instance?

Prophetic Voices

In the Autumn of 1997, a hard-hitting article by Bishop Reinhold Stecher of Innsbruck aroused great controversy in the church in Austria and beyond. He deplored the oft-repeated tendency of the ecclesial institution to subordinate the teaching of Jesus to administrative practices and the exercise of human authority. He pointed out that problems inevitably arise when we ignore God's desire for universal salvation, and the most profound theological and sacramental reality, in order to treat human regulations as though they were absolute. The bishop offered a number of examples:

… instead of making provision for the eucharist based on the spiritual health of the Christian community, we concentrate on purely human laws about who is authorised to do what – laws which ignore God's will that all should be saved, as well as the essentially eucharist structure of the community. Everything is sacrificed to a definition of church office for which there is no basis in revelation … The tendency to place human laws and traditions above our divine commission is the most shocking aspect of many church decisions at the end of this millennium. It seems, for instance, to disturb no one at the highest level of the church that literally hundreds of millions of Catholics are unable to come to the sacraments of forgiveness, which are morally necessary for salvation – and because they now cannot come, in a generation they will not want to come … The church's central authority remains completely undisturbed when the widespread amalgamation of parishes makes compassionate sacramental ministry to the sick impossible ... As things now stand, Rome has lost the image of mercy and assumed the image of harsh authority. We need fundamental changes of emphasis in crucial aspects of our pastoral practice, both with regard to Jesus' command to bring the gospel to all, and our treatment of the individual sinner.[2]

Distressing examples of a desperately serious lack of discernment within the Roman Catholic hierarchy can be drawn from a wide range of pastoral situations. Referring, for instance, to the heart-rending manner in which Catholics in war-torn countries, menaced by overseas debt and landmines, are also denied the eucharist for lack of priests, Dr Michael Winter wonders how long such despairing peoples will be required to suffer from the misplaced zeal of our twelfth-century legislators. 'Classical moral theology maintains that man-made law ceases to carry a moral obligation when its original purpose has ceased, or has become harmful. By restricting the priesthood to celibates, the twelfth-century legislators presumably had in mind the provision of good priests for the church. Serious theology has evacuated confidence in the basis of that law, with the result that its continued observance has meant that a vast number of communities have no priest at all.'[3]

That same Autumn, there were many comments and statements around Ireland following reports of President Mary McAleese receiving Holy Communion from an Anglican priest in Christ Church Cathedral, Dublin. In a review of the widespread reactions to the President's act, Fr Bernard Treacy OP found it:

> ... disappointing that some Catholic commentators re-fought the battles of four hundred years ago with ringing denunciations of the Reformation churches as rejecting belief in the real presence of our Lord in the eucharist. It was as if the work of the first Anglican-Roman Catholic International Commission (ARCIC 1) had never been undertaken. It was as if that commission's highly respected bishops and hardworking theologians, from both traditions, had never succeeded in producing the *Windsor Agreement on the Eucharist*. It was as if we had forgotten that document's carefully phrased endorsement of our two churches being in 'substantial agreement' about the eucharist ... Out of such discus-

sions have come many agreed documents which chronicle a growing convergence and deepening level of understanding. … Catholics who accept the Anglican invitation to 'draw near and receive the Body of our Lord Jesus Christ and drink his Blood', clearly believe that the quest for unity has now reached a point where there is a truthful option even if canon law does not provide for it. It must be taken that they honestly see themselves as witnessing to the convergence reached to date. We've been reminded that there is another truth, and a very painful one – it is that we are still quite a long way from the day of full institutional communion.[4]

In 1996, at Oxford, Archbishop John Quinn, former president of the United States National Conference of Catholic Bishops, delivered a forthright lecture on the need for reform and renewal within the Catholic Church, beginning with a new style of papal primacy 'open to a new situation'. Having commented on a whole range of disturbing current developments and practices within the institutional church, he quoted from an admonishing letter written by St Bernard of Clairvaux to Pope Eugene III: 'You have been more the successor of Constantine than the successor of Peter.' The article continues:

While the Vatican Council has brought a greater simplicity to the modern papacy, and John Paul II has introduced further simplifications, Bernard's comment readily brings to mind the tension between the political model and the ecclesial model at work in the church.

The fundamental concern of the political model is order and therefore control. The fundamental concern of the ecclesial model is communion and therefore discernment in faith of the diversity of the gifts and works of the Spirit. The claims of discernment and claims of order always co-exist for one cannot be embraced and the other rejected. They must always exist in tension. But it is always wrong when the claims of discernment are all but eliminated in favour of the claims of order, thereby making control and the political order the supreme good.[5]

Whilst still engaged in writing the final section of this book, it has been disturbing to receive from Rome the encyclical, *Ad Tuendam Fidem – For the Defence of the Faith*, with its aim of adding to the Codes of Canon Law in order to strengthen the teaching authority of the church. Many Christians are engaged in an authentic search for a deeper insight into how issues such as ministerial ordination, the teaching authority of the church, and the role of women, are experienced by the people of God at this time. They feel, at the very least, disheartened if not crushed by the style and content of this latest edict from Rome. The current correspondence in the Catholic press, certainly in England, seems to agree that debate on such matters is being discouraged and even stifled. There seems to be little appreciation of the *sensus fidelium*, of the Holy Spirit at work in the hearts and minds of those who make up the body of the church, in discerning the truths of revelation for our times. Indeed in his attempts to clarify the situation, the internationally renowned theologian, Avery Dulles, appears almost apologetic, and disappointingly casuistic:

> The Pope's apostolic letter was a routine piece of tidying up. He added a couple of codicils to the Western and Eastern Codes of Canon Law to bring them into alignment with the new profession of faith promulgated with papal approval in 1989.

Dulles discusses the three different levels of official teaching and the degrees to which people can respond:

> ... the assent of faith, firm acceptance, and religious submission of will and intellect ... with just penalties to be imposed at the discretion of the authority in question – the Holy See, the bishop, or the religious superior, as the case may be ... for those who reject second level teaching ...[6]

The language and tone, both of the encyclical itself, and of Fr Dulles' article, are not likely to open the doors of understanding for many faithful church-goers, nor do they speak of trusting the faith-filled hearts of all who struggle to find meaning within the church, and clarification of the church's unique mission for the world. In contrast, it is encouraging to note that the 1998 National Conference for Priests for England and Wales considered that, '... the recent theological instructions from Rome undermine the credibility of the church and are even a "cause for scandal".'

A letter sent by the delegates to the Symposium of European Priests meeting described,

> ... the growing anxiety among priests and laity over 'increasingly restrictive and sanction-based directives which come from the Holy See and the Roman Curia.' Vatican documents which had attempted to stifle debate on 'unresolved' theo-

logical discussions were described as alarming. It is understood that the priests had in mind Cardinal Ratzinger's com-
mentary on the Pope's recent apostolic letter, *Ad Tuendam
Fidem*, amongst other texts. The priests' letter goes on to say
that efforts by the curia to outlaw discussion on matters such
as the ordination of women have become 'grave impedi-
ments to people accepting the credibility of the church as an
institution.' In contrast to its criticism of the Vatican, the letter praised the bishops of England and Wales for recognising
that there are people in the church who feel 'hurt, angry, or
excluded.' It quoted the bishops' September 1995 document
Meditation on a Jubilee Church, in which the bishops conceded
that, 'We find ourselves sometimes excluding people whom
Christ may well have invited into his company.' In the light
of such 'reflective leadership', says the letter, many people
are 'totally puzzled' by the 'attitude of fear that seems to un-
derlie certain statements from Rome.'[7]

As Archbishop Quinn has recognised, there will always be tension between the political model of church and the ecclesial one,
but it seems crucial that this tension becomes a creative force for
growth. Perhaps the church needs to hear more than ever the
voices from the margins, in order to find its true identity.

Airless places
It is so important to be single-minded and brave in our search
for authenticity in these matters. Because of the presence of
'original sin' in all of us, there is a constant temptation to elitism
of all kinds in our communities. Within our church this often
takes the form of a deadly institutionalism and equally destructive clericalism. People trapped in such airless places are never in
a hurry to self-appraise or to offer themselves and their beliefs
for the evaluation of others. But the charge committed to us, by
our Saviour, is too precious to take any risks:

I am quite certain that the present Catholic Church differs in
significant ways from what Jesus was talking about when he
spoke of his church. His church is not measurable by statistics or human boundaries. It is made up of people who live
by his teachings. These may be found, in today's world, either inside or outside the boundaries of a particular church.
Sometimes a woollen garment being knitted has to be completely unravelled in order to remove an error that was

stitched into it. The error of patriarchy goes so far back in the Roman Church that a complete unravelling and new start is required. Jeremiah, the prophet, gave the example of the potter having to do a similar thing: 'whenever the vessel he was making came out wrong, as happens with the clay handled by potters, he would start afresh and work it into another vessel, as the potters do.' (Jer 18:1-6)[8]

It takes deep soul-searching to discover the real intentions of our hearts. And it is an old search. Am I for Paul or Apollo, for the 'old' or for the 'new' Catholic Church, for the Roman Catholic Church or for Christianity, for the God of Christians only or for the God of all people? There is always resistance to opening up our true motivations and secret desires, if we ever really know them, to others. Institutions carry a heavy weight of communal egoism and collective pride. The church has always seen itself as a 'cut above the rest'. It is convinced of its uniqueness. It has a history of keeping itself at a distance from so many ecumenical projects and councils of churches. Such convictions of being exclusively special need careful and prayerful discernment in the light of Jesus' many assurances to all and sundry of the impartiality of God and of the equality of all individuals and peoples before divine compassion.

Shapes of Ministry
The preaching of the gospel is not about the building of ecclesiastical empires and enclaves that refuse to be humble with each other, nor about maintaining an ecclesiastical structure at the expense of a prophetic voice, nor about placing more burdens on the shoulders of those who are searching for some consoling community to join, nor about implying a dualism that places 'ordinary' human life over against explicit 'Christian' living. When seen against the backdrop of authentic revelation, the mission of the churches is bound to take a renewed shape and emphasis. Such a fundamental Mission Statement must inform and reform all the theories and practices about Christian preaching, teaching, sacramental celebrations and ecumenical processes with which we are familiar.

In creation spirituality, God has been speaking the truth about the world since the beginning of time. We are not inaugurating this truth. We are not initiating it. We are simply announcing a truth that always was. God has been loving us through geological history. We're just the lucky ones who have come along now in a moment of time to bring it to consciousness, to give a word to it, Jesus. He is the revelation of the heart of the Father. Jesus is revealing what has always been going on inside of God – and is going on inside of God towards Islamic people, Jewish people, Buddhist people, Hindu people. We don't have any corner on the market of God ...[9]

A recent meeting of the National Conference of Priests (UK) left space on its agenda to contemplate fundamental developments. In a summary of the findings, the chairman, Roderick Strange, wrote, 'Asked why she was held in such high regard in India, Mother Teresa is said to have replied, "Because I converted no one". She helped them find God and be good Hindus, good Muslims, good Buddhists. Is that a clue for us priests? A new priesthood for a new evangelisation, less intent on formal conversions, more anxious to offer service and give life. If the nature of that new style of priesthood is unclear, we must be patient. One risk must be taken – to hold on to the question.'[10]

This whole quest for a recovery of the mind of Christ and of the vision of the early church for our Catholic leaders today, will take ages, given the resistance to it by so many of our clerics. It will be a difficult and testing period. It will, like wisdom, make a bloody entrance. Without a spirit of repentance and humility it cannot happen. But, if there is ever going to be a new springtime, another Advent, it is a challenge we dare not ignore. It is a time for imagination and courage to take the lead as we explore the valid questions that are being raised, and which have profound implications for styles of leadership and concepts of ministry.

At a time when many priests feel under stress and dissatisfied as never before, women and married men are confined to limiting ways of ministry and service. As long ago as the last century, Cardinal Newman called for an educated laity, not meaning simply people with academic qualifications, but people who would take an active and thoughtful part in the life of the church. He saw the vitality for the church in people who were able to take initiatives and who were ready to explore ways in which the gospel could be preached in new situations. Not that any of this was completely new. Even back in his day, Cardinal Newman was concerned that,

... the church of his own time demanded of the laity only docility and obedience, rather than originality and activity. Times have changed and what the church calls for now is for collaborative ministry and for a central place to be given to adult catechesis ... The bishops (in *The Easter People*, their response to the National Pastoral Congress in 1980) said, 'the last synod of bishops taught us clearly about the absolute priority of a continuing adult formation and education in the faith ... any genuine renewal of the life and work of the church will in the end largely depend upon commitment to this work. The precise way forward is not yet plain, but it is obvious that we must walk in this direction. We willingly accept the practical implications of personnel and resources that may be proved necessary'. (para 145)

These are strong words. Yet we have to admit to our shame that the last twenty-five years have not seen any sustained growth of adult education in the church in this country. We have not really paid heed to the vision that is expressed in these documents; and it is all the more regrettable because the National Pastoral Congress was an exceptional event, and its recommendations were not made by a small select committee but by hundreds of delegates from all over the country. It truly represented the mind of the church in England and Wales, and the bishops gave it their whole-hearted support.[11]

There is no doubt that a certain apathy has developed, and the initial enthusiasm of those heady days after the National Pastoral Congress has been replaced by a cynicism in some, and by a departure from the church by others, who despise the meagre resources and minimal practical commitment to these ideals in the last twenty years. This is even more puzzling at a time when the ordained priesthood itself is in such decline both in morale and numbers. A three year research project conducted by Mgr Stephen Louden as part of his doctoral thesis, disclosed that one in three Catholic priests working in parishes feels 'burned out' by their priestly ministry. For the purposes of his survey he described 'burn-out' as '... the end result when very highly motivated and committed priests lose spirit mainly because of stress and tension'. Indeed only 10% of those who responded to the survey felt they were dealing 'very effectively' with parish life, whilst as many as 23% felt 'at the end of their

tether'. Mgr Louden suggested that one reason is the lack of appreciation and affirmation expressed by parishioners, and this,
together with little feedback from their bishop and colleagues,
led to tension and stress.[12]

Because there are now fewer priests than there were thirty
years ago, and because priests' work in recent years has increased and has become more complex, the report identifies
these factors as contributing to the stress experienced. Mgr
Louden notes that seminary recruitment in some parts of the
Western World is down by 90%, partly because of

> ... the link the church makes between vocation to the priest-
> hood and the vocation to celibacy. Some theologians have ar-
> gued that the two are not necessarily linked; young men at-
> tracted to the priesthood may not feel called to celibacy. This
> has to be a reason why some young men are not presenting
> themselves for the priesthood. Another reason why England
> and Wales have fewer priests is that a large number left in the
> 1960s and 1970s. Priests who pressed for change at that time
> came to feel frustrated, and felt their only option was to
> leave. 'Their criticisms did not produce policy changes in the
> church', Mgr Louden recalled. 'The church's reaction was,
> "Let troublemakers go". Many bishops welcomed the opport-
> unity for priests to get out, and they were given an excuse to
> neglect structural shortcomings as they watched the most
> dissatisfied priests depart: they considered neither protest
> nor departure a legitimate form of criticism.'[13]

As if to illustrate that this phenomenon has not disappeared, in
the same issue of *The Tablet*, Fr John Wijngaards, well-known in
England in the field of Christian communication, announced his
decision to resign from active ministry. In his view the Vatican's
latest teaching against the ordination of women 'in spite of there
being no proven objections from scripture or tradition that the
mind of Christ excludes them,' robbed him of the possibility of
remaining in full communion with the Catholic Church.

Describing the 'great damage to the Body of the Church,'
which he believes has been done by such official teaching, Fr
Wijngaards said: ' Millions of believers have stopped attending the eucharist on account of it, turning for spiritual consol-
ation elsewhere. The teaching authority has lost its credibility
even among loyal pastors, who often struggle to limit the
damage inflicted, by offering their faithful a more sensitive

pastoral guidance than Rome does. 'Most alarming of all,' he added, was 'the inevitable corruption Rome causes in all levels of responsibility in the church by forcing on all a complicity of silence.' Concluding his statement, Fr Wijngaards announced that he had no intention of renouncing his 'right and duty' to express his theological views. He would remain a 'conscientious and orthodox Catholic' until the day he died ... He would remain a missionary 'though in a different manner than before.'[14]

How well I recall, from my early days as a young priest, being inspired by men like Charles Davis, Hubert Richards, Peter Hebblethwaite and many others, less wellknown, who felt forced to journey along that very road, as they opted for integrity of conscience, after much prayerful heart-searching. What a loss to the life of the church has the absence of their ministry proved, and what a long road the church will need to travel, in humility and repentance, to seek forgiveness for some of the hurt and damage caused to so many lives. Surely at the end of this millennium, and to usher in the new springtime for which the Pope prays, we will not make the same mistake twice! Instead, could we throw wide the doors of welcome and healing, and in a spirit of true repentance, recognise the church's own failings? In the final analysis, it is the church itself which is wounded and incomplete, without the service and witness of so many holy women and men who at present are alienated from our communities. Can we at least open up the whole discussion of priestly ministry in such a way that the real questions of today are faced honestly? Can we acknowledge the confusion and paradox that exists, rather than reacting out of fear and a fierce desire to control? Only such an open attitude can create the climate for dialogue, out of which fresh images and new life will come.

There is no doubt that in these times of change and challenge for the church, there are, too, signs of hope. As the soul-searching continues, some in leadership positions within the church rise up as beacons of hope, as guiding stars leading us towards the example of Jesus. In a spirit of humility, and with great courage and vision, they are striving to respond imaginatively and creatively to the problems, seeing in the crisis, opportunity. Their prayer is to honour the genuine search within human hearts for a church that proclaims the dignity and worth of all people, a church that is constantly in the process of self-purification in order to conform more closely to the mind and heart of Jesus.

Bishop Willie Walsh is amongst those who are endeavouring to read the signs of the times and encourage a faith-filled and trusting response. Writing in *The Furrow*, in 1995, in an article entitled, *Strength in Weakness*, he makes a plea for diverse views within the church to be aired. He acknowledges his own nervousness in expressing controversial views on particular issues, especially when these views might be 'somewhat out of line with traditional views on these matters'. His anxiety stems from the hurt his remarks may cause to those who have served the church loyally for many years, and also from his own very human fear of being misunderstood, or misrepresented. More important than these feelings, however, is the need to create a climate where honest dialogue can be pursued, where tension can exist between 'the theologian, analysing, probing and testing and the bishop, who sees his role as official teacher'. 'Differing points of view presented honestly and listened to with open minds may not achieve unanimity but they will surely lead us in the direction of the truth to which we all aspire.'[15] Bishop Walsh's commitment to this kind of dialogue has drawn him into another controversy within his own Diocese of Killaloe. In an attempt to give birth to a new way of being church for the next millennium, he has decided not to replace an out-going priest in one parish, but to ask parishioners to take on their rightful responsibilities. He is using the crisis of the shortage of priests as a positive invitation to reflect deeply on the whole notion of local church and ministry within it.

'For over a hundred years,' he said, 'we have had a clericalised church and the situation in Killanena-Flagmount offers the people the chance to take responsibility rather than before where people took a very passive role, as the priest was the figure of authority.' Part of the restructuring in the 500 strong parish has been the dismantling of the old parish council, whose membership remained unchanged since 1981. In its place is a new 16-member council from 102 nominations. Parishioners now look after finance, the care of the aged, preparing the liturgy, faith-development and care of young people.'[16]

It is a sad reflection on the effectiveness of the church as a hierarchical and patriarchal institution that the bishop's plans have met with much resistance and a certain amount of anger, as well as enthusiasm. Many people have become dependent in an unhelpful way, which does not reflect the dignity and grace of the baptismal calling to priestly service. The negative response also demonstrates how little adult formation has been taking place over the years, a factor acknowledged by Bishop Walsh. The way the church tries to shape collaborative ministry, urged by the bishops so strongly, at least theoretically, in *The Sign We Give*, will give witness to its commitment to a renewed understanding of the church's mission. At a very basic level, a radical change in the use of resources, and in pastoral planning strategies will be required to provide the necessary formation and training opportunities for lay people. There is also a real urgency about redefining the whole nature of what takes place in seminaries. Most crucial of all will be how closely in touch with the expressed needs of all its people are those in authority within the church. Only by listening humbly to each other will the Spirit of freedom and hope breathe new life into tired hearts and enable new models of priestly service to emerge and a civilisation of love to be realised.

In a resource paper for the National Conference of Priests in 1996, Fr Kevin Kelly, the moral theologian, shared hope-filled insights from his experiences in an inner-city parish in Liverpool. He describes the essential role of the diocesan priest as sharing in the pastoral work of the Good Shepherd, and that this means ministering pastorally just as Jesus did. For Jesus this meant laying down his life for his sheep. Fr Kelly says,

Jesus was killed because his pastoral ministry was unacceptable to the religious authorities of his day. Though he urged people to listen to their teaching, he did not let his pastoral ministry be restricted by sticking rigidly to the letter of their human regulations. This is not to suggest that Jesus did not appreciate the value of good human laws. However, for him, all human laws were interpreted in the light of their basic pastoral purpose of serving the good of his sheep. The religious pastors who opposed Jesus rendered the law lifeless by failing to understand its purpose. Their regulations left people feeling excluded and lost, like sheep without a shepherd. Much of the art of pastoral ministry lies in interpreting good laws in such a way that they are life-giving for the sheep under one's care. That is where pastoral sensitivity comes in. Pastoral sensitivity is a mind-set rather than a set of rules of practice. The good pastor, like the good artist, needs to know the basic skills of his trade and the rules of thumb to be followed. However, like Jesus, his main concern must be the needs of his sheep – and each sheep is unique. What is good pastoral care for one person may not be so for another.[17]

Fr Kelly all too readily recognises the difficulty faced by many priests when they experience the gap between the demands of their pastoral experience and the official regulations of the church. He is aware, of course, that priests are not ordained to 'do their own thing', but are called to obedience. However, obedience in this context means that pastors must really listen to the deepest needs of the people in their care, and discern how best to respond. When pastors develop the art of listening in this way, they are hearing and obeying the voice of God in others. When this begins to happen, a vibrant way of ministering together begins to unfold and new models of priestly ministry emerge.

The recent experiences of both Bishop Walsh and Fr Kelly serve to highlight the degree to which there is need to be in tune with what is happening in people's lives, and for dialogue that starts from that grounded place. Fr Kevin Hegarty, writing about the challenge facing the church, describes another recent survey by the Market Research Bureau of Ireland. One of the many worrying factors that emerged was a significant decline in church attendance, especially amongst 18-24 year olds, of whom only 37% now attend Mass regularly. The main reason given for the decline was the lack of relevance to daily life.

Modern Irish Catholics are less likely to accept church teaching when it fails to correspond with their human experience. That is why so many supported President Mary McAleese's reception of Anglican communion at Christ Church Cathedral. In a country where Christianity has often been disfigured by denominationalism, and where now the most serious attempt in over 70 years at north-south rapprochement is under way, it seemed to them right that the President of Ireland should accept eucharistic hospitality from another denomination, especially as church leaders so often assure us that much more unites us than divides us ... This church in crisis is not well-served by the quality of its leadership. For too long the Vatican has appointed in Ireland bishops who are safe. Such stolid attributes are hardly enough for episcopal ministry in an increasingly urban and diverse country. We need leaders who can transform the situation, rather than simply keep the system running. There is so far little sign of that. Priests and people do not have confidence in the consultative process that takes place before the appointment of a bishop. In the current conservative atmosphere in Rome, no liberal priest will be appointed, no matter how administratively efficient, theologically literate or spiritually authentic.[18] Signs of dissent but also of hope are to be found all around. The need to read these 'signs of the times' and to discern the voice of prophets is urgent. My hope is that this book will contribute to, and expedite, the ongoing conversation about how best to critique and purify the Catholic Church's self-understanding in the light of the life and work of Jesus. If it is ever to achieve this aim, and to be taken seriously, it will need the honest, courageous and dedicated action and reflection of 'ordinary layfolk' and other saints, scholars and mystics, and the protection of many angels. Perhaps it will also need to place itself in the company of 'sinners', those on the margins – the *anawim* – if it is to reflect the pattern of Jesus.

On the threshold of a new millennium is a very challenging and privileged place to be. Most people experience an urge both to gather up the past into some kind of discerned harvest and to set springtime seeds for another harvest in the future. Against the mystery of Passover, Christians especially are drawn to celebrate endings and beginnings. Within the church, Pope John Paul II has brought to the forefront of our priorities, the Jubilee issue of revisioning our story and of constantly renewing our original vision. The church must always be endeavouring to reform itself. The Pontiff calls for both a return to sources and a breakthrough into a new Advent.

Resetting the Compass

Losing the Way
Some of our truest tears are shed at the sight of the difference
between the dreams we once carried and the reality we now experience. Somewhere along the way the dreams broke down, or
they were stolen, or they were not cared for, or they were taken
for granted. Today's tears, in the context of the breakdown of
our churches, are about the difference between God's dreams
for us, as revealed in Jesus Christ, the one, sufficient sacrament
of human and divine unity, and the present sorry state of a dis-
membered body of scandalously separate and desperately
struggling little collections of denominations, blind to the sinfulness of their present situation. How does this happen? How do
the singer and the song get so radically separated to the detriment of both? How do the holiest of our leaders become so
trapped into maintaining an often bureaucratic and political
church-system which rarely results in the building of a human,
compassionate body of dedicated lovers? How can something
so simple and loving be twisted into a complicated and demand-
ing system? Where are the points of divergence?

There are various stages in the evolution of God's self-revelation where the original design can get lost, where wrong turn-
ings can be taken, where the first purpose can be gradually side-
lined, where a deadly dualism can set in. Dualism is a terrible cancer in the various bodies of divine revelation: it is the pernicious
virus that destroys the clarity of God's desire and decision to become human. And it continues to be a festering wound in the
body of the churches today.

Because dualism is so full of sin and so antipathetic to the
true heart of God's revelation in Christ, and of Christ's embodiment in the Christian Church, I want to explain it further.
According to Edward Schillebeeckx, dualism denies the intrinsic
value of the created order, a value enshrined in a once-powerful
Jewish-Christian tradition of the blessedness of all creation. It
denies that God willed the world as it is, or willed human beings

as they are. To be finite, such views would hold, or to be vulnerable, to fail, to die, arises from a basic human flaw or from some primal sin. Therefore, dualism would insist, the true form of our humanity is set in a previous lost paradise or in a future age after this world has ended. Dualism would hold that to be human is to go radically astray, to be wrong-footed from the start, to be flawed in our finitude, from a first sin at the beginning of time. It refuses to accept ignorance, mortality and mistakes as the normal condition of humanity.

This dualism is, to my mind, is the main reason for the disturbing difficulties that face the Catholic Church today. Bede Griffiths, for example, saw the essence of all religious progress as one from 'dualism' to 'non-dualism'.[1] Another fine European theologian, Dorothee Soelle, defines dualism as that which sees human power and creativity as somehow detracting from God's power in our world, as though mature parents would be jealous of their children's self-esteem and self-confidence. Human creativity can never detract from the power of the divine presence, since its source is one and the same.

She senses the need to develop a spirituality of creation. Old religious language, outdated literalism and conventional images of God and humanity, must develop, for instance, from 'otherness' to 'sameness'; from 'infinite distance' to 'mystical union'; from 'God as wholly other' to 'God within us'; from 'obedience to God' to 'empowerment by God'; from 'Father, Judge' image to 'depth, source, creative-being'. Dorothy Soelle writes of three essential dimensions of a spirituality of creation – the sense of wonder, the human capacity to perceive beauty, and the presence of joy. Bishop David Konstant, my own bishop, addressing Catholic Teachers in Birmingham in 1996, makes just this point.

If I were asked what particular quality I would want to find in a teacher in one of our schools, I think I would say that I would be looking for someone whose vision of the world and of creation is holistic. You should be able to see everything all of a piece, not separated into different compartments. Faith and living cannot be kept apart from each other, they need to be fully integrated. Our vision should be such that we are able to see the beauty and harmony of creation. This vision in part arises from our understanding of God as creator and the place that we have in this work as indicated in the account of creation. But the vision was completed by the incarnation.

When God became one of us the whole of creation was revealed to be already stamped with the presence of God, and
in a more intensified way became destined for God. In the
lovely words of Gerard Manley Hopkins: 'The world is
charged with the grandeur of God.' This is St Paul's vision of
a world which is itself waiting for completion, as if the work
of creation still continues, a work in which we all have a part.
'We know that the whole of creation has been groaning in
travail together until now.' (Rom 8:22) Teilhard de Chardin
saw the world as growing towards its end point under God's
guidance and through our sharing in this movement. The
Christian's vision is of the world created good, in which all
can work together for good; it is a vision of a world wherein
we are stewards, and in which everything is purposeful.
Hence the need to integrate wholly what we believe with
how we live.[2]

All Directions point to God

Encompassed within the besetting sin of dualism is the process
whereby the original vision gets lost. Let me refer to a few of
those 'moments' when the focus shifts and the image becomes
blurred. In the first place, I often wonder if we lose sight of God
sometimes because of the intensity of our total focus on Jesus.
Sometimes we act as though there were no more dimensions to
God other than those revealed in Jesus; as though immanent
Sonship in time and transcendent Fatherhood's eternity were
one and the same; as though the only authenticity of the historic
religions of the world lay in their implicit and anonymous dependence on the Christian revelation; as though the major belief-
systems of all time had nothing genuinely original to offer to us,
as Christians, about the nature of God. There are many difficulties and challenges around this very sensitive, and very explosive issue waiting to be explored by the Catholic Church.

(The need for this debate) comes from new knowledge of the
human religious world and of our continuity with that. This
raises questions about the theological core of the Christianity
that emerged out of the ecclesiastical debates and council decisions of the first five centuries; namely that Jesus of
Nazareth was God the Son living a human life. For from this
there follows the world-centrality of Christianity as the only
religion founded by God in person. It is here that the strain is

now being felt. For Christianity's implicit or explicit claim to an unique superiority, as the central focus of God's saving activity on earth, has come to seem increasingly implausible within the new global consciousness of our time.[3]

The tendency towards exclusivity inherent in most organisations, is endemic to the human condition. There is a widespread ideology of exclusiveness. The insistence on exclusivity has a powerful and attractive motivation at many levels of human searching and idealism. But it has no place in a Christian spirituality or ideology. It is not, however, too difficult to see how it has infiltrated the market-places of consumerism and the sanctuaries of the churches.

The notion of a Godhead based in the heavens, talking only to a particular group of people, has been very much part of the Jewish and Christian traditions and is basic to their understanding of revelation and their self-identity. All of this arises because revelation is always filtered through human experience and, therefore, linked with certain people, at certain times and in certain places. To be unique seems more appealing than to be a part of. The challenge now is to be more flexible in our understanding of the Mystery, to reflect on whether we have fashioned too small a God, to be humble enough to allow for a kind of divine compassion beyond our human experience, to re-examine our understanding of theologically doubtful concepts such as 'meriting salvation', 'earning grace', as well as more scriptural ones such as 'pure gift', and 'unconditional loving'. In other words, the challenge is to re-create and liberate our current limiting images of God into more dynamic, energising and feminine ones.

This challenge holds the possibility of better dialogue with other religions. Rather than communicating from positions of exclusivity – we have God on our side; we have truth and you haven't – dialogue could be along the following lines: as we listen and pay attention to the reality of God in our cultures and our worldviews and our experiences, these are the insights we have come to. We realise we cannot contain the notion of God in our limited worldviews, but we offer our insights to you for your consideration. At the same time, we wish to learn from your experiences and insights for we believe God is working in and through all of us.[4]

What I'm trying to explore here is the attractiveness of the good news of Jesus, the love and meaning at the heart of incarnation, before establishment contingencies and political pressures and human sinfulness eroded the clear outlines of the countryside of the first gospel. After the heady and halcyon days of the Second Vatican Council, I remember writing about the end of Christian triumphalism, of Catholic suspicion and aloofness in matters ecumenical. Dialogue has replaced confrontational dogmatics, I wrote, because, according to Vatican II, 'in a universal family of humanity all peoples comprise a single community ...'[5]

Even if at the moment we seem to be experiencing a disappointing, fearful and sad 'backlash' to such feelings, a prayerful consideration of the Catholic Church's self-understanding at that time, is still bound to vibrantly colour our perception of our role today. An intense, if not intrusive and misguided type of evangelism, to be found within most of our mainstream Christian churches today, has partially succeeded in closing so many of the famous windows that Pope John XXIII so prophetically opened.

Nevertheless, the genuine and universal quest for goodness, truth and beauty which is the irrepressible, essential and most enduring part of our humanity, and which has given rise to, and is the foundation and motivation of all the great faiths and ideologies, can never be overcome. 'From ancient times down to the present, there has existed among diverse peoples a certain perception of that hidden power which hovers over the course of things and over the events of human life ... Religions to be found everywhere strive variously to answer the restless searching of the human heart.' (Vatican II: *Non-Christian Religions*, Pt 2)

In recent times the concept of 'anonymous Christianity' has come to the fore, especially in Karl Rahner's thinking. It would be wrong to use this debatable, blanket term as an excuse for not exploring further the rich diversity of other religions and cultures. Neither should the striking similarities between creation myths, salvation histories, ethical systems and anthropologies lead us to fear the finding of a common denominator with our own beliefs. The more open Christianity is in this respect, the more truly creational and incarnational it becomes, for the character of unity-in-diversity, and the exclusion of dualism, must always be the hallmark of creation in general and of human beings in particular. 'The growth of communication between the various nations and social groups opens more widely to all the treasures of the different cultures ... Thus, little by little, a more universal form of human culture is developing; one which will promote and express the unity of the human race to the degree that it preserves the particular features of the different cultures.'[6]

Jesus – Sacrament of Possibility

In the second place, I wonder whether, at another level, we lose sight of the simple revelation of compassionate harmony that Jesus embodied in himself, in light of the scandalous divisions and rivalries between our Christian denominations. There are still Christians who believe that their own particular persuasion has the edge on others, in terms of God's pecking order. One way of revisiting and reclaiming the lost heart of the Catholic Church is to continue our examination of the original vision of Jesus during his enfleshed time on earth. What was he trying to do? What dream was he at pains to realise? In what cause did he invest his best energy? It is so important to spend more time in trying to understand these questions.

It is true to say that God became human so as to reveal the divine potential within all human beings and all creation. The incarnation tells us so much about humanity as well as about God. It is the everlasting sacrament of the possibility and capacity of each person for unity with and for becoming like God. Jesus Christ is both the ready, open, human ear, waiting for the voice of its transformation and the loving whisper of the inviting, saving God. All of this totally orthodox theology is a necessary preamble to recovering the lost soul of the Catholic Church. While such theology has never been in question among the saints and scholars of our centuries of debate, it is remarkable how little of it has percolated through to the homilies, the catechisms and the catechesis of our day. However, we are pursuing here a vital pointer to the essence of the revelation that is Jesus, and to what should still be the main emphasis of the mission and message of the Catholic Church.

Christ completed and perfected what creation began by being at once 'the way forward' for the final and irrevocable breakthrough of humanity into God, and, at the same time, 'the way in' for the ever-approaching, self-disposing love of God for us. He was, too, the ultimate locus for the consummation of these two movements – a consummation that summed up all that was graced potential in humanity – making him the first of creation whose own existence throws light on the true meaning of created humanity.[7]

With the purposes for writing this book in mind, there is neither the space, time nor necessity for developing in great detail the theological implications of these revelations. The implications are, however, of immense importance for the Catholic Church's self-understanding of its role. This self-understanding will affect, for instance, the thrust of its seminary training, of its official promulgations and preaching, of its catechesis and celebration of the sacraments, of its attitudes towards the value of the ordinary, daily ups and downs of the 99% of lay folk who make up the Body of Christ.

The immanence of the Word, now, for us, is what we must continue to grapple with. This doctrine of immanence, of incarnation, of Word-fleshing, turns our normal ecclesiastical approach to Catholicism upside down. It does this because it is non-dualistic. Such an intrinsic teaching can terrify a system. The true Christian, like the child, the mystic and the poet, is a menace on the assembly-line, or, as John O'Donohue puts it, '... the mystical frightens the institution because it creates such an undeniable window for the wild light of the divine to shine through. Amidst the quotidian routine of rules, prayers and promises, the touch of this wild light is the most urgent dream of every heart. This light brings such illumination and transfiguration that it threatens to displace the centre and unmask the functionary as a peripheral custodian.' This doctrine of revelation shifts the focus from 'the sacred' to 'the secular', from 'the holy' to 'the merely human'. It forces us to redraw all our maps regarding what we're about as priests, religious, catechists and ministers. It demands that we reset our compasses when it comes to trying to explain the directions and meanings of life and death, of failure and success, of the ordinary and the extraordinary. Much of Karl Rahner's theology is devoted to revealing the graced nature of life itself as we live it, and the way in which the sacraments celebrate the fact that this routine, daily life is already full of God, but, because of the originally flawed nature of all humanity, needs continual purification, re-focusing, refining and re-direction.

Grace is simply the last depth and the radical meaning of all that the created person experiences, enacts and suffers in the process of developing and realising himself as a person. When someone experiences laughter or tears, bears responsibility, stands by the truth, breaks through the egoism in his life with other people; where someone hopes against hope, faces the shallowness and stupidity of the daily rush and bustle with humour and patience, refusing to become embittered; where someone learns to be silent and in this inner silence lets the evil in his heart die rather than spread outwards; in a word, wherever someone lives as he would like to live, combating his own egoism and the continual temptation to inner despair – there is the event of grace.[8]

Jesus came to reveal the love and meaning at the heart of creation and of our own individual and community lives. The incarnation was meant to unfold the tapestry of significance in God's first plan to create a cosmos, a universe, a world, a humanity. The point of the Word-made-Flesh was to make clear, once for all, that God is to be discovered, experienced and celebrated in the fabric of each day's living; likewise with the church and likewise with the sacraments. The goal of Jesus' ministry was to establish the sacredness of our so-called secular life, the possible experience of God in every experience, the end of an unenlightened dualism that makes universal atonement and completion impossible. Every sacrament is intended to witness to that truth, not to perpetuate, as so often happens, the godless divide between these two worlds.

From the evidence of the Hebrew scriptures, through incarnation and the Christian scriptures, through the centuries of Catholic history, this initial insight has not changed. The work of Jesus Christ is to liberate people from their inherent sinfulness, to help them see again in spite of the virus of blindness that is never far away, to set their hearts free to do the one thing that hearts are best at doing – loving.

Jesus understood his ministry in terms of setting people free. We need to be clear about this. His life and death were not concerned with changing God's mind or winning back God's friendship. Rather, his living and dying were about changing people's minds and hearts. This is a different context in which to understand salvation. In Jesus' preaching, salvation is connected with setting people free from fear, ignorance and darkness, and changing the way they imaged and thought about God and themselves ... Jesus' call to 'repent' is not so much about a movement from personal sin to not sin-

ning as it is about a transformation of the way we see God
and us, incarnation and creation. At that time people thought
that God was not close to them. Jesus called them to change
their way of thinking. Convert! Repent! God *is* here – in your
loving, in your caring, in your generosity, in your compassionate visiting. And more! God is *always* here, even when
you are conscious of your failure, your sin, your low status in
life, and when everything seems to be going wrong.[9]

In their evangelising and missionary work, Christian bodies
such as the Catholic Church are called to make significant and
even radical shifts in their understanding of the nature of the
'good news' they present. This re-focusing amounts to what is
sometimes called 'a paradigm shift', like the whole new mind-set
that happened after the Copernican revolution. The salvation,
redemption, completion, wholeness achieved in Jesus is the realisation, unique to Christianity, that to be truly human is already
to be divine, that the first creation was already an incarnation of
God, that the full and ordinary life of ordinary people is God's
delight, that nothing, except sin, is outside the presence of God.

We are led to conclude, from contemplating Jesus' life and
preaching, that the divine and the human are intermingled,
and that to see a human person live a totally loving, gracious
life is to see the face of God. The Wisdom of God finds expression in human beings. Of course there is more to the reality of God than this, but if we do not proclaim and celebrate
this basic insight about ourselves and where and how we experience the divine, we are not being faithful to the understanding that dawned on the first Christians at Pentecost.[10]

A Divine Destiny

The need to rescue people from a sinful, threatening world is
still written deep into the Catholic psyche. The sin/redemption
focus of our understanding of incarnation still colours our sacramental catechesis, teaching and preaching. Society is often written off by church authorities as 'a culture of death' from which
people need to be removed into the safety of a community that is
energised by a different life-force and vision. What is continually
being overlooked, in our self-understanding as church, is the
original joy of God's first creation, while in no way denying the
awful reality of the sinfulness of the world. The cautious and
often negative emphasis in many current Roman Catholic statements is unnecessarily at severe odds with a world that is fired

up with optimism and enthusiasm for its future in a new millennium. This unbalanced interpretation of revelation is, I'm sure, one of the chief reasons for our diminishing numbers and for the loss of young people from our communities.

To come to grips with the dualism that underlies our current sacramental theology and sacramental celebration we need to re-examine a christology that has slipped from the church's mainstream approach to salvation and revelation. If Christian revelation is about God – a God who is not only transcendent but eternally immanent – then equally it must be a window on the nature of humanity, for in Christ, as we have seen, the divine offer of love and complete human receptivity are united. The locus of revelation, therefore, is the living experience of humanity and its meaning in the light of Christ.

What a difference it would make if all our liturgical seasons, our remembrance of the saints, our celebrations of the sacraments, our ferverinos at devotions, were more aimed at affirming the potential and actual splendour within the humanness of those in our gatherings. To be sure, it would be disastrous to assume that human nature, left to itself, would find its own way safely home. Given the original sinfulness of the human condition, the need for salvation is beyond question. What is questioned is the dualistic emphasis, found so often in Catholic sects, on the fallenness, the badness, the capacity for evil of human beings. Jesus, on the contrary, strives only to emphasise the goodness, the potential for divinity, in all people. He is the one who reveals the beauty and compassion within an already and always graced humanity.

> The truth is that only in the mystery of the incarnate Word does the mystery of man take on light. For Adam, the first man, was a figure of him who was to come, namely Christ the Lord. Christ, the final Adam, by the revelation of the mystery of the Father and his love, fully reveals man to man himself and makes his supreme calling clear. It is not surprising, then, that in him all the aforementioned truths find their root and attain their crown ... He blazed a trail, and if we follow it, life and death are made holy and take on a new meaning.[11]

This discussion is an attempt to build a bridge between the present redemption-based *raison d'être* of the church and a more creation-centred one; to build another platform for an edifice to the glory of created and redeemed humanity; to balance our well-proclaimed darkness with our passion for the possible lightness of being. Once again, in our endless searching for discernment regarding this building and balance, to whom shall we turn?

Jesus: God's Human Face

Jesus Christ is the summit of the history of human self-discovery; he is not qualitatively different from the human race, but is rather the fullest expression of self-actualisation which is the vocation and potential of all people, by virtue of their being created in God's image. 'The light that appeared in Jesus,' observes Rudolf Bultmann, 'is none other than that which had already shone forth in creation.' In Christ, the law of human evolution has come to fulfilment; in him humanity's quest for 'being-human-in-God', as Hubert Halbfas puts it, has found its goal; in him we have overcome our fallenness. The big evolutionary breakthrough has happened; the man, Jesus Christ, has demonstrated the ultimate power of true loving as a real possibility for all, not simply as one amongst many stages in the evolution of the world, but as the highest point towards which everything is moving. The main mission of the churches, then, is to proclaim that the triumph of love has been assured for every person, people and culture in the history of the world, because this victory happened, once, in the fleshed Word.

> Jesus came to reveal to us in superabundance how loving is the fundamental power in the universe ... He came to tell us that we need not fear, that we could take the risk of vulnerability required by loving reconciliation. Thus it is in and through Jesus as the revelation of the loving trustworthiness of God (and the cosmos and life that God has created) that we overcome the effects of the sin of the human race.[12]

Because of his deep wisdom, experience and holiness, Pope John Paul II has a vision of creation and salvation that will not be compromised. In 1980 he said, 'Man must be viewed as a distinctive and autonomous value, as bearing in himself the transcendence of personality, with all that it ultimately implies. Man must be affirmed for his own sake, and not for any other motive or reason; solely for himself! More than this, man must be loved because he is man; love is due to man by virtue of the special dignity which is his. All these affirmations concerning man lie in the very substance of the message of Christ and the mission of the church.'

Because the spirit of Jesus is in all people, then everyone's true spirit is life-giving and healing. St Luke's famous summary of the purpose of the incarnation is often seen as a kind of messianic mission statement. 'He has sent me to bring the good news to the poor, to proclaim liberty to captives, and to the blind new sight; to set the downtrodden free, to proclaim the Lord's year of favour.' (Lk 1:16-19) The potential to live out this responsibility, the ability to be priests and prophets of human transcendence, belongs to everyone by virtue of their birth and of their baptism. This is the transforming good news that Christian churches are mandated to announce ceaselessly, undiluted and uncorrupted.

The whole of humanity is destined to be the New Adam, not in a purely abstract sense, but incorporating, as Teilhard de Chardin saw it, the totality of matter, culture and creation, the value of which has been irreversibly emphasised in the Word made flesh. This reality of God made human, participating completely in creation, is affirmed in the Christian tradition from earliest times. We are called to convince people of their divine destiny; to fire them up with the goodness of their lives; to excite them with the possibilities of which they are capable; to impress on them the unique responsibility they carry for the salvation of their community and of the whole world.

Tertullian of the second century, no New Age, pantheistic guru by any standards, wrote, 'It is in the flesh that salvation hinges.' An eleventh-century saint of the Eastern Church, Simeon, said, 'These hands of mine are the hands of God; this body is the body of God through the incarnation.' And later, St Theresa made a similar and now famous affirmation: 'Christ has no body now on earth but yours; no hands but yours; no feet but yours; yours are the eyes through which to look out the compassion of Christ to the world; yours are the feet through which he is to go about doing good; yours are the hands with which he is to bless people now.'

The way to human fulfilment and healing is to penetrate right to the heart of the world, in all its sufferings, ugliness and desolation as well as its joys, beauty and integrity. In Christ, Hans Küng suggests, our humanity has undergone transformation; this is not something tacked on to our human existence, but the revelation of its intrinsic meaning and value. George Maloney develops this idea. 'Man stands at the centre of the cosmos. Deified man, in whom God lives and through whom he acts to fulfil the world, is the mediator between the disparate and disjointed world and the unity that has been achieved perfectly in God-Man's humanity through the incarnation. There can be no transfiguration of the material cosmos except through human beings who themselves, by grace, have been divinised.'[13] As Christians we can never separate faith in God from faith in humanity, trust in God from trust in human beings, and the healing grace in Jesus from the healing grace in all of us.

Only Connect ...

The perennial quest among people like myself these times, is for a way of connecting the sacred and the secular, the natural and the supernatural. Only when dualism no longer pertains will the true nature of the incarnation be allowed to run free. We are all well aware that it is only in Christ that this reconciliation has taken place. In him the seeming opposites of the things of heaven and the things of earth are harmonised. This mystery is the inspiration of theology and poetry throughout the history of Chrisitanity. It is meant to be the rich source of our christology, ecclesiology and sacramental theology. But so often the reverse is true. The church is seen as an unworldly, and therefore irrelevant, system that stands in stark contrast to a threatening world.

What is needed is a way of holding these realities together, of revealing what Hugh Lavery calls 'the really real'. It seems to me that what we call 'grace' has the capacity to achieve this challenge. The truly traditional theology of grace within orthodox Christianity has enough breadth and depth to carry some of the essential meaning of the infinite mystery of the fleshing of the Word. Misunderstood, the same doctrine can become an agent of dualism.

It is common, unfortunately, for preachers to talk about the sacraments in terms of offering grace to graceless people. This presumes, to a greater or lesser extent, that those who do not belong to the sacramental life of the church are without grace. There is a hollow ring to that supposition. It carries no echo, except that of sadness or self-doubt, within people's spirit. In such a proclamation there is no good news. And this, in turn, contributes to the phenomenon of the faithful departing from our communities. These are the people who have given up on formal religion but who long for an authentic spirituality. They have given up because they see no relevance between their lives and their religious practices, between nature and grace. Instead of finding inspiration, strength and empowerment, they experience confusion and irrelevance.

But grace does not designate a 'supernatural' area standing above and beyond created nature: it refers, instead, to that significant ground of all being which circumscribes and supports the horizon and depth of all everyday experience. The liturgy is rich with expressions of this truth. The Eucharistic Prayers and the Prefaces, the form of our sacramental celebrations, the prayers of the Roman Ritual, all point to the universal presence of God in and around everything, as the fountain, source and sustainer of creation, 'of all life and holiness.' (Eucharistic Prayer III) Indeed how remarkably striking are the words that ring out with joy and confidence in the preface of Christmas III:

Today a new light has dawned upon the world;
God has become one with humanity
and humanity has become one again with God.
The eternal Word has taken upon himself our earthly condition
giving our human nature divine value.
So enchanting is this communion between God and humanity
that in Christ the world bestows on itself
the gift of God's own life.' (*my translation*)

Grace is the innate capacity each one possesses to relate, forgive, encounter suffering, create, invent, imagine, endure, explore – indeed to do anything which is a positive option for love and growth. Grace is the context, capacity and transformation bound up in every moment of being and becoming, in every desire and achievement of authentic self-realisation. While we are forever obliged to believe in the absolute giftedness of grace, an obligation we can only celebrate humbly and with great joy, we can affirm too, with equal force, in the words of the unique theologian, Piet Fransen, that 'grace sets our deepest humanity free, precisely because it restores our most authentic humanity to us and by this means, *humanises* us to an eminent degree ... Properly speaking, we do not receive grace; we do not possess it as something foreign to us, or as something entering into us from the outside; for *we are our grace*. As Caesar wisely observes in Thornton Wilder's *Ides of March:* "I seem to have known all my life, but to have refused to acknowledge, that all, all love is one, and that the very mind with which I ask these questions is awakened, sustained and instructed only by love".'[14]

Disclosure Moment

For instance, just now I've come in from visiting some parishioners who had requested a visit for a variety of reasons. As I drove through the mid-day streets of our little town here in Garforth on this brisk February day, I was struck quite strongly by a vision of where the immanent God was really and fundamentally present. My moment of disclosure was not as radical and visionary as many of those we read about, but it is very much in my soul as I write these lines. I was passing the library at the corner of Main Street and Church Lane where several elderly people were returning and acquiring some books, tapes and other means of communication. It was then that I had a glimpse of the holy nature of their joy in reading, their search for knowledge, their use of imagination in the novels and poetry they entered into, the lift and life of the stories of great people and great events that they revisited in print. I thought of the sacrament of Confirmation, of the gifts of the Holy Spirit, of knowledge and wisdom and learning, all incarnated in these Wednesday people. And I saw all of this as a kind of expression of the divine on the streets of Garforth, a scrap of God's autobiography in space and time, a split-second continuation of the incarnation, a diary of human and divine becoming at an ordinary street corner in an ordinary town. I remembered some lines from W.B.Yeats.

> My fiftieth year had come and gone,
> And I sat, a solitary man,
> In a crowded London shop,
> An open book and empty cup
> On the marble table-top.
>
> While on the shop and street I gazed
> My body of a sudden blazed;
> And twenty minutes more or less
> It seemed, so great my happiness,
> That I was blessed and could bless.[15]

I parked my car and went to Medicare chemist shop around the corner. I had a prescription for my nose. I have difficulty with my breathing. While waiting in the queue I had time to revisit and continue that moment of disclosure about my awakened and startlingly clear sense of God at work and at play in all that was happening around me. There was a man who looked very pale and ill, shuffling around with no light in his eyes. There was Mary, whom I knew and greeted, waiting for her phials of insulin to keep the life flowing in her. A father, off work for the day, or maybe out-of-work for longer, was holding the hand of his daughter whose eyes were red and swollen from some painful-looking infection. Again, I became so strikingly aware of a deeper mystery at hand, of a rumour of angels around the place, of a stunning fabric and texture to what, at first glance, seemed so mundane and commonplace. The drugs, the tablets, the medicine were all from the store-house of nature. I thought of the Celtic belief that God places somewhere in creation a cure for all the ills of life. And the people were serving each other, talking to each other, comparing notes with each other, consoling each other.

I had never noticed it before but the place, it seemed to me at that moment, was full of grace. There was no need for conversion here: no need for a re-direction of human nature; no need for a call to repentance from sinful ways. This is where God is happening, I thought. This is where the most fundamental and real presence of the divine is to be found. I could see St Mary's Church of England church through the window of the pharmacy. (Our own Roman Catholic Church had not yet been built.) What the churches do, I realised, is to affirm the incredible holiness of this queue of people, to confirm the deepest mystery of an everyday line of needy citizens, waiting, sometimes patiently, sometimes not, for their name to be called to the counter, to be given the white packet containing the insulin, or the tablets, or the pain-reducing medicine.

In the same breath and at the same time, did I hear another voice surrounding the attendant's voice, calling the same name but at a deeper level? When Mary the diabetic desperately searches for help and healing, did I think of an answering grace in a white packet called insulin that guarantees Mary's quality of life? When the little girl longs for her inflamed eyes to be cured, did I think of Bartimaeus pleading for his sight back, and wonder whether what Jesus did then in one way, he is now doing in this very shop, in another?

And the pale man with no light in his eyes – what about him? He is given the tonic to redden his blood and lighten his step and straighten his back and shoulders. His lost zest for living is restored to him. He will soon bring a new presence and joy to his home and family. What else is this but divine grace? Is not this the real raw material of human living, together with every healing touch on earth, that is caught up and celebrated as holy in our sacraments, particularly in sacraments such as reconciliation and anointing? Is, therefore, the meaning of revelation, of church, of sacrament, to point to the more profound reality of what is happening in the homes and lives of all people, in the shops and streets of all villages, towns and cities. Why, I thought, has the negative wedge of an ecclesiastical dualism split wide the healing of the world from the healing of God? From what fear, from what dualistic mischief does our resistance and reluctance to acknowledging the holiness of such saving and amazing graces arise?

Driving home, I saw at least four adults, two men and two women, pushing prams with small babies in them. There was such an aura of completeness about them. As I looked at them through the windscreen of my car (a distancing window, incidentally, through which, as a celibate, Catholic cleric I seem to have looked out at the world for so much of my life) I had a sense of their totality, of their self-sufficiency and of quiet, satisfied fullness. What, I asked myself, is my role regarding these people? What can our churches offer to such inhabitants of our town? (I suspected that most of those I met were not churchgoers.) And then, once again, it began to become clear to me.

My role is not, in the first place, to get them to become practising Christians, Catholics, or into any other structured form of religion. It is not to tell them first about Jesus so that they might join our churches. It is not to encounter them as though God was not already deeply at home in their lives. It is something else. It is simply to try to understand and name their experiences for them. If they are open to such a journey, to such a disclosure, to something of the mystery of their lives, to something already incredibly beautiful in their relationships with husbands, wives, partners, children, parents, friends, neighbours, to the hardships and struggles of each day's living, then part of my role would be to walk with them, listen to them, learn from them and, wherever possible, share, name and celebrate with them the deeper realities, the richer revelations about the love and meaning at the heart of their sometimes routine, sometimes surprising lives.

When our small community travels through the quiet sabbath streets of this village-town to celebrate the Christian eucharist around our present make-shift school-altar, what is symbolised in the bread and wine is the totality of the humanity that is happening, day and night, within and around the hearts and hearths of the citizens and homes of Yorkshire and beyond. God's sublime secret revealed again and again on a rickety table in a schoolroom near Leeds. Mystery at home in a nursery. The sacrament is about showing forth the inner sacred meaning of what is always happening, about focusing on the unrecognised divine depths of routine moments, about affirming the sanctity of all human experiences, about making manageable, in symbol, the mysterious dimensions of all relationships, of witnessing to the continuing unfolding of the reality of the incarnation during the course of each new day and each new night.

In such affirming and revelatory dimensions of Christianity, what can never be forgotten is the redemptive, salvational power of what the church has to offer to the world of life and to the life of the world. However the phenomenon of sin and evil is described by various philosophers, psychologists and theologians, there are few who deny its presence. There is a destructive force, an ambiguous drive, a negative energy permeating all existence. A brief glance at any day's news, or into one's own or another's heart, will produce more than enough evidence of a deadly virus.

Not only in the ways outlined in the previous few paragraphs, is the mission of Jesus, of church and sacrament, of the Christian presence in our town, to reveal the sacred meaning at the heart of life's experience. It is also to serve the people of God, that is all our citizens, by a reviewing and critiquing, a remembering and evaluating, an examination of consciousness, so as to honestly discover the damaging, negative and diminishing aspects of our actions and reactions, our choices and decisions, our silences and our speaking out.

There are models and modes of contemporary spiritualities that deny, pass over or minimise the need for the refining, purifying and healing of our 'natural' ways of being. The Christian contribution to the enriching and strengthening of each person's life and each community's existence in the real-life situations I imaginatively entered into today, lies in its acknowledgement of the fatal flaw that runs through humanity and all creation. This 'fault' carries immense power and force; it can be incredibly destructive; it can develop an evil energy; it is a reality in every moment of every human experience.

And so, as well as celebrating, as we have just seen, in my glimpses of a moment in the life of our Garforth community, the God-likeness of all creatures and of all creation, the church and sacraments, with equal commitment and endeavour, set out to encounter, encompass and redeem the strange truth, the perennially humbling phenomenon of what we call original sin. What life and resonance, what healing and wholeness, what love and meaning, what satisfaction and relief does such an understanding of Christianity, such an interpretation of the role of the church in any area, bring to hurting and needy individuals and families, to communities at home and abroad in sore need of justice and freedom!

Sacraments of what happens

In the early Christian era this experience of the Spirit of the Risen Christ was vivid and immediate and far less structured than it later became. Men and women presented the evidence for the continued presence of Christ, not so much in the formulations of a structured church as in the quality of their own lives. In the joys and hopes of constant and daily struggle, they built a community of love and trust. 'By this we know that we have passed from death to life, by the love we have for each other.' (1 Jn 3:14) And commenting on this, St Augustine added that the love with which we love each other is the same love with which God loves us. Culminating in the Second Vatican Council, the emphasis began to move from a predominantly institutional understanding of the church to a more vulnerable, experience-based and people-centred community of the baptised. This shift in emphasis arose from the changing perception of the relationship between the church and the world. The recovery of a theology of creation plays a huge part in this changing perception.

The world is the graced arena in which human beings strive always to become more and more truly human. It is the history within which God became incarnate and established forever its essential value. In Christ, God accepted the world definitively, so that everything in it was shown to be decisive for the salvation of creation. Nevertheless the decisive nature of the created world must be actualised by human beings themselves in the process of history. All activities – discovery, invention, technology, artistic creativity – should be positively directed towards deeper humanisation, for through incarnation the world's welfare has become our dearest responsibility.

To promote the central place of the world's intrinsic value as a prime focus for our energies is not to threaten the Lordship of Christ in our lives. Rather this is the very mission that we are called to carry out in the name of Jesus, the decisive point of his domination in history. Grace is freedom; it bestows upon things the scarcely-measured depths of their own being. It calls things out of all their sinful alienation into their own. It calls the world into its perfect worldliness. The church is the sign-community, the community that is aware that God has already placed in the hearts of all people the real possibility of becoming 'other Christs'.

The Church in the Modern World, the Vatican II document, makes clear that 'by her relationship with Christ, the church is a kind of sacrament of intimate union with God and of the unity of all humanity,' (para 38) In Origen's words, 'Our Lord Jesus Christ, the word of God, of his boundless love, became what we are that he might make us what he himself is.' Thus, the task of the sign-community is continually to highlight and celebrate the presence of the Spirit everywhere, to announce that incarnation has happened, and corporately to express its full implications and meaning for every human being.

But how far have we drifted from that original vision, from that positive and optimistic vindication of the ultimate potential of human nature? Why are we regarded as the enclave of those who do not trust the sincerity of other denominations' protestations, who suspect the goodness, the truth and the beauty of those who belong to other religions or to none? Has it something to do with a dualism that sets the unbaptised heart over against the 'saved' one, as though God distinguishes between the initiated infant and the non initiated, as though birth itself does not grace one with a divine belonging, as though to be human is not to be blessed, as though simply 'to be' is not enough to be called holy?

> Christians cannot boast that they have themselves an excel-
> lent way of life, for they have little to point to when they
> boast. They only confess this: we were blind in our distrust of
> being, but now we begin to see; we were aliens and alienated
> in a strange empty world, but now we begin to feel at home;
> we were in love with ourselves and all our little cities, but
> now we are falling in love, we think, with being itself, with
> the city of God, the universal community of which God is the
> source and governor. And for all of this we are indebted to
> Jesus Christ, in our history, and in that depth of the spirit in
> which we grope with our theologies and theories ...[16]

So often, and so tragically, there is little evidence of a change of heart on the part of an institution that is too deeply influenced and directed by well-intentioned leaders, most of whom can only operate out of an all-pervasive and deadly clericalism.

The church must *affirm* the world within which it moves, insofar as the world's enterprises tend towards real humanisation. Conversely, wherever people's actions tend to damage and do violence to the love that is ever-present, then the church must function as *protest* against such regression and alienation. Always, the ecclesial community, the specific church, must serve the needs of humanity by helping the realities of the world to find the true and authentic source of their own being, and by reflecting in its own activities the quality of love that it seeks to signify.

> The essential nature of the church, therefore, is to be this mystery of love, of the divine love revealing itself and communicating itself to people. All the sign-language of doctrine and ritual has no purpose but to reveal and communicate this love. This is the light in which the doctrine, the ritual and the organisation of the church are to be judged ... The Kingdom of God, the reign of the Spirit, has to take shape in this world ... (The church) has continually to renew itself, to discover again its original message, to define it in the light of the present day, to manifest its power to transform people's lives.[17]

Whether we use the word 'sacrament' in terms of Jesus Christ, of the church or of the individual rites that vary between traditions, we are talking about celebrations of ordinary and extraordinary life, about validating the authenticity of human experience and about the individual and communal need for purification, discernment and transformation in the vicissitudes of our fragile existence. The first step towards a deeper understanding of sacraments is to see them in the context of a world already permeated and filled with God's presence.

The art is to enable people to become what they already are. The phrase 'Receive whom you are' accompanied the offering of the eucharistic bread at the communion of the Mass in the early years of Christianity. *You are the Body of Christ.* Grace is life fully lived. God's basic gift to people is the lives they live and the good earth from which they make their living. In *The Furrow*, James Mackey writes:

> The life which is now being called God's primordial and perennial grace to man is precisely the life of everyman's everyday experience. It is man's working and eating, walking in the fields or on the seashore, playing for his team or dancing in his club, sleeping with his wife or talking with his

friends, suffering the slings and arrows of outrageous for-
tune or holding out a helping hand to his fellow man, deciding what is best with the best guidance he can get and getting
up for Mass on Sundays. All that is grace.[18]
Instead of superficially perceiving those 'outside the church' as
somehow unfinished or incomplete, or even nameless or neutral, or worse still, as blind and lost, perhaps, following the sensitivity of Jesus to all that his Father has created, our church will,
one day, find its very meaning and mission in proclaiming the
essential holiness of all people, the sacred heart of all creation. Is
God diminished when God's family is sanctified? Does the
church lose when the world grows more truly healthy? Is not the
very work of the Spirit to reveal the innate worthiness and beauty
of matter? Is it not only in the arena of the life of the world that
sin and evil can be encountered and transcended?

All Creation is Holy

Christopher Kiesling examines the notions of grace and nature.
'Christian faith is born of the experience of Jesus Christ, a man
who was born, lived, suffered and died like other people, yet in
whom God was reconciling all things to himself. Through Jesus
Christ, people were given the insight that in ordinary human existence, its joys and sorrows, its hopes and disappointments, its
daily activities like eating and relaxing, conversing and enjoying
companionship, its use of things and interaction with people,
God is at work transforming people into his children in whom
he wishes to dwell in a communion of life.'[19]

The Vatican Council's document, *The Church in the Modern
World*, makes it clear that in the past we over-emphasised the
notion of two distinct worlds, one sacred and one profane.
Gregory Baum, a 'peritus' at the Council, expresses his special
insight in this way:

The radical distinction between the sacred and the profane
has been overcome in the person of Christ. In Christ it is revealed that the locus of the divine is the human. In him it is
made manifest that God speaks in and through the words
and gestures of people. The Christian way of worship, therefore, can no longer consist in sacred rites by which people are
severed from the ordinary circumstances of their lives.
Christian liturgy is, rather, the celebration of the deepest dimension of human life, which is God's self-communication
to people. Liturgy unites people more closely to their daily

lives. Worship remembers and celebrates the marvellous things God works in the lives of people, purifies and intensifies these gifts, makes people more sensitive to the Word and Spirit present in their secular lives. The sacraments of Christ enable people to celebrate the deepest dimension of their lives, namely, God's gift of God's self, in a way that renders the dimension more powerful.[20]

I never cease to be amazed at such glimpses into the meaning of revelation. And whenever we share it with others, the reaction is similar. After talks, workshops and presentations about such an understanding of the mystery of incarnation, invariably there will be those who say something like, 'What you have said is not new. We have always known it in our hearts. We have never doubted the sacredness of our lives, of our child-bearing and our daily work, of our struggles to survive and grow, of our efforts to forgive and start again. Our hearts have always told us that these are holy tasks. All that's new is that now we have heard it said.' What a deep transformation it would trigger off around the Christian world were this good news to be proclaimed wherever the people are gathered around the table of the Lord!

And yet to lose hope would be to doubt the very mystery to which we are committed. Let us briefly examine the heart of our story again. The hidden involvement of God in the humanising of people has become fully, definitively and unconditionally manifest in Jesus Christ, the Word made flesh, and it is this Christ that is proclaimed and celebrated in the church. In the church we have not only the source of salvation for those who belong to it, we see also in the church God's redemptive plan for the entire world of people. In the church is proclaimed and celebrated the mystery of redemption from within that summons people everywhere. Edward Schillebeeckx writes in *The Church Today*, that what the church has to offer us explicitly is already implicitly present in human life as a whole; it is the mystery of salvation. The church reveals, proclaims and celebrates in thankfulness the deepest dimension of that which is being fulfilled in the world. He is sure that the church is, in fact, the world where the world has come fully to itself, where the world confesses and acknowledges the deepest mystery of its own life, the mystery of salvation fulfilled through Christ.

And so we understand the individual sacraments as privileged moments of ultimate meaning, as windows of deep disclosure, as holy x-rays that reveal the true condition of a person's or a community's inner, spiritual health. Leaving aside an often misleading or even damaging and dualistic catechesis about the sacraments, what they basically do is to take the earthly realities of our human existence – birth, reconciliation, sickness, love, the need to worship, commitment, death – and to the eyes of faith they show forth the deeper meaning hidden within, the silent activity of the Spirit, gradually sanctifying and redeeming every aspect of daily life until the time when God will be 'all in all.' In his famous *Christ the Sacrament*, Edward Schillebeeckx reminds us that whatever is lived out in an everyday manner outside the sacraments, grows to its full maturity within them. The anonymity of everyday living is removed by the telling power of Christ's symbolic action in and through his church. Therefore, the sacraments cannot be isolated from the organic unity of whole, human, persevering Christian life.

To take one example: Referring to someone who comes to celebrate the eucharist, Karl Rahner writes:

> He offers up the world under the form of bread and wine, knowing that the world is already constantly offering itself up to the incomprehensible God under its own forms, in the ecstasy of its joy and the bitterness of its sorrow. He looks, praising, at God's ineffable light, knowing that this vision takes place most radically where eyes weep tears of blood, or glass over as they see the approach of death. He knows that he is proclaiming the death of the Lord, in as much as this death, once died, lives on always in the world, is built into the inmost centre of the world, and is truly enacted again in that man, who whether he knows this expressly or not, 'dies in the Lord'. He knows that he is proclaiming at Mass the coming of the Lord, because the Lord is already realising his coming in the world in everything that drives the world on towards its goal. He receives under holy signs the true Body of the Lord, knowing this to be worthless were he not to communicate with that Body of God which is the world itself and its fate; he partakes of the one Body so as to remain always in communion with that other Body in the reality of his life.[21]

To be sacramentally literate, according to Hugh Lavery, we would move beyond the constraints of time, space, numbers and immediacy. While always relying on the tangible elements of the earth for their matter and form, the essence of sacrament, whether as applied to the Saviour, to the church, or to baptism or eucharist, is to point away from itself, as Jesus did, to move out into a wider field of reality, to embrace within its symbolism that which could otherwise never be brought home. Where reconciliation is concerned, for instance, there is a need to clarify the fact that this sacrament does not confer a different kind of forgiveness from that which human beings exchange among themselves. It is not a 'second' type of atonement between church and penitent, between God and sinner. Nor is it a holier, more divine reconciliation, above and beyond whatever human appeasement takes place. Not everyone is aware of the true significance and necessity of the communal celebration of this sacrament.

What is celebrated is the forgiving presence of the indwelling Blessed Trinity in each human being. This is first expressed and shared in whatever ways are appropriate to the people concerned. It may be within a community, a family, a friendship or within one human heart. What is important to believe is that wherever and whenever it happens, there, and only there, is the event of grace, the power of the Spirit, the infinite and complete energy of God. Nothing else is needed. At that moment the Godhead is fully fleshed, the incarnation continues, the Holy Spirit is audible and tangible. There is no need for a two-tier hierarchy of forgiveness, one human, one divine. To hold this is to be radically heretical. And yet, throughout Christian countries, churches, parishes and schools, our liturgical preaching and sacramental catechesis often conveys a confusing two-tier, double-decker approach to grace and nature, to the human and the divine.

And where sacraments are concerned there is much more to be said. Here we are not just concerned with preventing dualism being reinforced, because of the approaches adopted in much current religious education. Neither are we limited to promoting and ensuring an intrinsic and incarnational understanding of this most radical tradition so central to Catholic belief, but more to explore sacramental theology in all its richness. Of the many characteristics that we, as Catholics, may legitimately be proud, the robustness, totality and uncompromising doctrine of sacramental reality must be our finest. A forgotten aspect of the meaning of sacrament is the universality of its symbolism. When an individual or a community, for example, enters into the rites of reconciliation, all words and gestures of forgiveness, and all efforts at making or maintaining peace are celebrated. It is not so much a matter of 'squaring it with God' yet again, after having broken a law, as of celebrating the powerful Spirit of God at work in the community, bringing healing and harmony to broken and discordant places. We need the sacrament to focus us on this difficult reality, to reveal the divinity within the act of dying to oneself, which is one way of looking at forgiveness. To truly forgive is beyond fallen nature. Only through the help of God, already within us all in possibility, can we overcome the proud ego, the condition of original sinfulness. The sacrament is so necessary to identify, to nourish and to celebrate that indwelling presence of our Lord and Saviour.

The sacraments do not confer a grace that was absent. Sacraments proclaim and enable us to own a love that is already present to us. A sacrament celebrates the Lord's giving, certainly. But his giving is not confined to the sacrament. What we need to focus on within the sacrament is our taking the love of God home with us, with a fresh awareness of that love. And that new awareness is the substance of *the grace of the sacrament*. Before reading the following informative summary from Christopher Kiesling's *Paradigms of Sacramentality*, it might be helpful to explain that a paradigm is an example which holds within it the essence of meaning, against which concepts can be examined and understood. (Further explanations of 'paradigm' are found at the beginning of *The Ministry of Women*, in Part Two.)

Baptism as incorporation into the Christian community is a paradigm of the sacramentality of all entrance into human community – family, city, nation, labour union, political party, school, bridge club. Confirmation is a model of all commitment to worthy human associations, causes and ideals. Penance is paradigmatic of all human reconciliation, whether between members of families or of other communities, between proponents of opposing ideas of government, between nations at rivalry.

Further, anointing the sick is paradigmatic of the sacramentality of all care of the bodily and mentally ill, the economically and culturally deprived, the down-trodden, the rejected. Ordination is paradigmatic of the sacramentality of all human responsibility for the welfare of others, especially their common welfare, of all human leadership and government, whether in the narrow circle of the family or the wide circle of international life. The eucharist is paradigmatic of the sacramentality of all self-sacrifice for others and for the causes of justice, love, freedom and truth. It is paradigmatic of the sacramentality of every meal which people share and of all human sharing, whether economic, cultural or spiritual. Marriage is paradigmatic of the sacramentality of every human encounter, every human friendship, every human love. It is paradigmatic too of the banalities of daily social life of every kind. (The following section develops this theme at greater length.) The Word of God (in the sense of the Bible, the oral traditions behind it, and the words of God's spokespeople behind them) may be added to this list as paradigmatic of the sacramentality of all human speech and communication.[22]

Unless we are aware of the sacramental nature of all reality and of the fact that our whole Christian life is worship, we cannot fully appreciate the constantly revealing mystery of the incarnation, of the church and of the individual sacraments. What has been said up to now is that the world and all it contains is created out of the extravagant and unconditional love we call God. The breathtaking mystery of creation, past and present, is an incredibly beautiful sign of compassion, communicated to people, and reflecting the wisdom and loveliness of God. This, in itself, makes the world already holy and sacred. And then, this presence of the Spirit and the Word which were there in and from the beginning, as St John reminds us, is fleshed in Jesus Christ, consecrating again from within, a nature and an earthly reality that was sorely in need of salvation. 'Make ready for Christ,' shouts Thomas Merton, 'whose smile, like lightning, sets free the song of everlasting glory that now sleeps, in your paper flesh, like dynamite.'

Original Sin and Original Blessing
By this stage there must be many readers wondering about the place and reality of sin in such an overview of revelation, and about its consequent implications for the redemptive role of the church today. Even apart from the fact that millions of Catholics still take the Adam and Eve story quite literally and understand their actions in the garden to be the only reason for the incarnation, the Christian doctrine of original sin must always play a central part in any theology that seeks to probe ever more deeply into the mystery of the relationship between God and humanity. Even before we examine the nature of what is called original sin, it is clear that most practising Catholics cannot con-

ceive of any reason for the Word-become-flesh other than that of the fate-filled happenings involving a snake and an apple. This is so because most of us have been brought up with such a notion. That is why almost all our self-awareness, as church, has to do with redemption and salvation. The drift and thrust of most of our cautions from the Vatican, of our weekly homilies and of our sacramental catechesis, for instance, is almost totally centred on strategies for encountering, coping with or escaping from, a strange and threatening world. Many a new day will dawn before the hoped-for paradigm shift outlined in these pages will once again become the traditional norm for Catholic doctrine, liturgy and life.

From the earliest Christian times the issue of original sin, personal sin and the sin of the world was hotly debated whenever a theology of creation was proclaimed. There is no need here to go into the history of a debate which surfaced on many an occasion throughout the centuries, beginning within the lifetime of Jesus, then with Irenaeus, Scotus, the mystics, Thomas Aquinas, St Francis, Teilhard de Chardin, liberation and feminist theologians such as M. D. Chenu, Edward Schillebeeckx, Rosemary Ruether, Roland Murphy, Sally McFague and many, many others.

Yet it is important to outline a few pointers regarding the misconceptions that surround this most influential of teachings. In fact there are those who would hold that our present Catholic understanding of church is distorted out of all proportion by the profoundly inaccurate and misleading interpretations accorded to it. What is so significant is the fact that the recent and widely available theological revisioning of the doctrine has made little or no headway into the popular homiletic and catechetical content of current practice. There are many reasons for this regrettable loss of impetus for a potentially new springtime for Christianity. Other than to submit that this is an immensely costly oversight for the relevance of the church to hundreds of thousands of young and old today, this is not the place to examine such reasons in great detail. A few general indicators may be sufficient for the moment.

If a creation-centred approach to the Christian mystery of the incarnation is now, once again, being heralded and proclaimed as the turning-point in the current mixed fortunes of our apparently diminishing church, and if a renewed theological balance about the love and meaning at the heart of life is ever to be recovered, then a new way of thinking about the sacrament that is

Jesus, that is church, that is baptism, that is eucharist, is to be restored. This shift in consciousness and awareness never comes
easy. What is carved into the psyche for centuries will not be re-
shaped in a day. And even when the re-thinking begins, there
will be many doubts. For instance, many of those trusting believers who become open to the possibility of another way of
perceiving the whole history of salvation and continuing re-cre-
ation, often carry an abiding anxiety that the proponents of this
kind of theology may be in danger of minimising the sheer mal-
ice and evil that is rampant throughout the world and that is
also a deep-seated possibility in the heart of everyone. Is sin regarded, they ask, as nothing more sinister than an unavoidable
difficulty which is part and parcel of a developing consciousness
and cosmos – a necessary obstacle in the course of the human
journey to its promised end?

The Happy Fault

Karl Rahner maintains that the first Fall was not the only cause
of revelation and salvation. Eminent theologians hold that the
most basic motive for revelation was not the 'buying back' of
humanity from damnation but that the incarnation was already
the goal of the divine plan even apart from any divine fore-
knowledge of freely incurred guilt. The incarnation may be seen
as the most original act of God anticipating the will to create and
then to redeem (if necessary), so that redemption from sin
would be 'included' in the first desire of God for the *hypostatic
union*, for another way of being God's self, which necessarily
called for creation and its conservation. All that is important
here, from the point of view of the church's teaching, is that the
victory of the Logos over sin should not be denied. But it is
freely permitted to regard the incarnation in God's primary intention as 'the summit and height of the divine plan of creation,
and not primarily and in the first place as the act of a mere
restoration of a divine world-order destroyed by the sins of
mankind, an order which God had conceived in itself without
any incarnation.'[23]

This understanding of the meaning of incarnation is of vital
importance to our questions about the role of the church in the
world. Once it is clarified that we are not merely a 'fallen race',
that Jesus Christ came not just to blot out our sins, that the sacraments are nothing but a protection from our own relentless ten-
dencies towards evil, then everything changes. The church can

be seen to exist so that our inherent sacredness can be recognised and affirmed; so that the image of God can be brought to
perfection within us; so that the divinisation of our humanity
can be achieved. The *Dogmatic Constitution on Revelation* supports this theological stance when it sees Christ as both the completion and salvation of God's first loving desire. (Documents of
Vatican II, *Dogmatic Constitution on Revelation*, articles 2 and 3.
Also *Pastoral Constitution on the Church*, article 22). 'The restoration in Christ of Adam's natural humanity is a gift, but for Christ
nothing supernatural is involved. Christ in his humanity is precisely what God intended from the beginning, no more and no
less. "Life", in the Pauline sense, therefore, is not a grace that
raises human nature to a higher level, but simply human nature
in its perfection.'[24]

Before we leave this discussion about the main reason for the
incarnation, let us look again at the notion of sin, personal and
original.

In none of the Hebrew or Christian scriptures can you find a
clear-cut distinction between personal and original sin. There is
no perfectly innocent human being because, living in a situation
of sin, all become personally entangled in it. Monica Hellwig,
holds that sin is a break with the right order and harmony of
God's world which sets things awry in it and complicates life for
everybody. To strike another is to arouse anger and evoke a
whole chain of violent acts. To be unfaithful in one marriage is to
cause a faint, diffuse anxiety in all marriages. To cheat or de-
fraud or betray a secret, even once, is to start ripples of fear and
distrust through the whole society. There is a world of sin
around. It is into this that each baby is born. St Paul speaks, not
of original sin but of 'the sin of the world'. Baptism prepares us
for the encounter with this sinful state.

It is not the arbitrary edict of God that people should pay the
penalty for the supposed sin of those who went before them.
Nor is the transmission of the sin in the act of procreation itself.
It is because of the way we are constituted that our lives are so
largely shaped by those who have lived before us. As individuals we are not made out of nothing but out of history. No one
really starts with a clean slate.

It is important to distinguish Christian awareness of the mystery of evil, the 'sin of the world', from the idea of individual
blameworthiness prior to any personal sin. The idea that 'baptism forgives original sin' is unknown to the church of the first

few centuries. St Paul presupposes that the gift of God's life precedes the mystery of evil, even apart from baptism.

The term 'original sin' arose with St Augustine and his defence of infant baptism. Scripture does not suggest that the 'sin
of the world' is passed to each person by generation. It seems to
suggest, rather, that it is passed on by society, culture, upbring-
ing and the experience of human relationships. Seeing the cor-
porate personality of original sin, the writer Tresmontant has
suggested that it is not so much the race inheriting the sin of an
individual as the individual inheriting the sin of the race.

There is general agreement among our best scripture scholars that the story of Adam's sin is a message about humanity,
not about the beginning of humanity. It concerns the way that
people stand before God all the time, not a historical description
of how the first man and woman fell before God. It is only now
that the damaging confusion of myth and history regarding the
Adamic narratives is being addressed.

Theologians are agreeing that the central emphasis on original sin has grown out of all proportion in the Christian scheme
of things, negatively affecting and distorting the church's understanding of its role and mission in the world.

Juan Segundo draws our attention to the two kinds of theology
that attempt to explain some of the key 'moments' in salvation-
history. There is a fatal flaw in a theology that attempts to link
too closely the fact of creation with Eden, the fact of a Fall with a
couple called Adam and Eve, and the beginning of salvation
with Jesus Christ. On the other hand, the new, incarnational
theology looks for the meaning of original sin in terms of the fact
that people sin and become corrupt; the sin of Adam is in our
own selves. It lies in the deliberate choice for the impersonal, the
alienated, the egotistical and the incomplete. It is a 'going
astray', a recklessness, a madness, a sickness, as scripture puts it.
Something goes wrong in us, an imbalance sets in, a good drive
grows 'out of true'. Resistance, tension, friction and concupiscence in themselves are neutral, necessary and given. But out of
alignment, the great human spirit runs amok in confusion, destruction and, eventually, evil. 'These forces of resistance and
concupiscence,' writes Segundo, 'in their specific meanings and
contexts intended here, are not erased by baptism but rather
given the communitarian possibility for opting for synthesis'.[25]
While redemption ended the 'enslavement to sin', it gives us a
greater responsibility in our decisions. Baptism, then, is seen as
the sacrament of community, and of personal growth within it.

These, then, are some of the pointers I wish to clarify regarding the central doctrine of original sin, particularly within Catholicism. In general they have to do with the purpose of creation in the first place. Put deceptively simply, was it for Adam or Christ? If individual salvation from original sin, and all sin, through baptism and through graced membership of the church and participation in its sacraments, is not the only or main reason for a Christian presence in the world, what then is the heart of the good news that the ministry and mission of Catholicism carries? In one of his recent talks to teachers, Cardinal Hume took this line of approach:

> In the past Catholics have been accused, perhaps with some justice, of stressing personal sinfulness and guilt and of over-emphasising the need for individual salvation. Today, we need to proclaim not only these, but also the fact that an individual is made for communion and community. We are also called to save the world and witness to the kingdom. There is no 'secular' realm from which God is absent. His presence in the world may be hidden and even denied, but God is everywhere. Therefore we must seek God in all the experiences of life and in all that is ... The truth is that the church, as *communio*, has not a purely spiritual character but is intimately involved in the building of the kingdom in the human city. The new heaven and the new earth are not only to be longed for in the next life, but are to be established here and now.
> It is one of the errors of our age to have established false dichotomies between religion and life, and between sacred and secular. The real distinction is not between religion and life, but between what is real and what is illusory; between a life lived in the truth and a life based on false hopes. Our faith reveals the truth about God and the truth about humanity, and so it is that St Irenaeus could say: 'The glory of God is the human person fully alive.'[26]

What is significant about these words of the Cardinal is the fact that he is interpreting the phenomenon of original sin, not in narrow historical and individualistic terms, but in the wider terms of a world in dire need of wholeness and healing, of the need for completion and fulfilment. He sees the mystery of incarnation as not just about the later putting right of something that went horribly wrong at the beginning, not just the desperate saving of an almost lost cause through the sin of our ancestors, but also about the vindication of the first creation, the affirmation of God's presence in everything that is, the delight of God in what God has made, whether or not there was some kind of historical fall.

In this instance, the role of the church is about the emphasis on original joy and blessing as well as, or rather than, on original sin and guilt, on affirming the glory of creation rather than on continually cautioning about its ambiguity and falsity, on pointing out the love and meaning to be discovered in daily life rather than on creating a dualistic dichotomy between the natural and the supernatural. The church exists, in part, to clarify the fact that if there is any line to be drawn, it is not the boundary-line between church and world, between good people and 'bad' people, between death and life, between angels and devils. What is clarified is that such a line is drawn, if we agree to use such unsubtle terminology, between authentic and inauthentic living, between sheer greed and a magnanimous attitude, between the truly human and the falsely human, between trusting and suspicion, between hoping and being cynical, between forgiveness and revenge.

For centuries, there has been a major element in our Roman Catholic belief system that sees the church as in conflict with the world, as a beacon of truth in a tunnel of deceit, as a recipe for life in a culture of death, as the holy mother of truth in competition with the father of lies, as a ship of saints in a sea of fools. But grace, as we have seen, is not like that. In recent months I have been privileged with free access to weekends with healing groups of substance-addicted and sexually-abused people following twelve-step programmes or other survival strategies. For them, salvation lay between opting for truth rather than for lies; for honesty rather than for pretence; for reality rather than for fantasy. The healing was palpable, the energy was undeniable, the growing was almost tangible.

These people had little time for the church as such – in fact they would hold that very institution responsible for much of their deeply-moving distress. Many of them deplored the clericalism that seemed immune to the raw reality of their human frailty in the face of relentless abuse. To be in the presence of people who had laid down their masks, who had no interest in making any impression other than the indelible mark of a shocking sincerity, who carried the strange freedom of having nothing left to lose, whose hope sprang from some pure, primal and natural energy, is to be renewed, inspired and made holy. Is this, I wondered, what every eucharist is meant to be about? Is this the

searing and sacred reality of redeemed humanity that hall-
marks the gatherings of Christian pilgrims? To people such as
these, and to the victimised and abused parts of all of us, it
makes a heaven or a hell of a difference whether the church in
which we find ourselves points to humanity as a sin to be atoned
for or holds us all up as a blessing to be celebrated.

Finding True North

North Yorkshire is a pleasant place of surprises. Yesterday the whipping waves were leaping white with playful fury against the dramatic headland visible from Whitby Abbey. The cold winds, too, were joining in the ferocious fun. They whistled through the Abbey's holy ruins like invisible invaders, reminding the few intrepid visitors of the stormy history of that still elegant edifice. And today, a few miles away in Rievaulx Abbey, by the river Rye, the home of Abbot Aelred, the greatest spiritual writer of his day, the September sun has brought back the peace to the countryside.

The dales and moors of Yorkshire are truly magnificent. Little wonder that the religious orders of the middle ages chose this expanse of land, this area of rolling pasture and swirling waters, for their abbeys, monasteries and priories. Within a few hours of travel you can explore the living albums of the spread of the Christian story among the ruins of Kirkham Priory, Byland Abbey, Mount Grace Priory, Fountains Abbey and many more.

At Whitby Abbey I found myself standing at one of the crossroads of Celtic and Roman Christianity. It was here, at the Synod of Whitby in AD 663, that the divided English church finally gave way to Rome and accepted many of the practices that shaped religious beliefs in this country forever. The Abbey had just been founded, by the extraordinary Abbess Hilda, on some land bequeathed by King Oswy of Northumbria in thanks for his victory over King Penda of Mercia. Like Iona Abbey and Lindisfarne, Whitby Abbey marks a unique turning-point in the missionary compulsion of organised Christianity.

Pagan Promise: Between Creation and Incarnation

I could not help comparing the peaceful embracing by the Celtic pagans in Ireland of St Patrick's version of Christianity with the acrimonious and often bloody encounters, a few centuries later, between the Roman episcopal style of church and the Celtic monastic tradition. On the one hand there was, as far as we know, around the fourth and fifth centuries, a cautious welcome by the Irish pre-Christians for a story about a God who became human to reveal the sacredness of all life and the beauty to be found in all kinds of light and darkness. They had many traces in their communities' myths about an incarnation that would end in a death and resurrection. On the other hand there was, again as far as we know, around the seventh and eighth centuries, a long period of civil war and destruction when two aspects of the same Christianity encountered each other, with a fierce campaign of force by the eventual victors.

The question in my mind this afternoon is about the precise nature of our still desperate commitment to evangelise and convert today's 'pagans' to another way of life.

Between the great religions of the world, and particularly within them, we find some of the most awful stories of coercion and intolerance in the annals of humankind. And even today, within Christianity, there is a dangerous compulsion towards an extreme kind of evangelism that can hardly be reconciled with the approach of Jesus Christ. I must admit here, as a Catholic priest, to a deep ambiguity within me about this whole issue. Our Christian scriptures tell us that salvation is to be found in the worship of the heart rather than in the ceremonies of this temple or that. The kingdom of God is within. Our Eucharistic Prayers reinforce the same salvific emphasis when referring to all who seek God with a sincere heart. What then is the precise nature of the good news that we are undoubtedly called upon to spread?

Many of us belong, in one way or another, to the Celtic tradition of Columcille and Colman and a host of missionaries who delighted in travelling recklessly far and wide, to bring enlightenment and joy to the most extreme parts of the world. Like myself, many priests will have studied in colleges and seminaries that existed for the sole purpose of overseas mission work. Poor people in numberless countries have saved their pennies to support the 'nuns and priests' who left home, families and careers to 'save the lost'. While there is no denying the desire of Jesus Christ that his church should serve, heal and liberate all people everywhere, bringing the message of reconciliation, hope, justice and peace to our earth and to all its inhabitants, it is not at all clear what such an enterprise really means today. The recent re-emergence of a traditional theology of creation, and a more enlightened understanding of mission, calls us to examine much of what took place within the missionary imperative of past centuries, and suggests a very different approach to the commandment to 'preach the gospel to every creature.'

One of the significant shifts in contemporary missionary techniques is the acceptance of inculturation as an essential element in the proclamation of the gospel. Pius XII touched on it; John XXIII stressed the plurality of cultures into which the good news must be received; Vatican II *(Ad Gentes Divinitus)* considered the relationship between religion and culture. For Paul VI what mattered was 'to evangelise man's culture and cultures ... right to their very roots' *(Evangelii Nuntiandi)*. Most insistent of all has been John Paul II. 'A faith,' he says, 'which does not become a culture is a faith that has not been fully received ... not fully lived out' *(Osservatore Romano*, 28 June 1982). Elsewhere he refers to inculturation as 'particularly urgent in evangelisation today' *(Redemptoris Missio)*.[1]

A current Christian incarnational theology of creation defends and proclaims the sacredness of all that God has made. There is so much of God in everyone and everything that exists. Albert Nolan reminds missionaries about the dangers of a 'holy arrogance' in their zeal for souls. He asks them to remember that God's footprints are already discernible all over those unbaptised hearts and foreign lands, long before the missionary arrives. God's image is clear in every creature because every creature is the fruit of the divine womb. If this is so, then is our mission, at home or abroad, to proclaim the holiness already within people and every creature, Christian or not, church-going or not, or is it to change them and turn them into another kind of being? To put it another way, does the church exist to spend itself in serving the potential for divinity within the world, or does it desire the world to be brought into the church for the church's own good?

Jesus called the twelve apostles, and then he gave them their instructions. He sent these men on missions, as the twelve, and he gave them the following instructions:

'Do not make your way to gentile territory, and do not enter any Samaritan town; go instead to the lost sheep of the

House of Israel' (Mt 10:9). Now, let me stop right there. There is always a tension, in the work of religion, between exclusivity and inclusivity. The conservative type overemphasises exclusivity; the liberal type overemphasises inclusivity. A person has to be a real artist, a real faith-filled person, to know how to hold them in creative tension. Jesus does, very well. In this particular line, he's emphasising exclusivity. In other words, a group has to have a sense of identity and boundaries before it can call people to it. We have to know who we are. We have to name ourselves ... (But) Jesus is talking about the kingdom which is beyond questions of exclusivity. 'Bring in the lepers, bring in the blind, bring in the poor to the banquet.' Jesus knew who he was. Only when we know who we are, however, are we meant to move out. So, the first thing he tells them is to find out who they are, what their group is. Once they have a sense of community, he can send them out. He says, 'As you go, proclaim that the kingdom of heaven is at hand. Cure the sick, raise the dead, cleanse those suffering from virulent skin-diseases, drive out devils. You received without charge, give without charge. Provide yourselves with no gold or silver, not even with copper for your purses, with no haversack for the journey or spare tunic or footwear or a staff ...'(Mt 10:7-10)

Jesus never tells his initial twelve apostles to set up a foundational, grounded place where people will come to them. That's the first stage of institutionalisation, and Jesus actually gives us no foundation for institutionalisation. It's clear that he is talking much more literally about a movement, and he uses every mythic image he can to keep us on the move, to keep us from institutionalisation. Jesus talks about a movement called the kingdom of God, and Paul turns it into a church ... At this point, at least, Jesus is not talking about local churches and people coming to us. He's saying that we should keep going out to them.[2]

True Christian compassion springs from an awareness of our interdependence and unity with everyone and everything. Pure missionary zeal is fuelled by this grace. It comes about from our sense of intimacy with the world, the earthly offspring of God's unconditional desire for unity. Is our mission then to guarantee, reaffirm and bless the Godliness of all life wherever we find it, and save it from the lovelessness and sinfulness of all that threatens it, or is it to impose a set of beliefs that is often alien or incomprehensible to those we set out to convert? In the early 1980s African theologians began to express anxiety that their people were praying in a liturgy that was not theirs and that they were being asked to live according to a morality that was not a conversion of their own previous morality. Because of the depth of concern about such matters, *inculturation* was given a prominent place on the agenda of the African Synod in April/ May 1994. Where do we find our model for laying the foundational principles of mission and evangelisation?

'As you enter his house, salute it.' (Mt 10:12) Let the grace flow through you. Give your blessing to everybody. We call it the gift of magnanimity. To bless others means to trust them, to empower them, to tell them, 'You're doing it right, trust yourselves. You've got the power; you don't need to rely on me for the power; the power is within you. You have already been given the gift of the Holy Spirit which has been poured out with generosity.' (And the people replied) 'You mean we don't need to jump through hoops? We don't need to buy some turtledoves and sacrifice them in the temple?' 'No. God forgives you as readily as this. God is on your side more than you are on your own side. Your job is simply to announce the gift, to give the gift of unconditional and free love of God, to keep telling all people that they are the children of God.'

Why is that so hard for us to do? All sacraments are metaphors. They're all just fingers pointing to the moon. But the moon was there before we started pointing to it ...3

I'm still thinking about the peaceful Pagan/Christian alliance in Ireland during the very early centuries and about the later, acrimonious Celtic/Roman encounters around the time of the Synod of Whitby. Am I right in thinking that Jesus Christ came only to purify, enhance and enrich the world into which he came? Is it in accord with orthodox Christian doctrine to hold that he came to reveal the love and meaning within the miracle of the first creation; that this first creation was, in fact, a primary kind of incarnation? Can a Christian hold that because the Word became flesh, once, sacramentally, in Jesus Christ, all flesh, therefore, reveals the Word; that the revelation of Jesus was about the divinity of the first creation; that he was the sacrament of the God indwelling in everything, in every leaf and every star and every creature? What does Christian mission mean if we start from the premise and the knowledge that every heart is already holy? And what does evangelisation mean against this background? And how do we, Catholics, rewrite a more appropriate sacramental theology and a theology of mission if such is the case?

The perennial question is about whether we make our God too small. Do we limit God to one (Christian) model of God's many self-revelations in the religions of the world, and then do we limit God to one (Catholic) version of the Christian revelation? Do we forget the empowering and challenging theology of creation that begins with Jesus, that is continued throughout the church's tradition, that is enshrined in the documents of the Second Vatican Council, and that has always been a central theme of life's mystics, poets and scholars?

Returning to the Beginning

The questions running through this book are about how the Catholic Church can recover the intention and the mind of Christ for today's world and how to prevent its (necessary) institutional presence from going desperately astray in its most essential aims and efforts. The imperative to self-preservation has led many an organisation to protect, defend and convert in a manner far removed from its first passion.

There are many who really worry that the church to which they belong has lost track of the beauty, magnanimity, universality, compassion, openness, trust and courage that marked out so distinctively the life of Jesus. Even in the face of our gradual erosion in terms of numbers at Mass and of ordained priesthood, of our seriously damaged image and credibility in many parts of the world, of the challenging voices of the 99% of those who make up the body of Christ, the Catholic Church, so many of us still refuse to accept the deadly evidence of the debilitating condition within our ranks, or any responsibility for the dry skeleton that we are in danger of becoming. In a world that is energetically bracing itself for a new millennium, teeming with creative and innovative ideas, it is rather heart-breaking that our presence is rarely requested.

These questions clearly apply, too, to issues closer to home. We are all familiar with an aggressive type of evangelisation that is far removed from the gentle spirit of Jesus. There are

many Christians deeply involved in dualistic and ultimately destructive campaigns. They have missed the most wonderful
point of the mystery of the incarnation. Most denominations
have a hard core of such 'enthusiasts', if not fundamentalists. In
their righteousness they seem to have no idea of the damage
they do to the essential meaning of incarnation. They draw a
deadly line between the experiences of 'ordinary, human life'
and the experience of God incarnate – between the awareness of
life as it is lived and the awareness of God's in-dwelling presence in all things.

Many people, including clergy, think that religion has to do
mainly with ideas and concepts and formulations. There is no
one to blame. We were trained that way. We get terribly trapped
in a shallow religion of legalism and ritualism. But true religion
is more than books. Spirituality is about more than the head.
Jesus was a person, not a doctrine. Biblical spirituality is very
different from institutional religion. Biblical spirituality is about
the way things are, about the present moment, about, according
to the mystics, the 'isness' of things.

> 'Ever since the creation of the world, the invisible existence
> of God and his everlasting power have been clearly seen by
> the mind's understanding of created things.' (Rom 1:20) We
> know God through the things that God has made. The first
> foundation of any true religious seeing is, quite simply,
> learning how to see and love what is. The contemplative in-
> sight is, first of all, learning how to see.[4]

But the matter goes further. When, for instance, a 'non-practis-
ing' mother brings her baby to be baptised, do we see the occasion as someone 'from outside' wishing to become 'saved' (de-
pending on the appropriate adjustments of lifestyle, pastoral
practice and Mass attendance on the part of the petitioning family)? Or, as priests, do we see our role as that of recognising the
presence of God in the parents and baby and of blessing and celebrating that presence in the sacrament of baptism? The Christian
community that welcomes the baby as one of the family, a beginning that will hopefully flower into committed membership, is
the community that holds this reverence for all of creation.
(How contradictory it is to read, in the current baptism rite,
'now you are a child of God' when the Hebrew and Christian
scriptures reveal that it is by virtue of birth we become children
of God.)

The mystics saw the birth of each new baby as another manifestation of God. 'Here comes God ...' they would proclaim at the moment of arrival. They saw every new baby as a guarantee of God's belief in humanity and in the future of the earth. Do we see the church as serving itself, or living only to confirm the holiness of the miracle of human love issuing forth in the birth of new life? Do we see 'the world' as the raw material for becoming 'church', or do we see 'church' as explaining and reassuring the holiness of life as it is? If we accept some validity for this way of interpreting the mystery of the incarnation, then there are many more questions to be asked about what we think we are doing when we are celebrating all the other sacraments. Do we approach these highly significant moments of human life from the point of view of trust in the sacredness of people's humanity and desires, or from an arguably dualistic and prescriptive agenda? Did not St Augustine say something about the love with which God loves us being exactly the same as the love with which we love each other?

When, in our diocesan or parish sacramental strategies, for instance, we outline the conditions for 'acceptance' of petitioners into the preparation programmes, the criteria that provide evidence of 'goodwill' and proof of 'regular practice', is there a danger of getting it all wrong? In a sense, are *we* not the privileged ones? Jesus seemed so delighted and honoured when the stranger, the sinner, the outcast, the foreigner, the undecided joined him for a meal or for a chat. He always played the role of the privileged servant. He saw the presence of his Father's love in all who came his way.

The church is the world where the world is most truly itself. In his *Christian Faith and the Future of the World*, Edward Schillebeeckx explores the orthodox theology behind such a statement. 'What the church has to offer us explicitly,' he writes, 'is already implicitly present in human life as a whole; it is the mystery of salvation. The church reveals, proclaims and celebrates in thankfulness the deepest dimension of that which is being fulfilled in the world.' These are the sentiments that would radically change our usual pastoral understanding of church and sacraments. Whether we describe them as personal encounters with Christ, or as rites of initiation into fuller ecclesial membership, or as peak moments in the life of the church, the sacraments basically take the earthly realities of our human existence, birth, reconciliation, sickness, love, struggle, and, to the eyes of faith, they show forth the deeper meaning hidden within, the silent activity of the Spirit, gradually redeeming and intensifying every aspect of daily life until the time when God will be 'all in all.'

New models for old

The notion of 'models' is great for abstract clarity and for developing concepts. It was used to good effect by Avery Dulles in his work on church and on revelation. When pushed too far, it can be too simplistic a device to cope with the complexity of its subject, and its uses become counterproductive. However, the strategy of 'models' or 'types' may help us here in discerning an appropriate process of evangelisation for the next millennium. Patrick Collins, CM, delineates three models of evangelisation as discernible within the Catholic Church – *sacramental evangelisation, charismatic evangelisation* and *political evangelisation*.[5] I will attempt to add a fourth model.

Sacramental evangelisation

There are many people today who agree that Catholics are over-sacramentalised and under-evangelised. This first model has contributed to that state of affairs. It is head-centred and aims at mental assent to certain doctrines revealed by God and taught authoritatively by the church. At the heart of this model lies the reception of the sacraments, regular attendance at Mass, obedience to the Pope and assent to all the doctrines of the faith. The required instruction, teaching and preaching is usually objective and lacking in an experiential dimension. To be personal about one's own experience of grace would be considered a form of subjectivism and self-promotion.

This is a fair description of the approach to priestly work adopted by the seminaries in which most priests, including myself, were 'trained'. Fr Collins believes that 'it is probably true to say that this model of evangelisation still predominates in the church of today. The present Pope puts a lot of emphasis on the need for instruction in objective truth. He obviously feels that the modern experiential approach to religion, with its distinctive models of evangelisation, is in danger of devolving into relativism and subjectivism.' In my opinion, this approach has had its day. Developed in the classical era of essentialist spirituality,

it is not well suited to the needs of the existentialist era in which
we live. There is overwhelming evidence for this conclusion in
the results of current research and official enquiries.

Charismatic evangelisation
Many of us will have some acquaintance with the model of
evangelisation known as kerygmatic or charismatic. Advocates
of this approach do not see the reception of the sacraments of
initiation as a sufficient basis for a vibrant life of faith and trust
in Jesus the Saviour. They seek for a way of promoting a heart-
felt awareness of the Lordship of Christ through a conversion
experience or through baptism in the Spirit.

Fr Collins explains that 'Evangelicals and charismatics believe that the *kerygma* (the good news) must be proclaimed and
backed up with testimony of how one has experienced its saving
truth oneself. *Life in the Spirit* Seminars, *Cursillo* weekends and
Alpha courses are good examples of this model. Evangelicals
also believe that the truth of the proclamation should be demonstrated not only in the witness of a holy and joyful Christian life,
but also by means of charisms such as healing and miracles.'

This approach is very biblical, personal and expects a sharing
of witness and faith-journeys. Certain strands of the popular
RCIA programme (for adults wishing to become full members
of the Christian Church through the Roman Catholic tradition)
follow these lines. Nevertheless, this exciting and dynamic
model, which brought a much needed joy and renewal to the
rather dry church of the first half of this century, is no longer
widely relevant. It belongs to a diminishing band of adherents
who tend, in their enthusiasm, towards individualism, subjectivism, personal feelings and private prophecies. Interested enquirers are often discouraged by the extremism of self-styled
charismatic movements who declare little interest in the official
teaching of the church in matters of liturgy and theology or in
the gospel call for action regarding universal justice, equality
and peace.

Political/developmental evangelisation
Unlike the charismatic model, the political model of evangelisation is urgent about precisely those gospel issues of fairness, justice and universal compassion. It shifts the emphasis away from
mental assent to doctrines, from personal rather than community

dimensions of Christianity, to gospel-inspired activity. It strives
to liberate people and communities from all that oppress them
such as personal and structural sin which are inextricably
linked. It holds that Jesus' kingdom is a thoroughly political notion. With Jon Sobrino it believes in a political love, 'a love that is
situated in history and that has visible repercussions for human
beings.'

This model of evangelisation is pragmatic in orientation, relatively new, and owes a good deal to the liberation theology
which has emerged from third world countries. It has been influenced by Marxist thought and by Catholic social teaching
such as found in Pope Paul VI's encyclical, *The Development of
Peoples* (1967). This liberation can take different forms. It can be
seen in structural terms, namely, that there are laws and institutional arrangements in society which are oppressive, evil, and
alien to gospel values. By showing compassion and love in these
practical ways, not only do these evangelists witness to the good
news, they themselves are evangelised in the process.

The liberation at the heart of this third developmental model
of evangelisation, especially in Western countries where there
are large middle classes, would have its meaning in terms of the
oppression which might be seen as psycho-spiritual, having to
do with inner hurts due to physical, emotional or sexual abuse
by members of the family or the wider community. Only compassionate love can prompt the practical and therapeutic action
that aims to alleviate such human suffering. As a result, human
development courses, counselling and therapy can also be seen
as an aspect of evangelisation.

Fr Collins introduces a third aspect of this political/develop-
mental model. 'As St Paul points out in Romans (8:19-22), the
good news is for all creation. But at the moment there is an ecological crisis as a result of the ruthless exploitation of the natural
world and the consequent rise in levels of pollution and global
warming. It could be argued that people who draw attention to
these problems, and those who try to alleviate them, are engaged in a form of evangelisation which often complements the
therapeutic kind already mentioned ... This approach interprets
the healing ministry of Christ in a contemporary and holistic
way.'

Incarnational model of evangelisation
For all its intellectual clarity and moral rigour, the terrible cold-
ness that the first model has developed into, has wreaked too
much havoc on countless numbers of God's people, and has
ended up in dangerously distorting the lovely revelations of
Jesus. In the second case, for all its spontaneous energy and at-
traction towards hands-on healing, the charismatic model is too
superficially self-oriented, too fundamentally exclusive and is
based on a rather dualistic theology. The third, developmental
approach seems relevant to the needs of our times while being
totally true to the gospel. It is experiential and practical in orientation. It is not afraid to get its hands dirty. It has no truck with
an elitist, triumphalist church. It is neither hierarchical, institutional, individualist nor clericalist. It believes that the poor are
the special people of God. It respects them and, without pious
sentimentality, it respects the potential of the poverty within all
people.

The model of evangelisation that I would opt for is near
enough to this developmental approach. There are several em-
phases to ensure. Stripped to its essentials, the good news is
about the amazing identity of each person and about our relationship with the mystery we call God. The only kind of conversion that I can give myself to these days, is that of recounting to
all and sundry the love-story of creation, the powers within humanity, the unconditional love of a beautiful Creator and Lover.
For me, evangelisation is about telling everyone I meet what
Jesus has revealed about the divine value of everything we do
and suffer and hope. This incarnational model of evangelisation
would set all the preaching and teaching of the church, the catechesis and celebration of the sacraments, in the context of a liberation from oppression, external or internal. It would enable the
blossoming of our humanity when lived in the presence of an indwelling God, the healing from the hurt caused by our own sins,
those of others and the sins that have become almost a standard
part of our social structure today. The good news I want to bring
to people is about the challenge to network with others all over
the world in a 'mystical body', a divine family, a company of angels, to heal and redeem and inspire a new beginning in a dying
church and a fragmented world.

Challenge to Change: Recovering a Passion for Life

This is the inspirational, incarnational vision that leads people back to the community that welcomed them wholeheartedly and delightedly in the first place, without placing any more demands to fulfil, or hoops to jump through, than Jesus did. But when will this understanding of sacrament be the norm? When will our sacraments be celebrated by the mass of grateful searchers for healing who will thereby find new love and meaning in the routine of their lives? How long will it take our ministers and teachers, our priests and parents, to insist on this primary purpose of church and sacrament?

> In the historical development of the Catholic sacraments, layers of theorising about the meaning and effectiveness of the rituals have removed them from the level of immediate experience for most believers. In addition, 'the sacraments have become so "churchy", so separated from the lives we live at home and at work and at play, that we no longer spontaneously relate them to the other symbols that surround and affect us.' (T. Guzie) Many Catholics no longer see their religious practice as a vital part of real life; this results in the loss of the transformative power of the sacraments, with which we might change the culture and restore the planet.[6]

When parents and children approach the Christian Church for baptism or first communion or marriage, do we fail to recognise that they are already ablaze with God's glory? Do we see them as lacking something that we, in the church, have to offer so as to alter their lives, or do we wish only to reveal to them the beauty they already carry, and to bless it, purify it and celebrate it with others in the family of Jesus? The kingdom of the Blessed Trinity is already within them; they are already made in the divine image, God's work of art; the instinctive, natural, human love that draws them together, that issues in a baby, that enables them to forgive and protect each other, to acknowledge their vulnerability and weakness, makes them co-creators with God and heirs to God's everlasting joy.

That is the good news we can share with them. We can honour their humanity because God did so in taking on the condition of flesh and blood. We can point out to them the holiness of their work, the divinity of their creativity, the spirituality of their struggle to survive in sometimes almost impossible situations. We in the church testify, confirm, guarantee and sacramentalise that amazing truth. Without such an institutional, public and required practice, the deadly reality of original sin would play havoc with hearts and minds so susceptible to the wiles and temptations of our deeply flawed nature.

It is not baptism that makes us members of God's family. To be baptised is not to enter the world of grace, because the grace and love of God is already there; it is freely given, it surrounds our existence, and we are all in contact with it from the first moment of our conception. But to be initiated into the family of Jesus is a different matter ... Sacraments proclaim and enable us to own a love that is already present to us. A sacrament celebrates the Lord's giving, certainly. But his giving is not confined to the sacrament. What we need to focus on within the sacrament is our taking the love of God home with us, with a fresh awareness of that love ...[7]

In an earlier book, I outlined some models and images for a developing understanding of priesthood today.[8] It follows quite naturally to imagine a human-hearted church in a similar way, to apply these same images to the mission of the church at the beginning of a new millennium.

As a *Farmer of Hearts*, the church becomes the explicit sign in the world of the holiness of each human heart, recognising there the same dream Jesus had for the abundant life. Such a church provides conditions for the nurture and growth of each person, recognising the rich yield that is harvested when gifts are used and celebrated. People's lived experience is honoured as providing the rich and varied tastes, colours and textures of this abundant harvest, rather than the bland monoculture which results from clericalism. The weeds of sin are noticed, but more vibrant is the church's blessing of any attempt, however small, to sow the seeds of love and hope. It follows that pastoral care, evangelisation and catechesis would reflect this vision.

A church which is a *Prophet of Beauty* seeks to proclaim the truth about the graced nature of all creation, about the dignity of each person, and about the eternal mystery that lies in the depths of each human heart. It is a sign in the world of the otherness of things, celebrating the multi-faceted ways in which the beneficence of the Creator is revealed, not only in the grandeur of nature, but also in the humdrum of daily existence. The church becomes a community of fellow mystics who trust in, and reveal to each other, the glory within humble lives, who inspire belief in each person's capacity *to perform even greater works* than Jesus, as he himself promised. (Jn 14:12) Liturgy and sacraments are crafted by the community to affirm and celebrate the divine beauty within all of life's experience.

A church which is a *Healer of Fear* makes manifest, in a wounded and broken world, the marvellous good news of the paschal mystery. By its life of prayer and deep faith, the church witnesses to the fact that once and for all on Good Friday it was only fear itself that stayed nailed to the cross, that even at the bleakest times healing and transformation are always possible, through the power of the Holy Spirit. As such the church is a beacon of hope in a society where pursuit of success and power are dominant. The church affirms by the way it reaches out to and embraces those on the margins, the wounded, the *anawim*, that it is in our very woundedness, at the point of our pain, that we are transformed. This witness is especially true of the institutional church of our day, which has had to bear many scandals and own its own weakness and sinfulness in real humility, but at the same time always trusting, with deep conviction, that within the heart of such pain is the seed of resurrection glory.

Close beside this, as an image, is the church as a *Soul Friend to Community*. Where the church is proclaiming the communion of all life and each person's need of a caring, nurturing community, it recognises that this will not be realised without holy women and men within the church listening compassionately to individual stories, and honouring, too, the intricate movements within their own soul. Whenever people have enough courage and trust to risk 'bearing their soul' to others who listen in an altruistic spirit of healing and compassion, then grace flows beyond those concerned and the whole community is enriched. This is nowhere more dramatically expressed than when the church celebrates, in the sacrament of reconciliation, forgiveness as the place where liberation and growth take place.

Then, as *Weaver of Wholeness,* the church is able to gather all the multicoloured strands of people's lives, their faults and failings as well as their gifts and strengths, and weave a tapestry of truth and justice, whose pattern emerges as an ever-loving, extravagant and merciful God. Through all its rituals and sacramental celebrations, the church has the golden key to unblock the door of resistance, enabling grace to flow freely to reveal the heart of a compassionate God.

Two other images which are vital for a Christ-centred church are *Voice of the Silent*, and *Sacrament of Compassion*. If the church is custodian of the Word of God, entrusted to speak this living gospel to the world of its time, it follows that it first needs to hear the Word within its own heart. This means a continual process of renewal and growth and calls for a real dependence upon the cutting edge of the scriptures to form and inform, to inspire and energise, to enflesh the Word, to discern the movement of the Spirit. The extent to which the church is able to recognise its own inner poverty in its compassionate interaction with the world, will reflect the extent to which a two-way ministry can operate. In other words, the church will embody in its vision and mission, the need it has itself to be healed and blessed by the 'little ones' of this world. It is not simply that the gospel imperative demands that the church stands alongside and acts in solidarity with the poorest of the poor, the refugee, the down and out, the drug addict, but that the church discovers the secret that it is the voice of such marginalised people which brings the wholeness and authenticity and transforms the church's own preaching and mission.

Fr John O'Donohue, addressing the 1998 National Conference of Priests in Ireland, coined the beautiful phrase *Minder of Thresholds* as an image for priesthood today. He grounds this in a theology of creation that proclaims each moment as holding new and endless possibilities, and the human mind as 'the place where the infinite and the eternal are glimpsed and felt. In this primal sense every individual is a sacrament, viz. an active and visible sign of invisible grace. Though the outer form and activity of our lives may fascinate, burden or distract us, in our deeper nature each one of us is called to be priestess and priest ministering at this vital threshold where the eternal transfigures time and where the divine heals the human.' This image provides a powerful insight into the role the church has in awakening individuals to their dignity and to their potential for ministering at this threshold of divine compassion. The church is the visible sign making divine presence explicit in the variety of situations in which people find themselves. Through its liturgy and sacraments it opens people to the mystery of ultimate presence, most especially in the eucharist, where, '… damage, shadow, negativity and limitation are urged towards real presence. The sad transparencies of human hunger become the Bread of Life.'9

The church ritualises and celebrates in sacrament the most crucial threshold moments of the human journey. The essential and very privileged role for the church at these moments is to reveal, through its human, compassionate accompanying, the intimacy of God's love in the depths of the human spirit. Honouring the significant milestones on our journey through life in this way would mean that sacramental celebrations would truly awaken each individual and the community to the possibility of transformation that lies at the heart of each unique experience.

The word 'minder' has connotations of looking after, protecting and guarding, whilst 'threshold' conjures up images of stepping into the unknown, of leaving something behind, of taking a risk. For the church to be a *Minder of Thresholds,* it would be in tune with all that is at play within a person's heart at times of significance and great change in life, and how those around, family, friends and community, are profoundly affected too. I'm thinking most especially of threshold moments of life and death, of marriage, that amazing act of trust when two people commit themselves to each other for life, and also of the less dramatic, more routine daily thresholds when we pick ourselves up, begin again and need the nourishment of the Bread of Life and the communion of each other to continue. How the church understands its role in enabling people to cross such intimate, vulnerable, challenging and profound threshold moments will inevitably be reflected in its pastoral vision.

If we accept models such as these as appropriate for the whole institutional church of today, then we must face a radical revisioning of many of our unexamined assumptions regarding the meaning of 'being church'. This whole renewed way of looking at the meaning of the incarnation, the revelation that was Christ, the purpose of Christianity, the significance of church membership, will have immense consequences for our pastoral procedures regarding, for instance, parish policies towards the celebration of the sacraments, with particular relevance to 'admission' strategies for baptism and first eucharist, the role and content of the RCIA programmes, the critiquing of evangelising programmes such as Alpha and others, the decisions we make about those who may not receive communion, etc. Such a development and transformation of our understanding of the message of Jesus will also have important implications for our definitions of sinfulness, unworthiness and conscience.

Priests and parish leaders who follow a more open approach to such matters, whose first reaction to a request for some kind of involvement from a seemingly 'unsuitable' parishioner is one of gratitude, who see themselves in the role of rather inadequate servants, testify with joy to the continuing participation of so many enquirers in the life of the parish. Where the rules are not so hard and fast, where the searching hearts of 'hit and miss' members are honoured and trusted, where the holiness of each tiny sign of goodwill becomes the deciding factor, where the human welcome of Jesus is the first experience of the one who seeks something from the sacramental church, then, as sure as spring follows winter, our communities and congregations will grow. Anyway, in the light of people's attitude to Christianity today, we are scarcely in a position to take a 'hard line'. Many pastors will testify to the harm done by the harsh judgements on damaged people by the 'hardliners' of the past.

I could put in a phone booth the people who have left the church because of Hans Küng or Leonardo Boff, but I could circle the globe with the people who have left the church because of the arrogance of the institutional church, because of the arrogance of Rome, because of my arrogance. We try to hold on to the grace of God and dish it out only when we think other people are worthy, only when we think other people are law-abiding and have played the game our way.
Brothers and sisters, the pain is too great in the world. The pain is too great to be niggardly with the grace of God. The discouragement is too great in the church, right now, to waste time criticising the church; we don't need more criticism or negativity. We have the power to trust our own experience and to trust our own journey and especially to trust our own heart. It is in our heart that truth resides and grace is available and God is offered ... Live it, love it, give it away with joy and abandon. There are many people starving on this earth and too many people spiritually starving in the church ... to those of you who are women, I tell you that human consciousness finally has reached the point of honouring the feminine. But we desperately need, in our church, the recognition of feminine consciousness. It is the only thing that is going to, humanly speaking, balance out this church and lead us to the next stage.[10]
Strong and healthy then, our communities and the enquirers

will grow because the spirit of Jesus will fill our churches. Vibrant and creative they will become because, in losing our fearful and protective attitudes to church membership, in ending a very common perspective which places church over against world, we will embrace all people with any love in their hearts into the centre of our family, knowing that only *through* that experience of belonging, not *before* it, will hearts be changed. Is it too much to believe that from within the experience of this kind of loving acceptance a new church is bound to emerge, a church bearing all the Calvary wounds and the resurrection joy of Jesus? For the church, too, the only way of recovering the vision of Jesus is to begin living it today.

Spirituality: Personal and Ecclesial
We have considered some of the reasons for people's departure from the church. One of the most common, I think, concerns the lack of nourishment available at the weekend liturgy. There is an inner hunger, consciously felt or not, for spiritual meaning in a materialistic world, for some explanation why bad things happen to good people, for reassurance and guidance about relevant issues in their lives, for affirmation and encouragement about new beginnings after old falls. Not only is this hunger not being recognised or met, they say, but people's heart-felt searching is not even perceived or understood.

> When will religion learn? It seems that in two thousand years we should be getting the point by now. Jesus did not come to create enclaves of righteousness. The gospel is not intended to create in-house groups that can feel morally superior to other people. It's meant to create free people who have an excess of love. That's how we recognise people filled with the Spirit – magnanimity and excess. If we have to hold on to it and protect it and define it and defend it, it isn't grace, and it isn't God. God does not need our protection. God just needs instruments and heralds.[11]

And so, many of these disillusioned souls decide to 'go it alone', to find their spiritual sustenance elsewhere, to renew their energy through their friendships, their community events, their hobbies and interests. They do not need, they claim, to be members of the church, on any level, any more. In fact, they hold, belonging to a church that is out-of-date, irrelevant and dualistic is, far from providing new life, new hope and healing, more of a negative, limiting and burdensome experience.

Today we are experiencing a serious breakdown of a church culture built around conformity, uniformity, blind obedience to authority, religious attitudes that border on superstition, notions that the sacred is separate from human experience, and strict control over people's thinking and acting ... (Among middle-aged people this new mood) is evident in their refusal to be tied to a Sunday Mass obligation under the pain of serious sin; in their refusal to allow church authority to discount their experience and sincerity; in their refusal to tolerate liturgies which do not nurture their faith or affirm God's presence with them; and in their refusal to work any longer with a system of governance which is not able to break new ground because it is locked into a theological worldview steadfastly resistant to change ...[12]

Karl Rahner has no doubt that the Christian of the future will be a mystic or he or she will not exist at all. This forthright statement has found its way into all kinds of theological hypotheses about the future of the church. Does this mean that the nourishment of the mystical dimension of the church is our most important calling just now? Is this the only aspect of our church that will surely live on and grow and save the world? And, before that, the individual human heart must cherish the mystic within it. This is something we often forget – that human experience must precede any tidied-up doctrines, that all true theology begins with individual or communal experiences, that it is only in the light of the human, mystical experience of God, which is the real basic phenomenon of spirituality, that theology, validated by scripture and the church's teaching, acquires its ultimate credibility.

It has already been pointed out that the Christian of the future will be a mystic or he or she will not exist at all. If by mysticism we mean, not singular parapsychological phenomena, but a genuine experience of God emerging from the very heart of our existence, this statement is very true, and its truth and importance will become still clearer in the spirituality of the future. For, according to scripture and the church's teaching, rightly understood, the ultimate conviction and decision of faith comes, in the last resort, not from a pedagogic indoctrination from outside, supported by public opinion in secular society or in the church, nor from a merely rational argument of fundamental theology, but from the ex-

perience of God, of his Spirit, of his freedom, bursting out of
the very heart of human existence and able to be really experienced there, even though this experience cannot be wholly
a matter for reflection or be verbally objectified.[13]

When so many people find no relevance to their lives in the
teachings of the church, I'm sure that it is because we've forgotten the traditional truths explained by theologians such as Karl
Rahner. We have forgotten that human experience comes first,
as it did at the very foundation of the church, built, as it was,
around the human person of Jesus. It was only after the friendships, the forgiveness, the human intimacy with their loving
companion, that the first Christian gathering began to form. This
is the vital element that so many Catholics miss. They feel that
the church has lost its human heart, and so has lost its soul.

And yet, however much we wish that the institutional
church were different, and understandable as the 'going it
alone' of so many 'lapsed Catholics' seems to be, a strong case
must be made for the necessity of a church-context for the saving of our souls and those of others. If the spiritual journey is to
remain on course, if the discernment of spirits is to remain true,
if individual mysticism is to remain open to what Karl Rahner
calls, in his *The Spirituality of the Future*, the 'collective experience' of the Spirit, then there is a need for some place of belonging, some community of identity, some social rites of celebration
in so far as most people are concerned. However far a Christian
may drift from, or be driven to, as a result of the regrettable distance between the revelation that Jesus was, and the current
state of the Catholic Church, it is difficult to understand how a
Christian life, completely removed from a structured religious
company or institution of some kind, can continue to remain
healthy and balanced.

That is why we Catholics have so much work ahead of us, because, in general, without an organisation the revelation cannot
grow and spread. Jesus did set the criteria for an assembly of
some kind, a regular gathering, a eucharist people, a visible
sacrament. About that there is no doubt. Much of the vision may
have been lost, the compassion no longer evident, the trust at a
low ebb, but it remains the case that the people of God will always need a shape, a strategy, an identity, a common faith, a
name, a liturgy, a regular source for renewal.

Many of the thousands who are disappearing annually from

the churches of these islands are moving to joyful and intimate groups and house-churches less rigid, less formal and more life-giving than our own. Karl Rahner is well aware of this state of affairs. He wistfully recalls the time when the church was the object of an almost fanatical love, regarded as our natural home, sustaining and sheltering us in our spirituality, where whatever we needed was available as a matter of course and had only to be joyfully and willingly appropriated. The church supported us; it did not need to be supported by us.

Today all this is different. We do not see the church so much as the *signum elevatum in nationes,* as it was acclaimed at the First Vatican Council ... The church can be an oppressive burden for the individual's spirituality by its doctrinalism, its legalism and its ritualism, to which true spirituality, if it is really authentic and genuine, can have no positive relationship. But none of this can dispense the spirituality of the individual from having an ecclesial character, least of all at a time when solidarity and sociability in the secular field are obviously bound in the future to increase and cannot decline.[14]

The Soul of the Catholic Tradition

Because, then, we are social animals by nature, we forever need the context of community structure, with all its rites and trappings, its symbols and codes. No matter how sophisticated we become, these primitive traditions and imperatives will always be an essential part of the definition of our humanity. And since our spirituality, our capacity for divinity, is at the heart of our becoming, so will the ecclesial context for our journey together to God.

Having said that, there are special reasons why the Christian Church, particularly in its Catholic tradition, is the unique context for our exploration into Mystery. For those people who find new spiritual life in the creation tradition, it is of particular importance that the Catholic Church should recover the soul of its uniqueness. This uniqueness has to do with the essential meaning of the incarnation and with the implications of that mystery for our reflective lives.

The reason that the Catholic tradition (as with all Christianity) is vital for the nourishment of the searching, thirsting human heart, lies in its insistence on what is called the 'scandal of particularity' – the belief that in a certain place and at a certain time and in one person called Jesus, God became human. There is a raw earthiness about this belief not found to the same unrelenting extent in any other faith-system.

Many of the hundreds of thousands who leave the churches these years do so because their belief in the holiness of their own experiences is not validated by their required religious practices. Such alienated Catholics will not always express their often subconscious reasons for leaving in these explicit terms but they do find a kind of dualism and irrelevance in the liturgies and worship of which they have grown tired. This is such a shame because of all the religions of the world today, the Christian one offers the clearest authentication and validation of this spirituality of their hearts.

> Indeed, only Christ, as the Word of God made human, can offer a reasonable explanation as to how a transcendent God, totally Other, can also be experienced from within the world: consciously by mystics, unconsciously by graced individuals … The principle and instrument of all grace is the hypostatic union, the archetype of a new form of relationship between God and the human being and the foundation of the unsurpassable covenant made between them … Here lies the scandal of particularity: while the mystical practices of the other world religions are designed to facilitate the laying aside of material impedimenta so as to let being be reabsorbed into the world's origin, Christianity alone dares to contradict this programme by its assertion of a God who entered into and became a part of history, making his own body, on the cross, the unique bridge between the finite and the infinite.[15]

The word 'scandal' is traditionally used to emphasise the shocking nature of the assertion that God became human in Jesus Christ at a particular time. It is indeed a scandalous belief to the millions who reject it. And at the same time, Christian belief has never relented from its insistence on the total humanity of this Word-made-flesh. Here lies the key to the urgent and unending quest of a contemporary society bereft of true meaning in the whirl of their daily lives. It is precisely in the humanity of Jesus that the revelation of the significance of each one's earthly existence is found. (Vatican II, *Document on Revelation*, para 22) This revelation unblocks the vision of the eyes of the heart so often confused by the unredeemed dualism that is often presented as genuine Christianity. It pours love and meaning into all the aspects of human living, the diminishing forces as well as the quickening ones.[16]

If we, as Catholics, were only persuaded more vehemently about the priceless insights into our lives provided by the mystery of the incarnation, instead of wandering off either in despair or in a desperate search for a better belief-system, we would cherish the *splendor veritatis*, the brightness of our own truth that shines new hope into our lives. We would realise that everything we seek for in another country is already available in all its richness at home.

> Only in Christ, in whom all apparent opposites are unified, without mingling, can the partial insights of the various world religions reach a satisfactory account of the God-world relation, within a narrative that situates their own story of sin and grace between the beginning – the pre-existent Logos, and the end – his glorious parousia as the Word incarnate ... It is precisely according to her own revelation that the church is able to find nuggets of gold in these other religions. 'The Catholic Church rejects nothing which is true and holy in these religions. She looks with sincere respect upon those ways of conduct and of life, those rules and teachings which, though differing in many respects from what she holds and sets forth, nevertheless often reflect a ray of truth which enlightens all men.' (Vatican II, *Nostra Aetate*, 2) Jesus Christ is *totus Dei*, 'wholly God' but he is not *totum Dei*, 'the whole of God.' Without the Son we cannot speak of the Father, yet that speaking is never completely exhausted in history, for the Spirit constantly calls us into a deeper understanding of God in Christ, not least through the challenges of the other religions.[17]

There is something innate to the heart of humanity that finds a holiness at its own centre. Human beings carry a readiness for discerning the presence of God in their inmost selves. This belief in the rumour of an immanent divinity is central to almost all faiths. It is also at the heart of much of today's religionless longing and implicit spirituality.

The basis for a theological understanding of the religions of the world lies in the universality of God's presence and action in the world. These religions are human responses to God's all-encompassing presence and activity, where God works, as in all forms of created being, as the ground of being and meaning, and the source and end of being's fulfilment. However, this universal claim is based on the particularity of the incarnation and atonement in Jesus Christ: it is in the particularity of his unique epiphany that Father, Son and Spirit are disclosed as interacting with the world as the single source of creation, of reconciliation for an alienated world, and so for the fulfilment of creation itself ... In the radiance of the epiphany – light to enlighten the Gentiles and the glory of God's people, Israel – the church can see more, not less, even though the historic revelation is completed and we can expect no fresh truths but only the unveiling of truth's own face in the age to come. The church, en route between Pentecost and the parousia, can continue to find analogues of her own truth in the cultures of the unbaptised; not merely, indeed, echoes of the truth she knows consciously, but instruments for the fuller appropriation of its inexhaustible richness.[18]

How strange then, that the very guarantee of the validity of such longing and searching, namely the birth of God in human form which bestows an immeasurable dignity on all creatures and on all creation, should be so dimmed and dulled and distorted within the churches, as to be unrecognisable by those who need it, as the plant needs water. And how ironic it is that the Christ-moment was the culmination of these very intimations of the universal human spirit in its openness to the Other, regarding the possible humanising of a Creator God, and once this incarnation had happened, that the Christian formulations and doctrines of it are drawn from the life-experiences and heart-responses of those whose lives were intimately touched by the beauty of Christ. Just as the packaged loaves of bread in the shops were once small seeds that began their journey in the soil and were shaped into maturity by warm sun and nourishing water, before assuming their final and finished form on the tables of our homes, so too, the church has garnered the good wheat of truth from the divinely-crafted green fields of nature's waiting, human expectation and pagan culture for the better understanding and appreciation of the meaning of Christ, the final harvest.

In spite of the rampant individualism of a post-modern mentality, it still holds good that all those who have decided to 'go it alone' in following their true hearts, need to celebrate and be purified and invigorated by the ecclesial company of those other seekers of truth and beauty. Far from directing people away from the instinctive impulses and natural impetus of their discerning hearts, of which the Catholic Church in its fear of trusting human nature is often accused, the church, on the contrary, ought to cherish the growing multitudes who believe in the inherent goodness of all created things, while in no way ignoring the realities of what is meant by original sin. The church ought to proclaim itself as champion of the creation tradition and the creation theology which endorses such people's yearnings and embraces them into the company that re-focuses, expresses, refines, affirms, celebrates and intensifies such divine aspirations.

... For Damaged Beauty needs a New Design ...
So what kind of water will green the desert parts of our ailing church over the decades ahead? What kind of flesh will enliven the dry bones of a lifeless liturgy in a new century? What will be the characteristics of a courageous community undergoing a new lease of life and celebrating its vibrant compassion with great joy?

* Such a community would not emphasise fear. Its ideas and images of God would be full of unconditional love and compassion. God would be presented only as the intimate healer of our lives, not the one to blame for what goes wrong.

* Salvation would not be emphasised as the escape from hell or punishment but as individual and communal freedom – the freedom from darkness to light, from fear to trust, from ignorance to wisdom, forming a true communion of hearts and minds.

* Such a community would delight in the way God is present and reflected in its midst. It would encourage its members to heal each other and the whole world like Jesus did. Members would be encouraged to live out their baptism as priests and prophets. All parts of the community would learn to listen to each other.

* Never again would good, decent, loving human experience be divorced from the arena of the sacred. We would recognise and name our human loving as a sharing in God's self and a sign that God is intimately a part of who we are.

* All the liturgies would reflect the human condition of those present and absent – the joys and sufferings, the hope and despair. They would be creative and earthy, physical and relevant. They

would glorify God while lifting humanity into completion and redemption. 'Ownership' of sacramental arrangements would be widely shared.

* The meaning of priesthood would be explored so that the lay faithful would form the heart and head of the church in truly collaborative ministry. The challenge to make appropriate and courageous changes would be taken seriously rather than giving in to the fear of taking a risk. 'I have been troubled that an increasing polarisation within the church and, at times, a mean spiritedness, have hindered the kind of dialogue that helps us address our mission and concern.' (Cardinal Bernardin)

* A new humility would replace what sometimes appears as pride and arrogance in our leaders. The ever-present threat of insitutionalism and clericalism would be constantly discerned by the community. There would be a greater awareness of the competition and rivalry, cynicism and jealousy that are never far away. 'The good news we proclaim is about transformation – and even transfiguration – of the community and of the beauty of a unity which has a deep respect for the different and the diverse.' (Bishop Hollis)

* The human need for spiritual nourishment would be deeply recognised and appreciated. Mission and ministries would arise out of meditation and prayer. The enriching implications and realities of the incarnation for the abundant life of the individual and the community would be explored and proclaimed. This would entail much trust in each human heart and in humanity in general.

* A sense of mission would mark out the community. People would be called to nurture their vision together, to share their passion for the reign of God and to give their best energy to the forming of the Body of Christ in their midst. Enthusiasm, commitment and personal gifts would be acknowledged and wholeheartedly encouraged.

* In a willingness to relinquish its claims to exclusivity, in an admission that it does not hold a monopoly on religious truth, in an openness to the reality of God's presence everywhere, and in the belief that God's presence is constantly creative and beyond our present imagining, the Catholic Church will be a renewed beacon of hope and leadership in our world. 'All these combined could lead us *beyond* ourselves into awesome wonder as we engage the mystery of a God beyond all imagining, *into* our-

selves as we contemplate the wonder of who we are, and *toward* others as we accept the challenge of incarnating God's presence on earth as courageously and lovingly as the man who died on a cross two thousand years ago.'[19]

* The church in a new millennium must be broad enough to encompass undreamed-of technological achievements in the fields of genetic engineering, biotechnology, reproductive technology, etc. 'A spirituality suitable for the probable future must be broad enough to encompass the coming age of space, including the likely colonisation of the moon and closer planets within the lifetime of many of us, among yet other undreamed-of technological achievements. At the same time it must be able to address a world situation of increasing poverty, of likely global catastrophes in the ecological order, and of widespread famine and epidemic, as our ability to cope with political, medical and economic problems on our home planet is outstripped by the pace of population growth, environmental deterioration, and runaway social changes.'[20]

PART TWO

Pilgrimage Renewed

A Wider Spirituality

While the structures of religion are crumbling and while many fear that there is a widespread breakdown of moral standards, the need for some kind of spirituality, however we define that reality, seems to be increasingly discernible. The almost universal traces of what can generally be called a spiritual search is unprecedented in the history of the divisive dualisms that have gripped both religious and secular government for some centuries now. It is the curse of an all-pervasive dualism that has sharpened the appetite of those who hunger for the missing sense of spiritual wholeness and graced power. This hunger is for a wider, unified vision; it is about transcending the limits we place around our human potential, about a breakthrough from the negative habits that bind and control us, about an evolution towards the new becoming that is calling out to us, beckoning us forward in hope. In the long run, dualism, because of the gap it places between the human and the sacred, is a denial of the incarnation.

Like a hand-held torch that flits here and there in a dark room, now illuminating one special place, now another, the following reflections skip between various and neglected sources of God's presence all around us – sources of spirituality in each other, in matter, in the whole world, in all of creation. This chapter is about a spirituality that is wider than a salvation/redemption type religion would understand. It sees the 'saving of one's soul' in terms of universal healing and community transformation, as well as of personal concern. It tries to recover the sense of cosmic reality and holiness, a central dimension and fascination of contemporary society.

We yearn to reclaim the deep, primal sacred story of our evolving universe; of planet Earth as our cosmic home; in the diverse and magnificent array of life-forms around us; in the

largely untold story of the evolution of spiritual consciousness within humanity itself; and, finally, in the contemporary
desire to create a one-world family characterised by love, justice, peace and liberation.
The spiritual landscape we explore is both ancient and new.
For us as humans, spirituality is a natural birthright, which
over the millennia has been weaving a tapestry of elegance,
grandeur and beauty, with the inevitable scars of an evolving
universe. At this time of global transition, we need to re-con-
nect with that great tradition and reclaim it afresh in the context of our new evolutionary moment. Could any task be
more exciting? Could any be more relevant? And could any
be more urgent for the changing times in which we live?[1]

The term 'spirituality' is notoriously difficult to define. Among
many other characteristics, it has to do with openness, risk and
trust. Many hold that it happens at the margins of our awareness. It is at the boundaries of our consciousness, at the limits of
our normal thinking, that the burning is brightest. When the
Holy Spirit is involved, there are no definitive agendas, no blue-
prints for tomorrow. There is a God of surprises, a Spirit of
chaos and creativity that critiques, confuses and confounds
those who are too stuck in their religious systems. For the
church, many say that a new day is dawning and that a new passion for the possible is moving in towards the centre from the
vibrant margins.

At a time when few contest the truth about the breakdown of
the church system, as well as that of the social order where
human greed is destroying the natural resources of our world,
there are many also who are sure of a cultural and religious renewal, a global resurrection that calls for new qualities of heart
and mind in those who would understand and facilitate it. We
would be very foolish to ignore those counter-movements of our
years that herald in a timely, spiritual revolution to change the
emphasis and direction of the Christian presence in our rapidly
changing culture. There are innumerable signs and symbols of
this revolution. None of them are full of pure light. They all
carry their shadow-side. But they do reveal a significant trend, a
hunch we dare not ignore, a kind of *sensus fidelium* that points
towards a waiting truth. One of the truths revealed by many
thriving fringe church groups which practice meditation, yoga,
healing ways, creation spirituality, spiritual rituals, women's

workshops, therapy sessions for the abused, is that the mainstream churches, emptying by the week, are not supplying a
deeply-felt need for the nourishment of their own members or of
others who seek help.

Christian Metaphor – Boundary or Horizon?

Some decades ago, the Religious Experience Research Unit,
under the directorship of Sir Alistar Hardy, placed notices in the
popular newspapers requesting stories from people who had
undergone some kind of religious, numinous or spiritual experience. Among the many revelations that emerged from this
scholarly and still-continuing research, was the fact that church
membership and regular attendance militated against the fre-
quency and possibility of such moments. Instead of opening up
the faithful to a readiness for the transcendental, the dualism of
most official churches closed people's psyches to an experience
of the spiritual in nature and creation itself. Over-organised
faith became a *boundary* rather than a *horizon*.

This is all the more strange because everything that is authentic about and essential to the Catholic tradition of Christianity is deeply and beautifully sacramental. Of all known religions of revelation, it is most aware of the divine presence in
every aspect of creation. The story of God-becoming-flesh is the
most potent of all in sensitising the mystic in each one of us to
the immanence of the sacred. The transcendent God is not only
totally available to all in bread and wine, but in every heart,
breath, leaf, insect and molecule. A creation-centred and primordial theology of sacrament – of the sacrament that Jesus was
and is, of the church as sacrament, of the seven sacraments, of
the Word itself as sacrament – all offer a depth of spirituality to
green and excite even the most hungry, needy or jaded, human
spirit. I truly believe that once our churches begin to honour the
aspirations of our human souls, to nurture human creativity and
imagination, to overtly and consciously foster the richness of
humanity and to celebrate its gifted lay people, new miracles of
growth and healing will happen. Once these windows are opened
the view becomes longer and clearer and the horizons become
more enthralling and fascinating.

The Making of the Boundaries

Two issues relating to boundaries seem worthy of exploration.

The first concerns the unique centrality of Jesus in God's ways with the world. This uniqueness can be interpreted in a whole range of approaches to the meaning of the incarnation. At one end it assumes the shape of a closed fundamentalism that is often aggressive and even violent in the hard-line exclusivity of a fixation on the divine Jesus, based only on selected scripture texts. At the other, it is no more than a vague unscriptural, untheological support for an aquarian belief in a crucifixion-free caricature of a heaven-on-earth with the cosmic Christ. The question is raised here only because it will be raised again and again in the debates of the future. (*A Church with No Walls* in this book, deals in greater detail with this vital discussion). Two recent recipients of the Vatican's dreaded summons to Rome have theologised, in an apparently unacceptable way, about the place of other religions in God's economy of salvation. It is a most exciting debate. As well as the more familiar and thorny question about the supremacy of Roman Catholicism among other denominations, we now have to ask about the extent to which Christianity is supremely God's choice, so to speak, among the religions of the world. Karl Rahner's brave suggestion that members of the non-Christian mainstream faith systems were really 'anonymous Christians' has gained little ground, and for obvious reasons! Bede Griffiths was fond of referring to Cardinal Newman's belief that 'there is something true and divinely revealed in all religions over the earth'. But it is difficult to reconcile an uncompromising commitment to Christ with a reverence for other revelations. Diarmuid Ó Murchú pulls no punches here:

> In the popular version of our Christian faith, there prevails a type of theological imperialism which I feel I have often colluded with in the past and which I now perceive to be arrogant and oppressive. I refer to the Christian claim (to which Judaism and Islam also subscribe) that our religion contains the fullness of revelation, in the light of which all other religions are deemed to be somehow inferior . . .
>
> It seems to me that Christians have deviated quite seriously from the central message of the Christian gospel: the New Reign of God (Kingdom) promised to all a radically new egalitarian community characterised by justice, love, peace and liberation. In trying to enculturate this message over the centuries, we have extrapolated Christ from the Kingdom

vision and made him the subject of a personality cult … Jesus
did not preach himself; he told stories about the Kingdom of
love and liberation, and invited his followers to be salt of the
earth and light for the world, inspired by the same spiritual
vision. We need to transcend the narrow focus on the individual hero whom we have made so heavenly that we frequently betray the incarnational engagement which seems to
have been central to Jesus' own life and for which people are
hungering today.[2]

Another inviting and absorbing issue is about the place of matter, the earth, creation and its unfolding in the Christian story.
Over the decades I have puzzled about this and will continue to
do so, I hope, for many a day. It has to do with the God of creation, the God of Jesus and the God of the Catholic Church. They
are all drawn so differently. While there are, obviously, some re-
semblances between all three, they are still, to my mind, generally
irreconcilable. Sometimes I dwell on the wild imagination of a
divine artist who flamboyantly created the millions of incredibly
shaped forms of species, flora and fauna and human, extrava-
gantly absurd, amazingly and fundamentally amusing, one tiny
part of eighteen billion years of superbly-timed evolution,
which in itself is but one small fraction of an expanding cosmos.
So amazing is this playground of God that human resources of
imagination, mind or technology cannot cope with it, and all of
this is in the embrace of a patient, all-powerful and compassionate energy we can only call divine mystery. I find it, at times, almost impossible to hold that beautiful image in any credible
way, together with the seemingly limited, fearfully exclusive
and tamed image of God as portrayed by the institutional
Christian churches of today.

Like Teilhard de Chardin before him, Diarmuid Ó Murchú
reached for a rock as a symbol of an enduring reality, a reality
that has been around for a long time.

My species has walked this earth for an estimated 4.4 million
years … Anthropologists and archaeologists inform us that
we have exhibited distinctly spiritual behaviour and values
for at least 70,000 years. Perhaps, most enthralling of all, is
the highly artistic and creative spiritual ferment focused
around the great Earth Mother Goddess, that informed our
spiritual awareness as a universal species for an estimated
35,000 years (from c.40,000-5000 BCE).

As I sit at the rock face I ask myself: How is it that our theology and spirituality never refer to these realities? Why does our supreme religious wisdom choose to ignore the elegant divine-human co-creativity across the expansive wonder and beauty of creation? Why do most books on spirituality allude only to the Christian experience as if God did not even exist prior to Christian times? Is it possible that our anthropocentric needs have become so self-absorbing that we are in danger of suffocating ourselves in a religious enclave devoid of mystery, wonder and breadth?

Increasingly, I find myself in sympathy with the spiritual seekers who claim that formal religion, with its trappings and power games, is proving to be a major obstacle to spiritual growth and development. Religion sets limitations, and lures the seeker into dealing with issues which seem to belong to the perpetuation of the system rather than the growth of the person. The system in turn, instead of empowering the person to engage with the world in a transformative way, inhibits, and often directly militates against, the task of transformative justice. The anti-world polemic still dominates the formal religions.[3]

There is little joy in quoting such sentiments. In fact I carry a sense of guilt and unfaithfulness when I touch on these matters. But a stronger sense of urgency and trust and courage calls some of us to speak out in this way. Diarmuid Ó Murchú writes of the sadness and fear he feels when he thinks about these things. His sadness arises from the fact that a believing Christian like himself can deviate so far from what is perceived as the true faith. But he is only expressing the thoughts and feelings of thousands of Catholics these days in the face of certain leaders who pursue a closed system of salvation. This may seem a harsh thing to say but, I'm afraid, it is true. Ó Murchú's fear is that the wavering or unconverted might find his views attractive and then veer even further away from the way of orthodoxy. (My own guess is that an honest critique of our Catholic institution and our apologies for its most obvious faults and failings, will only offer more hope and faith to disillusioned millions.) He therefore thanks God and people for the inherited Christian faith which has sustained him and inspired him to follow the path he has chosen. I quote him at length because he wrestles so courageously with the questions from which most of us retreat.

I encounter two dominant Christian approaches. The first, and most prevalent, continues to be a closed, stultifying model often presented with a veneer of modernity and inclusiveness. Theologically, it goes something like this: Jesus Christ, as Messiah, embodies the fullness of God's revelation for humanity. Jesus is the measure and completion of all things, including the religious and spiritual aspirations of all time. Spiritual growth demands total submission to Jesus so that we can become totally like him in this life and live with him for ever after death.

This is called the boundary model, with its patriarchal, male, white Saviour firmly ensconced like a king on a royal throne (the dominant metaphor for much of the Christian era), and in whose name everything is prescribed and validated. Boundaries are set: theological, ethical, spiritual, ritual, within which orthodoxy prevails and outside of which one is considered to be unfaithful on a spectrum stretching from 'dubious' to 'outright heresy'. The great danger I see here is that in setting boundaries around the religious system, we also hem in the living Spirit and, theologically, we pursue questions which have more to do with our needs than an understanding of God's life in us or for us. Evangelical groups and movements adhere to the boundary model in a particularly vitriolic way, shielding the spiritually malnourished and petrified with an idolatrous God-image, largely designed on the childish fears of insecure human beings.[4]

The Mind's Horizon

Many other people, however, even though challenged and feeling uncomfortable in the face of open space rather than boundaries, will identify with an alternative horizon model. I have often preached on the opening prayer of the Pentecost eucharist about the vigour of the Holy Spirit as he/she sweeps into our lives 'with the power of a mighty wind, opening the horizons of our minds by the flame of her wisdom'. Ó Murchú writes:

As an alternative to the boundary, I propose the horizon model, one which embodies in a more integrated way the inspirations of many spiritual seekers of our time. We are dealing with an open system, focusing on Christ the primordial embodiment of God's New Reign in creation which continues to grow and develop until the end of time. Our starting point here is what the gospels call the New Reign of God, the trans-cultural faith community for which Jesus is the first and exemplary disciple. This is, above all else, a community of mission, catapulting its members into the heart of creation, where all creatures (and not just humans) co-create with God until the Kingdom comes to its fullness.

Our reflections raise even more profound questions for contemporary spirituality, recurring questions posed by many mystics down through the ages. The Jesus who inaugurated the Reign of God and continues to foster it as Risen Cosmic Saviour, is about something larger, more expansive and more inclusive than the church, but also about something more profound than formal religion. We tend to assume that Jesus came to establish a new religion, and we went ahead and invented a religious system in his name, a cultural strategy that may have been necessary to establish Christianity as a religious and moral force, but the price we paid was a fundamental betrayal of what gives heart and soul to the Christian faith in the first place ...

Could it be, therefore, that Jesus was not just about the transformation of religion, but rather about the end of religion? In evolutionary and cosmological terms, could it be that religion is merely a temporary reality that may well have achieved its purpose, and perhaps is now outliving its usefulness? The experience of many contemporary spiritual seekers suggests that large numbers of people are outgrowing the need for formal religion. They seek spirituality, but not religion. The retrieval of spirituality as the primary dynamic of human, spiritual growth may be the supreme challenge facing humanity in the next millennium. It is an exciting, but daunting, prospect.[5]

Many readers may well be shocked at this. Indeed, Ó Murchú has been taken to task for the vehemence of his black-and-white, overly simplistic distinctions between spirituality and religion, between sacramental community and formal institution, between heart and head. Let me quote from a letter written by Fr Sean Fagan, (and I agree with its contents) critiquing Ó Murchú's book, *Reclaiming Spirituality*:

I can understand Ó Murchú's anger. There is much in the church's history, past and present, that makes me angry and thoroughly ashamed of it ... Ó Murchú's basic weakness is

his anger at the institutional church and how this has damaged, if not destroyed religious life. He fails to see that tension between the institutional and the charismatic is not only
natural, but healthy and fruitful. But he also seems to forget
that the church itself is both charismatic and institutional.
Without the institutional church (with all its faults) we
would have no sacred scripture or sacraments ...[6]

Nevertheless, Ó Murchú has the courage to express his prophetic
vision and dares to ask the questions that most of us shrink
from, knowing well that it takes a long time of trial, error and
persecution, to discern the timing and turning, to hone and craft
the words, images and touchstones of our heartfelt hunches and
of the work of our God-given intelligence. There is no painless
plan for the work of the prophet. Even Jesus was killed for trying to express and to live his vision.

Above or Within?

Just as so many of the world's attitudes towards the powerful
Deity that controlled the mysteries of life, death and judgement
were radically altered at God's self-revelation in a small, vulnerable baby, so too with our attitudes towards our seemingly vast
and often-threatening world full of wars, destruction and
human evil. Many observers of the history of human growing
hold that, in recent centuries, one photograph alone did more to
develop our attitudes towards our earth, than any other single
event in war or peace – the astronauts' picture (1969) of the
world we live on, floating and turning like a small beautiful ball
of blue against the blackness of space. This was a moment of immense spirituality for planet Earth. It was a revelation about the
stirrings of the human soul – deep, archetypal movements of interdependence, belonging and, therefore, of compassion. In a
creation-centred church, this phenomenon of wonder would
have been celebrated with intense joy and thanksgiving as a
mini-miracle of insight into how God sees us and how delighted
God is with our beauty.

Among the many revelations from this most blessed epiphany
was the reminder that formal religion is a comparatively recent arrival, no more than 5,000 years old, whereas spirituality has spun
from matter for billions of years. As a church we have forgotten
that the reality of spirituality is wider than that applied to humanity. This is the reason for the dead weight of so many religious

traditions. The energy of the spiritual has been confined to human beings; the graced life-force that is part of the definition of matter has been presumed to be found only in conscious subjects.

Ironically, the redemption of spirituality is likely to emerge from where we would least expect – from the creation itself, especially as we relate with its daily impact in our capacity as earthly, planetary creatures. In this encounter, we begin to come home to our true selves, as the progeny of a reality greater than ourselves, without which our lives are seriously deprived of meaning and purpose. As we connect with the cosmic womb of our being and becoming, we will rediscover that our spiritual hunger is itself an expression of a sacred life-force, animating planet and universe alike. It is not we who make creation holy or sacred; rather, we are endowed with an innate yearning for spiritual wholeness because that happens to be the fundamental essence of the planet and universe we inhabit.[7]

James Lovelock recovered the hypothesis of the Earth as a person, Gaia, in which the delicate balances of all that keeps our universe functioning and orderly are somehow within the resources and intrinsic definition of our world. It is as though its internal soul is capable of self-renewal and self-organisation. We are all only at the margins of discovering this awareness – an awareness that came so naturally to those we call primitive, the native American Indians, the Celts, the Aborigines, the Maories and so many others. The divine presence and creative energy was felt and acknowledged, not around or outside nature and evolution, but at their centre. Nobody can match the elegance and authority of Teilhard de Chardin in his insight into this mystery:

Blessed be you, mighty matter, irresistible march of evolution,
reality ever new-born, you who, by constantly shattering
our mental categories, force us to go ever further and further
in our pursuit of truth.

Blessed be you, universal matter, immeasurable time,
boundless ether, triple abyss of stars and atoms and generations;
you who by overflowing and dissolving out narrow standards
or measurements reveal to us the dimensions of God.

Blessed be you, mortal matter, you who batter us and then
dress our wounds, you who resist and yield to us,
you who wreck and build,
you who shackle and liberate,
the sap of our souls,
the hand of God, the flesh of Christ;
it is you, matter, that I bless.[8]

The famous photograph filled our hearts with such sentiments.
Some of the reflections of the astronauts read like psalms of
praise or eucharistic doxologies. A space traveller from China
echoed God's great love for the world when he said, 'Seeing the
earth for the first time, I could not help but love and cherish her.'
Edgar Mitchell wrote that his first view of the planet was 'a
glimpse of divinity.' And Russell Schweickart's meditation is
profound and moving: 'You realise,' he wrote, 'that on that
small spot, that little blue and white thing, is everything that
means anything to you – all of history and music and poetry and
art and death and birth and love, tears, joy, games, all of it on
that little spot out there. You recognise that you are a piece of
that total life ... And when you come back, there is a difference
in that world now. There is a difference in that relationship between you and that planet, and you and all those other forms of
life on that planet, because you have had that kind of experience.'[9]

Ideally, our Catholic Church with its fine tradition of rites
and rituals, its elemental symbols and its endless source of
graced power in the true meaning of incarnation, would be the
champion and sacrament of a holistic holiness, of a creation spirituality, of an incarnational theology such as proclaimed by a
host of mystics, theologians and prophets throughout the centuries. These are the people who have revealed some of the rich
mystery of the Word-become-flesh, as they celebrate the potential divinity of all creation and of all flesh. The church has never
totally lost this tradition. It is there in all the sacraments, in all
the Eucharistic Prayers, in the beautiful Prefaces and Solemn
Ritual Blessings, in the Holy Days, the Rogation Sundays, the
devotions and the processions. But somehow this life-giving
emphasis has been mislaid, left aside in the perennial self-cen-
tredness of ecclesiastical anxiety and institutional defensiveness.
A huge part in the vision of a renewed and vibrant church turns

on a reclamation of the wholesome and whole-hearted trust in the goodness of humanity, of nature, of matter, and, most especially, of evolution.

It is the process of evolution itself, rather than any set of human experiences, that lies at the heart of our spiritual story. Out of the primordial silence, there erupted a massive, explosive burst of energy, which we now call the Big Bang. Where it came from remains, and probably always will, the eternal enigma for some, the eternal mystery for others. It seems important to note that it came out of silence, a quality of nothingness that contained the raw potential for the elegance and creativity we see all around us.[10]

Revealing the Power

So much is written these days about Celtic spirituality. Beyond the doubts and arguments concerning the precise meaning of the term, it is safe enough to say that within this fine tradition the presence of God, for most Celts, was a very tangible and daily experience. The secret of a radical renewal for today's churches lies in the proclamation of that good news. Beyond miracles and wonders, beyond fundamentalism and dualistic evangelism, beyond an authoritarian discipline and a last-ditch effort to anchor a drifting institution, it is in the revelation and celebration of the sacredness of every moment and movement of human life that the churches and world will be saved. The mystics and poets, of course, always had it. It is in the 'isness' of things that God is found. God is 'pure being' according to Thomas Aquinas, and Jesus is the one who, in his humanity, revealed that truth.

Jesus purifies us and liberates us into the awareness that the presence of God is revealed in the essence of everything, that all creation, everything that is in the heavens and on the earth, is penetrated with interconnectedness, according to Hildegard of Bingen, penetrated with relatedness, and is already full of grace and blessing. Like a sudden dawn that makes sense of shadowy outlines, revealing the beauty, symmetry and sheer delight of vast landscapes, so too, the understanding and believing in the nearness of God transforms our lives in the most amazing ways. One of these amazing ways is the conviction that all our truly loving emotions carry the fullness of God's essential being. This conviction is a huge threat to many Catholics. Yet no less a traditionalist than St Augustine held that, 'the love with which we love each other is the very same love as that with which God loves us.' It is in this sense that we redeem each other when we love each other. Written by a friend, I received this beautiful blessing last week:

Because I love you, you are eternal.
Because I believe in you, you are born anew each day.
Because you speak your dreams, you are a prophet of hope.
Because you reveal your shadow, my heart is made holy.
Because you bear your pain, your touch is full of compassion.
Because you let yourself cry, your tears water my soul.
Because you hold me close, I know the holiness of my body.
Because you laugh and play, you set free the child in me.
Because you believe in beauty, you open a window on ecstasy.
Because you are ready to forgive, healing happens all around you.
Because you have a passion for life, I believe all things are possible.
Because you write words of wisdom, my imagination catches fire.
Because we dare to trust, love is incarnate.
Because I love you, you are eternal.

I'm not writing these words on top of a hill overlooking the land and sea on a sunny day. I'm writing them behind a rain-lashed window by the side of my mother who is probably breathing her last few breaths. And the eucharist we celebrated at her bedside this morning was a sacramental gathering of every aspect of her life and love, including every laboured gasp of her present painful condition. During that Mass we reflected on the way that God's transcendence permeates the human reality of her marriage, motherhood and final surrender into the abyss of death.

Too often we keep the 'now' and the 'not yet' too far apart. Every sacrament collapses these differences between the present and the future. Every sacrament is a mysterious gathering of past experiences which are already part of our tomorrows. Nothing in our lives is ever wasted. Because our lives are the manifestation of God's essence on earth, because everything is grace, nothing is lost; all is harvested in the barns of heaven.

What a difference it would make to our faithful people if they were challenged each week to believe in their creative power, to use their God-inspired imagination, to trust in the healing energy of their humanity, to follow the purified yearnings of their hearts, to rejoice in the goodness of their lives, to celebrate their ability to bless and heal and save each other. We are called to be thresholds for each other through which we pass from aloneness to belonging, from sin to grace, from confusion to meaning, from being stuck to breaking through, from despair to the other side of pain. We are called to be, for others, safe bridges from fear to love. Referring to conditions in South Africa, the theologian Albert Nolan wrote:

> All these experiences of going beyond some limitation or restriction are experiences of God, because God is transcendence. God's voice is the call of transcendence that challenges us to go further, to do more, to try harder, to change our lives, to venture out into new areas and into the unknown ... God is out there calling us to move beyond the system, beyond sin, beyond suffering, beyond our narrow and limited ideas of what is possible.[11]

Another Perspective

In another book I have tried to outline the kind of theology of incarnation on which this kind of thinking and believing rests.[12] It is none other than an orthodox doctrine, thoroughly Christian, found in all truly classical theologies, and gaining widespread support in the work of our best theologians today. Unfortunately, and for all kinds of worrying reasons, such insights find little or no place in the current, official catechesis and Christian formation of these years.

This developing approach seems, in fact, to be more widely reflected in the best of contemporary, independent, secular institutes of spirituality and philosophy, where there is permission to draw up theological curriculums in the light of current trends in church-going and in response to ordinary people's spiritual needs, in a climate of alarming change and transition. There seems to be a fear within the ranks of most mainstream Christian churches, and particularly of the Catholic one, to take the incarnation at its face value – that God really did take a huge risk in becoming so vulnerably human, that a dualism which still insists on a radical separation between God and God's creatures is a contradiction of orthodox Catholic teaching.

Philosophical and spiritual texts tend to draw a sharp distinction between immanence and transcendence. This
smacks of dualistic opposition which is not merely unhelpful
but may be dangerous and misleading. The distinction is
often used by writers who seek to safeguard the 'beyond-
ness' of God, the God of pure mystery who is radically above
and beyond anything we can conceive or imagine. The concern seems stronger in the monotheistic religions, perhaps
because they propagate various notions of the embodiment
of God in our world, a feature that is most pronounced in the
Christian conviction that God entered fully into our world as
a human being like ourselves. The fear that we might im-
merse God too much in the world of our daily experience –
the immanence – is based on an anthropocentric tendency to
dictate who and what God should be for us.[13]

There is nothing to fear in thus addressing all aspects of our
faith, especially when so much is at stake for the future of both
church and world. Where the church is concerned we are witnessing the cost of forbidding even discussion on contemporary
concerns within our denomination. Truth is not glimpsed or
protected by such measures. Nor is faith best served by such
startling distrust. And there are much deeper issues that will
continue to challenge from within. 'Christianity,' writes
Rosemary Ruether, 'for the first time in history, is faced with a
large scale challenge to the patriarchal interpretation of religion
and to an increasingly coherent vision of an alternative way of
constructing the tradition from its roots.'[14]

Where new developments in our world are concerned, a
deeper trust in creation and in human invention would encourage a more confident and courageous stance on the part of the
church, in reading the signs of the times. In the editorial of
today's *Independent* (Jan 2nd 1999), church leaders are taken to
task for not providing guidance in the moral maze of choices
and decisions:

The real priests of the future are scientists and the real challenges for the future are scientific, in that the great dilemmas
of morality and politics are set by the expansion of human
knowledge (forever transcending the *status quo*). Above all
we face the choices posed by genetics. In the next century it
will be possible to clone human beings and, for rich people,
to select many of the characteristics of their offspring, includ-

ing intelligence. Humans will be able to control not just their future, but their evolution as a species.

These are not developments to be afraid of, although many of their consequences may be disturbing, not least because such knowledge also offers the possibility of solving the overriding problem left by the 20th century, of humanity's unsustainable use of the earth's resources. Too often, the lay person's (*and the Church's* – editor's insert) instinct is defensive and Luddite – ban cloning, impose a moratorium on testing, stop finding out how to do difficult things – instead of embracing the possibilities that the search for knowledge brings.

Leaving aside the almost impossible position in which the churches find themselves in having to deal with questions posed by the undreamt-of advances and developments at so many levels of human progress, having only a very inadequate and dualistic theology to work from, we find a similar scenario when we ask questions about spirituality at both individual and community levels. 'Can we continue to assume that religion contributes positively and constructively to our evolution and development as human beings? Is religion outgrowing its spiritual usefulness? Is the age of formal religion coming to an end?'

These are not just questions of some weird, new-age atheist or agnostic. They are very real questions of our time, largely confined to the inner searchings of the human heart and rarely spoken aloud for fear of misunderstanding, harsh criticism or outright condemnation. Pastorally, we tend to take such questions to the religious representatives of our culture (clergy, spiritual directors, theologians), but many of these people have a vested interest in maintaining the religious *status quo*, and because of their own spiritual and theological formation, may not be sufficiently receptive, vulnerable and informed to hear the echoes from the heart that accompany the spiritual search of our time. [15]

Primary Revelation

Many of us were weaned on a doctrinal diet of fear and suspicion of 'mere humanity' and of a soulless, material world; we were reared with a deep-seated guilt for somehow or other colluding in the death of Jesus with the ensuing threat of hell so clearly spelt out. It is not always easy for us to find a sure perspective from which to craft another more positive and hopeful overview of the meaning of Christianity, for a more loving understanding of humanity and of the gift of creation. Drilled into us at school alongside the penny catechism, and hammered home in the seminaries of the fifties and sixties, was the advice to distrust our bodies and our world because both were the source of temptation and even evil. Riddled with original sin, the quicker we escaped from this place of trial and testing, the better. While the extremes of such a terrible dualism are no longer taught or preached except by the fundamentalist or severely evangelical wings of our main Christian churches, it is still only just below the surface in the message and approach of many teachers, preachers and church rulers today.

This whole mindset arises from what is often referred to as the 'old cosmology'. The word 'cosmology' need not frighten us away or turn us off. It is not very clever to ridicule terms and concepts to do with the cosmic, the mystic, the prophetic. In the next few pages I hope to explore a few areas that may not be immediately familiar to the reader. I do so only because I fully believe that without such an exploration, the desire of the Pope (himself a thorough cosmologist) for a new Christian springtime, will remain unfulfilled. And so, at least a rudimentary understanding of cosmology – a dominant worldview – is necessary for all honest seekers after a healthy way forward for the Christian churches. There are many easily available sources for an accurate introduction to the subject in contemporary literature. The 'old cosmology' which profoundly influenced the churches during the last few centuries, was materialistic, dualistic and patriarchal. It no longer speaks to today's generation, either spiritually, scientifically or theologically. Thomas Berry refers to its influence over the past 200 years:

> During this time the human mind lived in the narrowest bonds it has ever experienced. The vast mythic, visionary, symbolic world, with its all-pervasive numinous qualities, was lost. Because of this loss, humanity made its terrifying assault upon the Earth with an irrationality that is stunning in enormity while we were being assured that this is the way to a better, more humane, more reasonable world.[16]

There are no band-aid solutions for our ailing church; no magic formulas for immediate health. Nor will our leaders' selective concessions here and there make any lasting difference. Redrawing some of the less significant boundaries will not change the immovable land-mass; tinkering at the liturgical or ecumenical edges will not alter the solid, resistant centre. That is why we need to explore deeply to find the church's true foundation, to find the place where the institution first began to lose sight of its vision and then risk losing touch with its soul. The theologians and the physicists help us to grasp some of the meaning, and some of the implications for the Catholic Church, of a new cosmology.

The new cosmology, the new unfolding story of the universe, overtakes and overwhelms all we ever knew about the planets in general and our earth in particular. Planet earth is understood to be a living organism, carrying within it all the immensely complex energies for its own gradual evolution and completion. When you listen to people like Thomas Berry and Brian Swimme, as I had the luck to do, you cannot fail to be fired up with their exciting insights and passion. New insights are reported, almost daily, in the papers. An amazing discovery lies in wait for those who invest even a little time and effort in looking through the physicists' windows of wonder. The New Story, as the current revelation is often called, is profoundly simple even though you may have to grapple a little with concepts such as interdependence, differentiation, interiority, communion and consciousness. This same New Story has the power to enrich and develop our Catholic theology and study of scripture.

One example may help to explain this statement. According to the old, dualistic cosmology, not much happened by way of revelation until Jesus arrived on the scene. Here, in Jesus, was the real beginning after the collapse of God's original plan for the world. And here, in Jesus, uniquely, was the fullness of revelation, denied to all other religions. In very general terms, a great deal of current church teaching rests on such beliefs. The new cosmology offers a radically different understanding.

It claims that creation itself is the primary revelation; that God's life and love become visible and tangible first and foremost in the unfolding of universal life. In all its aspects, including the polarities of light and shadow, creation and destruction, the divine becomes manifest; creation glows with the light and life of God. In this context, each of the religions is deemed to be a particular crystallisation of God's revelation for a specific time and culture. All of which suggests that the mainstream religions are destined to last for limited periods of time, and have a cultural significance for specific peoples rather than a relevance for the whole of humanity.

Spirituality rather than religion is the central concern of the new cosmology. It seeks to explore the spiritual meaning of the evolutionary process over the billions of years before humanity ever came to be ... The new cosmology is not seeking to overthrow formal religion with its claim of having special access to divine revelation. Instead, it seeks to re-locate God's co-creativity where it perceives it to belong primarily – within the co-creative process at large, and not merely within the minute time-span of the past few thousand years, during which the formal religions evolved.

In positing this fresh and challenging view of revelation, the new cosmology affirms a central conviction of the present work, namely, that the spiritual unfolding of life – at every level – is governed by a grandeur and elegance which we humans seek to control to our own detriment and usually to the detriment of creation also. This is a wisdom, which, fortunately, is out of our control. The supreme spiritual task of our time is to let go of our anthropocentric craving for dominance and superiority, and learn to live interdependently with our co-creative God.[17]

An awareness of interdependent co-existence is at the heart of the Hebrew and Christian scriptures but it is foreign to contemporary, greedy humanity. Where there is no communion between humans, there is little hope of any networking between people and the rest of the non-human creation that make up our planet. All of this kind of thinking forms the core of traditional Christian belief and, yet, so far have we drifted from our creation-centred and incarnational moorings that we do not recognise our original vision, and cry out in alarm when the compass is reset for such a horizon. At the heart of the new cosmology is the conviction that we belong to the universe, not the universe to us.

We cannot discover ourselves without first discovering the universe, the Earth, and the imperatives of our own being. Each of these has a creative power and a vision far beyond any rational thought or cultural creation of which we are capable. Nor should we think of these as isolated from our own individual being or from the human community. We have no existence except within the Earth and within the universe.[18]

All of this, in a renewed church, would be accepted and celebrated in Word and sacrament, with great delight by God's people who are encouraged to see themselves as facilitators and co-creators in continuing episodes of the New Story. Jesus is the one who reveals the love and meaning already filling the womb of the earth from the first moment of creation. He is the one in whom the paradox and breakthrough of evolution make sense. He is the blessed sacrament of the divinity within all matter, the emergence of the holiness of human life, the new consciousness of what was already, but half-hidden, within the miracle of the first being and of the first becoming.

In Jesus' life, death and resurrection, the New Story finds its coherence and credibility. Though chronologically later, it is in the incarnation of Jesus that the purpose of God's first creation is forever established. It is against the pattern of the death and resurrection of our Saviour and tremendous lover, that all the deaths and resurrections of the tiniest hearts as well as of the mightiest constellations, acquire an infinite value. And it is in this sense that the eucharist, with its earthy symbols of bread and wine, guarantee and confirm that our world is, indeed, the beautiful body of God.[19] There is no need to be afraid of this kind of thought and imagery. They are part of our Christian heritage. They are the mother's milk on which the Christian mystics were weaned. They fill the pages of our traditional Catholic rituals and blessings. They are wholesome and healthy, nourishing and safe, life-giving and liberating.

Far from being an agnostic or pantheistic development, the new cosmology evokes deep sentiments of love, respect, tenderness, care and creativity. It expands the narrow horizons of both traditional science and orthodox religion, and forges fresh connections with the long-lost feminine and intuitive values of our spiritual heritage. It invites us to outgrow the dualistic opposition of the sacred and the secular, the earthly and the spiritual, challenging us to engage with the God who transcends all our human distinctions and yet enters profoundly into our creative reality as human, planetary and cosmic creatures.[20]

The Ministry of Women

No one sews a piece of unshrunken cloth on an old cloak; if one does, the patch pulls away from it, the new from the old, and the tear gets worse. And nobody puts new wine into old wineskins; if one does, the wine will burst the skins, and the wine is lost and the skins too. No! New wine, fresh skins! (Mark 2:20-22)

To write about the role of women in the church, as it is today, is like trying to pour that new wine into old skins! We have to do away with old skins, break with old ways of thinking, let go of traditional, old paradigms of church, before being able to explore in a creative way, the role of women. The word *paradigm* is commonly used today to mean model, perception, theory, a frame of reference. A paradigm of church is the way we see the church in terms of understanding, perceiving, interpreting. It is the lens through which we see the church. The idea proposed here is that there needs to be a paradigm shift – a way of seeing the church from another perspective and looking at the role of women through that particular lens. A paradigm shift means that everything takes on a new interpretation, and change can only occur when we see things differently. Although we are concentrating on the role of women, that cannot and should not be divorced from the role of men. Change will be change for the better, and will be better for everyone. So, new wine, fresh skins! What will the new skin of a woman-friendly church be like?

A Church of 'Communio'

The church of the future will surely welcome, recognise, nurture and use every available gift and talent. Priority will be given to the full and active participation of all the people of God. In line with what Vatican II had said, *Christifideles Laici* recommended that, 'It is necessary that the church recognise all the gifts of women and men for its life and mission and put them into practice.' (Para 49) And again, 'The church seeks the recognition and use of all the gifts, experiences and talents of men and women to

112

make her mission effective.'[1] At the heart of this document lies the vision of the church as *koinonia* or *communio*. The meaning of these words comes from the New Testament and we can glimpse something of their meaning in words like partnership, shared life, joint partaking. Fundamentally we are talking about our communion with God, through Jesus Christ, in the Holy Spirit. Through our baptism we celebrate sharing in the life of the Trinity. We celebrate our immersion into the life of God, into the life of partnership. This partnership, communion, shared life, is first of all with the Trinity, but also with all the baptised. Together we are church, together we are the People of God, together we are the Body of Christ. We are baptised into partnership.

This oneness of the Trinity is where we find diversity of persons, each distinct, each equal, each having their own function and yet bound together by love. This, of course, is the perfect *koinonia* and it is what we, as church, are called to be. This truth takes us beyond distinctions such as male and female, clergy and lay. We look forward to a church where real partnership exists and where gifts, talents and skills are used no matter to whom they belong – male-female, child-adult, young-old, gay-straight, black-white, rich-poor, able-disabled, clergy-lay. Any talent that isn't fostered and developed is wasted, and that person fails to realise her/his full potential and the church, as a whole, is impoverished by a failure to recognise and use the talents of all her members. The result is that the whole body suffers.

God put all the separate parts into the body on purpose. If all the parts were the same, how could it be a body? As it is, the parts are many but the body is one. The eye cannot say to the hand, 'I do not need you', nor can the head say to the feet, 'I do not need you'. You together are Christ's body; but each of you is a different part of it. (1 Cor 12:18-21, 27)

What gifts and talents do women have to offer in this church, this *koinonia*? Let us begin by looking at priesthood. The *Catechism* describes the priesthood as a means by which the church builds itself up. *The Sign We Give* names the primary task of the priest as enabling communion to grow, rather than 'running a parish.' 'To fulfil this task, the relationships the priest develops will be of major importance. It is through the quality of relationships that he will most effectively invite people to make full use of their gifts and energy in ministries and other activities.'[2] Penny Jamieson, the first woman in the Anglican Communion to become a diocesan bishop, feels that some women are particularly skilled at exercising this relational style of leadership. She says, 'I have observed women, through the quality of these relationships, giving a church a strong sense of its worth and a strong affirmation of its being ... These leaders are skilled at recognising and affirming the gifts that God has given and they encourage their use, knowing the point at which delegation is possible. They co-ordinate the community, ensuring that all are working together and that the efforts of each person contribute effectively to the whole.'[3]

Carol Lakey Hess argues for a style of leadership that she calls 'caretaking leadership', which is marked by 'conversational education, hard dialogue, and deep connections.'[4] Sandra M. Schneiders says that feminist spirituality 'prefers networks to chains of command, webs to ladders, circles and mosaics to pyramids, and weaving to building. It wants discourse to be both rational and affective, dialogue to replace coercion, co-operation rather than competition to be our usual mode of operation, power to be used for empowerment rather than mastery, (and) persuasion to take the place of force.'[5]

We need look no further than the women in our existing communities who, outside of the church, are examples of the success of such styles of leadership. The church, if it is to survive, needs them. For years women have met in one another's homes, created networks of support, helped with one another's children and families, and formed and built up neighbourhood groups. They have been excellent builders of community and wonderful carers. Women have so much to offer in the field of pastoral care. In Penny Jamieson's experience, 'Women clergy have both a reputation and a good track record for being effective in pastoral ministry.'[6] She has also found that her womanhood is a source of grace when dealing with others on a pastoral level. She says, 'When I reflect on what I do – using the opportunities that my experience as a woman offers me – it seems to me that I am seeking to make space, "wombspace" if you like, where others can grow and experience the life-giving power of the Spirit.'[7] This 'wombspace' is a time to 'hold the space' when an issue has been named. A time to wait in patience and prayer. She likens her 'wombspace' to a sheepfold. They are both enclosure and room for growth. Priesthood in the Catholic Church is desperately in need of 'wombspace'.

As well as denying the skills of women, exclusion from this ministry has other consequences, described by Anne Thurston in her article 'The Ministry of Women':

> The startling fact of the incarnation has made it possible for the human community, male and female, to image Christ. For me this is the most compelling argument for the ordination of women. The absence of women presiding at the key sacramental moments in the Christian life has resulted in a lopsided symbol system. The verbal assurance of the equality of male and female is contradicted by the absence of the sign language, which affirms that equality. In that sense, arguing from the perspective of equal rights for women is not as critical as the argument which seeks to express more adequately the truth of the incarnation, that Word was made flesh, that *homo factus est* does not mean *vir factus est*, that God is present in the human community, male and female.[8]

In the same article she talks about the relational nature of ministry and also makes the point that ministry or service cannot and should not be divorced from those who are served. It is within the context of the community to be served that ministers receive their *raison d'être* and, therefore, 'If the needs of the whole Body of Christ are given precedence, then issues of gender and marital status necessarily become secondary, indeed minor considerations.'[9]

A friend told a story about her elderly parents who are traditional Catholics. They went to the funeral of a friend and a female Anglican priest led the service. To their surprise, they found themselves singing the praises of the priest. What impressed them was her warmth, her humanity, and her ability to relate to the congregation so easily and put everyone at their ease. As well as this, she preached a powerful sermon and proclaimed good news to everyone present. One of the greatest tragedies in the Catholic Church today is that so much of that potential remains unused, wasted, untapped or under developed. There is a real imbalance between the skills and talents women use in their working and domestic lives and the roles they take up in church life. In their daily lives women teach men in universities and Christian colleges and yet not in church. They proclaim, preach

and teach the good news or gospel of the Lord at home and in
the workplace and yet not at Mass on Sundays. They are in positions of leadership and authority in their work and yet excluded
from any real decision making in the church. Women can prepare the family meal at home and serve family suppers in the
church hall, but not preside at the table of the Lord. Women can
buy bread to feed the family, or bake bread, but cannot conse-
crate it during Mass. This is poignantly expressed in the words
of an unnamed poet:

> Did the woman say, as she held him for the first time,
>   in the dark of the stable,
>   after the pain, the bleeding and the crying,
>   'This is my body, this is my blood.'

> Did the woman say, as she held him for the last time,
> in the dark of the garden, after the pain, the bleeding and the dying,
>   'This is my body, this is my blood.'

>   Well that she said it for him, then,
>   For dried old men,
>   Brocaded robes belying barrenness,
>   Ordain that she not say it for him now.[10]

A Church of Equality

The church of the third millennium will treat women as equal
and empower them. They will use their gifts and talents and
work together with men in every area of church life. The influence of men and women working together with equal authority
will truly change the face of the earth. The church herself will
grow to be more relevant to the lives of everyone (including
women). Throughout the world the church will reflect those
gospel values of justice, equality and integrity. Women will
want to play a full and responsible role in the life and mission of
the church in the world.

But first, things will need to change! Women in the church
are over-represented and under-employed. Under employed
does not, of course, mean under-worked! In the church of today,
there are far more women in congregations than there are men.
Women perform many tasks within the church but are not allowed to participate in decision making at institutional level.
Their ability to help the discernment process is, therefore, greatly

diminished. Even religious sisters are bound by constitutions approved by men in Rome!

By the time the gospels were written, women were already being squeezed out of positions that could influence the whole church. There is still something feminine missing from the experience of being church today. But what is masculine and feminine energy? We are on shaky ground here. When we try to attribute certain characteristics to a given group, we are in danger of creating stereotypes, which are limiting and discriminating. Most of us are aware of men who have a well-developed feminine side, and women with a masculine side. What do we mean by that? We live in a world where gender stereotypes have robbed us of any essential knowledge of what it is to be masculine and feminine, and left us with caricatures. It is utter foolishness to talk about gentleness and nurturing as being the exclusive prerogative of women, and strength and leadership as exclusive to men. We can all think of examples of where the opposite is true. But how is energy experienced in large, exclusive groups? There is certainly a different kind of energy created when a group of men are gathered and when a group of women are gathered. The Chinese would call it yin and yang. They see life as the interplay between these two energies. If they are in balance, there is health, if they are out of balance there is illness. If we want a healthy, balanced church then there needs to be a dynamic interaction, interplay between male and female.

Tina Beattie in her book, *Rediscovering Mary. Insights from the Gospels*, says "The Catholic Church still clings to a vision of femininity and masculinity, male roles and female roles, man's authority and woman's submission, that makes it a deeply patriarchal institution. This is despite the fact that in the image of Mary as the archetype of the Mother Church, and in the feminine identity given to the church, there is also a matriarchal element in Catholicism. Journeying as we are between the incarnation and the fulfilment of God's kingdom on earth, Christians are called to strive as a redeemed community that reveals God's love to the world. This cannot happen until Christian patriarchy yields to a loving and egalitarian understanding of human relationships, a restoration to the vision of wholeness in Genesis, where man and woman together make up the image of God.'[11] At present there is an imbalance in the church, which leaves the body out of kilter and incomplete. The church of tomorrow will be able to hold these opposites in creative tension. This will happen by women sharing in the work of that restoration by striving to create in the church, conditions of justice and equality. Women need to continue to express the right to speak for and about themselves, to claim their right to mould and fashion the church, to have their voices heard and to have their views fully incorporated into the shaping of the church.

Women are already making valuable contributions in theology and spirituality but, unbelievably, the church still gives instructions that silence certain women scholars and stops them from even discussing the priestly ordination of women. Joan Chittister says, 'A woman's role obviously does not take her to the theological arenas of the church – the synods, the congregations, the councils – where, as a consequence, everything that is written about women is written without women.'[12]

She then goes on to say that many philosophers, psychologists and theologians argue that women are closer to life issues than men and yet women in the church continue to be denied the opportunity to make a difference. 'To publish documents on moral theology, ethics and ecology without including women in their development is simply to perpetuate the notion that men know what is good for everyone.'[13] Male-controlled moral formation, theology and spirituality makes judgements about things that men cannot and do not experience. The sign that the church gives is that she has little or nothing to learn from women in the church. An edict was issued that a seminarian may not have a woman as a spiritual director or theological guide and yet, 'It is hard to imagine an edict that insisted that no priest was fit to be a spiritual director to a nun. The church needs women at the highest levels of theological, pastoral, and canonical development not for the sake of women, but for the sake of the wisdom, the vision and the integrity of the pronouncements of the church itself.'[14]

An Inclusive Church

A new paradigm will embrace inclusiveness. The church will be a place where we can bring all our friends, knowing that they will be welcomed and included. Divorced and remarried friends, gay and lesbian friends, friends who are single mothers, friends who live with their partners, elderly friends, disabled friends, all of these, and many more, will be able to play a full

and active role at the eucharist. We cannot reach out to those
who are excluded, with a gospel of good news if we ourselves
exclude others. Many of our friends will be included and they
will be encouraged to share their stories and their wisdom.
Wisdom is not the sole exclusive property of theologians, acade-
mics and clerics, but comes from lived experience. All of us can
read a book and gather information. When we make sense of the
information, it becomes knowledge. This knowledge, when it is
integrated into the personal experiences of my life, can become
understanding. Understanding, when it is reflected upon, struggled with, lived, questioned, changed, discerned with others
and made my own, can become wisdom. You can sense this in
people when you are able to say, 'She knows what she's talking
about'. We need to recognise the wisdom that is present in every
member of the body. In the Body of Christ, all that is needed is
present, but we have to listen to the whole to make sense of it
and put the pieces of the picture together. We silence parts of the
body at a serious cost – the well-being of the whole body. We ignore parts of the body at the same cost. An inclusive church will
be a listening church where no one is silenced or ignored. There
will be no voiceless spectators   only active participants, both
male and female!

Each person has many facets to their being. For example, I
may be a mother, daughter, friend, partner and lover. The
church of the future will be a place where we can bring the
whole of ourselves and find acceptance. Richard Rohr, the
American Franciscan, often says, 'That which is not received is
not redeemed.' The church of tomorrow will be a place where
we are all received and, therefore, redeemed just as we are. In
any congregation there will be people who use contraceptives,
people who believe that women should be ordained, people
who question some of the church's teachings. No longer will we
have to leave these parts of ourselves at the church door in order
to get through a celebration. They, too, will be allowed a voice
and be received.

The use of inclusive language will be a reflection of the inclusive nature of the church. In scripture it says, 'I have called you
by your name' and men will recognise the insensitivity of congregations full of women having to identify themselves as,
'men', 'sons', 'brothers' and 'brethren'. They will recognise that
the use of inclusive language reflects the full humanity of

women and men in the light of the gospel. Language isn't neutral. It informs the way we think and creates concepts. God is beyond all names, but the church will seek to name the experience of God by using a wealth of imagery beyond the masculine, to assist the church in understanding the full nature of God. Various church groups and people who meet to pray together are already using these images. They name God as Ground and Source of Being, Laughing God, Pain Bearer, God our Mother, Nurturing God, Midwife, and Breadmaker ... the list is endless. When celebrating the eucharist, praying the office, or meeting in church groups in the new millennium, it would be unthinkable to use anything but inclusive language, and incorporate creative ways of imaging God which recognise that God is beyond any gender stereotypes.

Missionary Church

One of the convictions that will in the future shape the church is the commitment to mission. The vision of church as *koinonia* or *communio,* gives birth to a renewed and integrated theology of mission. We read in *The Sign We Give*, 'As the church lives communion, all people and all creation are drawn towards unity and community and thus enable the church to be part of transforming the world.'[15] The gospel will actually be proclaimed by the way that we live. The church as a sign or sacrament of Christ in the world will be characterised by inclusiveness, love, equality and partnership. We will truly be good news to those who are excluded, unloved, second-class citizens, or alone.

Women have a special contribution to make to the life and mission of the church. *Christifidelis Laici* states, 'If anyone has this task of advancing the dignity of women in the church and society, it is women themselves.'[16] The Synod Fathers note that it is women who are mainly the victims of discrimination and abuse. There is a paradox here as women do not have the power they need to overturn the domination of their oppressors. Fr Kevin Kelly in his excellent book, *New Directions in Sexual Ethics: Moral Theology and the Challenge of AIDS,* gives a comprehensive analysis of the ways in which existing oppressive structures, institutions and processes have damaging effects on women and children in particular. '... It would be a much more credible witness to the gospel if the church were renowned for its opposition to female genital mutilation, rather than it's opposition to the use of condoms ... It would seem at this point in history a Christian sexual ethic should be 'pro women' before it is 'pro marriage'.[17]

There are many other areas where the priorities of the church are experienced as discriminatory and damaging to women. Connections fail to be made between the plight of many women and the consequences of the church's teaching. Consider the message received by women and children when abortion appears much more important than child murder. How do we reconcile the fight to rid us of condoms rather than rid us of AIDS? The church is more vocal in its condemnation of the pill than of pornography and the sex industry. Again, the refusal to accept divorce rather than the refusal to accept male violence to women and children gives a clear message of priorities. The church must begin to see the connections between these things. Joan Chittister says, 'A UN fact-finding team estimates that more than 20,000 Muslim women were raped in Bosnia and then murdered or made to bear Serb children in order to humiliate Muslim men and perform an "ethnic cleansing". Rape has become an instrument of war, a form of penal punishment. But we heard nowhere near the same rage we heard about altar girls or the use of female pronouns in the liturgy of the Mass. A church that itself works steadily to keep women out of its male enclaves cannot expect to be able to teach the gospel of Jesus to the rest of the world. It becomes incredible.'[18]

In many places throughout the world women are still seen as subordinate to men. In places where this inequality is enshrined in social, political, religious and economic processes, the desperate plight of women, and as a consequence their children, is an example of systemic sin. There are many women in the church too, who, as a result of the church's patriarchal structure, have experienced prejudice, powerlessness, abuse, exclusion, domination and exploitation. They have begun to realise that this oppression is neither incidental nor accidental but systemic and structural. This is certainly a distortion of the gospel and their mission is the enormous and exhausting task of critiquing the cause of that oppression in order to create 'an alternative vision of a non-patriarchal future and a commitment to structural change to realise that vision.'[19] Their analyses are crucial in understanding the dynamics that allow oppression to take place, in order to challenge them. These women are also in a unique position to express true compassion and support to others experiencing such abuses.

Incarnational Church

'The Word was made flesh and dwelt amongst us.' The church of the future will continue to recognise that Jesus took on our humanity and the whole of creation, and all human experience is shot through with the presence of God. We will not need to look to church alone for the sacred. It is in our ordinary human experience that God is revealed and so all of our life is sacred, is religious. A belief in the incarnation includes the capacity to believe in a God who is revealed in the garments of humanity.

The people of God are already making a new church, recognising holy moments in their lives. Regina Bechtle says, 'Incarnation, with all its "in-the-flesh-ness", is a concept which women intuitively understand. With women writing spirituality, it is no accident that there has been an explosion of books about finding God in ordinary things, in simple pleasures, in home and family life, in sexuality and relationships – in the arena traditionally known as woman's world.'[20]

There are many examples of people celebrating their joys, mourning and grieving their losses, coming to terms with their disappointments, and sharing their hopes and fears. People are already involved in making sense of their individual stories by locating them within the 'story of life'. Sandra M. Schneiders says that storytelling, the narrating and sharing of experiences, is central to feminist spirituality. 'Storytelling is both a technique for consciousness-raising and a source of mutual support. By telling their own stories women appropriate as significant their own experience which they have been taught to view as trivial. By listening to the stories of other women, they come to see the commonalities and the political power in women's experience which they have been taught to believe is purely personal and private.'[21] This process will go on with or without the sanction of the institutional church. However, there are within the church those who see the good where it exists and bless it there. There is a need to acknowledge the existing rituals in people's lives and add the church's blessing. Where communities support and love one another, where freedom, human dignity and integrity are fought for and struggled for, God is there.

At a recent AIDS's service in Leeds, many people were visibly touched and deeply moved by the expression of emotion. One young man spoke passionately and eloquently about falling in love with his partner. The atmosphere was tangible. We were at one moment lifted by his joy at living life with such love, and in the next moment weighed down with him by the pain of his loss at his partner's death. We laughed and cried, but more, we felt at one with him. We could identify our story with his. We knew that at moments he expressed things for us all. He put words and meaning to the pleasure and the pain, which helped us to understand. He enabled us to experience life in a different way and grow by that experience. As he spoke we felt a love for him and his partner, for their love, their honesty, their integrity. We were honoured to have been there to hear his story. The service went on to include many traditional elements of liturgy, but all of them experienced in a new way, shot through with relevance, insight and meaning. People were expressing deeply personal experiences and finding understanding, acceptance and support and healing in one another.

Many people would not recognise in this service anything relating to church. A new church will be able to recognise and encourage this type of liturgy – liturgy where, through the tangible love and support of one another, we are able to experience the incarnate love of God. God will be made flesh to us in one another as we hold, support, embrace and touch each other's lives. There are, throughout the church, services such as the one described. The new church would, however, be able to bless and honour these services without having to contain and control them. It would be able to acknowledge women as taking on equal roles in the liturgy and ministering according to their giftedness, not their gender.

Too often people are alienated from the church because they have special needs that cannot be met within the rigid confines of existing liturgical and clerical structures. Women who have experienced sexual abuse by men are one such group. Sometimes they need the support of other women and may even feel unable to receive the sacraments from men. They may be unable to identify with an almost exclusively male, father God. There is an opportunity here to be creative in finding alternative ways of expressing God's image. There are so many places where this imagination and creativity is already being fostered and encouraged in the preparation and celebration of liturgy. It is touching people's hearts because it resonates, finds an echo in their lives. Sad to say, there seems to be little room for this kind of creativity in the celebration of the Sunday eucharist in so many places.

We need to look anew at the signs and symbols we are using, to ensure that they are relevant, that they truly speak to the nitty gritty of our everyday lives. There is a hunger in all of us for this and today people are 'making church' and creating liturgies to satisfy this hunger where they feel comfortable. They are finding their own signs and symbols. In various places around Leeds, 'shrines' have been created around trees, along the roadside, beside fences, to mark the spot where a loved one has died. These 'holy' places are covered with flowers, candles, pictures, prayers, toys, etc. Relatives and friends, who would never dream of coming to church, make regular pilgrimages to these shrines. Making connections between faith and life, life and faith, finding signs and symbols that speak to our hearts, storytelling, celebrating bodiliness, creating different forms of expression – these are all characteristics of feminist spirituality. This spirituality, expressed through liturgy and ritual, is flourishing in congregations of women religious and various 'women's groups' or groups led by women. Sandra M. Schneiders says that another characteristic of feminist spirituality is, 'The emphasis on ritual that is participative, circular, aesthetic, incarnate, communicative, life-enhancing, and joyful is a deliberate rejection of the rigidly unemotional, overly verbal, hierarchical, and dominative liturgical practice of the mainline churches.'[22] This creative energy of women needs to be recognised and used. Just imagine how a Sunday eucharist could be if only this energy was unleashed! Surely, this is an area in which women have so much to offer. (See *Reclaiming Ritual* below.)

Creating new skins: Steps to change
How can we create that new skin before the wine is lost and the skins too? How can we create that new paradigm shift before women become too disillusioned and leave the church and the church is lost too? There is hope. Is not one of the lessons we could learn from science that true community has to be based on creative co-operation, interdependence and interconnectivity? Everything in nature is interconnected – everything is related to everything else. We are connected to the stars. A supernova explosion gave birth to every element in our bodies. The church

needs to become a synergistic community where difference is valued, where the energy between different people creates something new. The church is full of different people with different gifts and talents. These differences could be the sources of creating new and exciting forms of church. Parishes could become communities that are truly fulfilling for each person, places that nurture their giftedness, self-worth and self-esteem. This church can come into being if the hierarchy enters into synergistic communication with all those who, at the moment, do not have a voice, including women. To quote Stephen R. Covey:

> When you communicate synergistically, you are simply opening your mind and heart and expressions to new possibilities, new alternatives, new options.
>
> ... You're not sure when you engage in synergistic communication how things will work out or what the end will look like, but you do have an inward sense of excitement and security and adventure, believing that it will be significantly better than it was before. And this is the end you have in mind. You begin with the belief that parties involved will gain more insight, and that the excitement of that mutual learning and insight will create a momentum toward more and more insights, learnings and growth.[23]

For this kind of change to occur, our male priesthood must be prepared to listen and create rather than pontificate, defend and protect. As long as our leaders write pastoral letters and encyclicals based on fear, setting up even more rules and regulations, and writing them in a language that is outdated and meaningless, then the spirit of possibility and creativity will never come to birth. There is much to be done, but we can be confident that we have all the necessary resources. In working for a new church there is no benefit in swapping a master for a mistress. The intention is to strive for the equality of men and women. There will be tension because we are not the same, but out of that tension can come a new kind of creativity which in reflecting masculine and feminine energies is more balanced and harmonious. Women are not better qualified than men are; they are equally as qualified as men for all the different ministries within the church. To enable people to accept this equality, we need to change the attitudes of both sexes.

There will be fear in moving towards new models where power and control have to be let go of, particularly by men. We need to acknowledge that the existing priesthood is becoming increasingly difficult to sustain in its present form. The new church will be more supportive of its clergy as a whole, and not maintain a structure which can set them apart from the people. Priests on pedestals have a long way to fall, while those who are a part of the community can more be supported. Structures need to be nurturing and power needs to be shared. Many priests are already finding collaborative ministry more life-giving than when 'power' is exercised solely by themselves. We have a telling illustration of the possibility of a 'new order' in South Africa. It seemed impossible that black people in that country would ever gain their freedom and liberation from oppression and share in the governing of their own country, but it is now a reality. Although there are many problems in the New South Africa, there are many wonders and miracles too.

Nelson Mandela must surely be a sign of hope for the church that the oppressed need not become the oppressors, that the struggle to overcome bitterness and resentment can be won, and that faith is ultimately rewarded. 'Like the Berlin Wall and South African apartheid, the church's patriarchal sexism appears immovable, but it is built on the sand of oppression, and history is on the side of liberation and justice.'[24] It is particularly pertinent that Nelson Mandela in his inaugural speech used the words of a black woman. May the same spirit, which inspired her with such courage and hope, inspire us too as we strive to build up the Body of Christ in the beginning of the third millennium.

Our deepest fear is not that we are inadequate.
Our deepest fear is that we are powerful beyond measure.
It is our light, not our darkness, that most frightens us.
We ask ourselves
Who am I to be brilliant, gorgeous, talented,
Fabulous?
But who are you not to be?
You are a child of God.
Your playing small doesn't serve the world.
There is nothing enlightened about shrinking
So that other people won't feel insecure around you.

We are all meant to shine as children do.
We are born to make manifest the glory of God
That is within us.
It is not just in some of us,
It is in everyone.
As we let our light shine
We give other people permission to do the same.
As we are liberated from our own fear
Our presence automatically liberates others.[25]

The Sacrament of Humanity

In a recent poll conducted by local radio as part of a programme about making a millennium time capsule, listeners were asked to name the most popular people this century. It came as no surprise to find that Diana, Princess of Wales, Mother Theresa and Dr Martin Luther King were the winners. What these three vastly contrasting people, with different backgrounds and cultures, had in common was their compassion, their human touch. Each in their own unique way found themselves alongside some of the most vulnerable victims of our divided world, whether it was the poor and dying in Calcutta, landmine victims or those suffering from Aids, or those discriminated against because of the colour of their skin. It is fascinating that the compassionate witness of these three people captured the heart and the imagination of listeners. They have each become symbols for our age of some of the best aspirations of the human spirit. This they have achieved by becoming passionately and actively involved in the human struggle. It would be true to say for each of them that the more immersed they became in that struggle, the more meaning their own lives held. Their memory is sacred to so many today, not because of office, status, wealth or religion, but because they cared.

For all three, their Christianity was conveyed to the listeners through human service. The fact that these three people were famous and enjoyed a high public profile, simply highlights what happens in a million quiet ways in different places all over the world. This chance encounter with local radio also illustrates one of the major tenets of this book, that it is only in and through our human dealings with each other that Christ is made present in our world; that indeed the church is called to be a *Sacrament of Humanity*. It is difficult to imagine that, if the same group of listeners were asked if they had evidence that this was the predominant vision of church today, there would be a resounding,

'Yes!' It becomes ever more urgent to realise how very far the church has strayed from the human path that Jesus trod, how out of touch with people's ordinary lives it is. The church, with its emphasis on dogma and its patriarchal structure, can no longer satisfy the immense thirst for spiritual renewal, and the hunger of people to find meaning in life. Unless it can make a radical shift in direction, unless it risks becoming immersed in the ecstasy and the despair, the ordinary and the momentous moments of people's lives, it will increasingly become an irrelevance.

The dynamic has to change. The church must travel in a spirit of humility, to journey alongside people wherever they are in their pathways through life. Fr Tony Philpot expands on this:

The church is not there for its own sake, to keep itself in being and assure its own future; it is there for the sake of the world, especially for all who do not believe. How easy it is for us to navel-gaze, to become fixated with our own area of concern or responsibility, and neglect the big picture. How easy it is for us to indulge in in-house chatter and gossip, and forget why we are there. Collective narcissism is not attractive, and we sometimes go in for it ... Until we are a true community, or a network of true communities, and until those communities have an uncritical heart for the broad sweep of humanity, and something constructive and empathetic to say to it, and are known for it, we will always be perceived as marginal to this world's real concerns. We need to think more about the millions of people without faith; and the millions who are undernourished and under-educated; and the millions of people who are suffering the wretched results of war, whether civil or not. The question of immigration and how the European Union treats its immigrants, is a moral issue of enormous importance. The question of abortion is not just another piece of RC obscurantism; it is about the most fundamental of human rights, and a civilisation which floats on a sea of abused rights is terribly, terminally precarious. These are the big issues – not the reordering of our churches, and the perennial questions of guitars in church, flowers in Lent and the staffing of the fete. I long to see a Catholic Church that will confront them squarely and intelligently.[1]

If this is the kind of presence the Catholic Church needs to be in the third millennium, where is it to find the heart for such a mission? Where does it need to start in recovering its lost soul? It seems to me the only starting place is the place Jesus started – in the loving trust he placed in very ordinary people, women and men like you and me, at times weak and sinful, at other times courageous and strong. It is in the loving, trusting, compassionate, forgiving hearts of all God's people that the church will find again its way of being in touch. When considering the church twenty-five years on from Vatican II, Archbishop Rembert Weakland, echoes the need for:

> ... a recapturing of the attitude that the church is but a humble partner, an imperfect society, engaging this world in dialogue ... We must recapture the courage that is needed to be prophetic toward a world that is waiting for the values of the kingdom. Most of all, we must recapture also the hope that was ours twenty-five years ago. If it was naïve then, it now can be the mature hope that has come from experience and a certain amount of disillusionment. I realise that this new humble attitude must be accompanied by deeds, and that means a new simplicity of lifestyle based on the gospel and the beatitudes, a lifestyle that might at times seem to be countercultural to the hopes and ambitions of many in the world.[2]

Fishing and Forgiveness: the Starting Point

One of the lovely images given to us by the Johanine scholar, C. H. Dodd, was that the church was founded on an act of forgiveness. He bases this, of course, on the beautiful account in John's gospel of the risen Jesus meeting with his friends in the half light, just as dawn was about to break, after they had had a fruitless night fishing. The encounter is full of the most direct, simple but intensely profound truths. There they are, a group of friends at sea, feeling a deep sense of loss, of fear and anxiety. Amongst them was Peter, their leader, the strong one, the one they all looked to, the one on whom Jesus had promised to build the church. Peter was a man who had realised his own frailty and experienced deep fear. He had completely lost belief in himself and had wept bitterly. After all, he had denied his truest friend, not once, but three times. This man was on the painful journey of self-knowing, learning the difficult lesson of forgiveness – forgiveness of himself which can only happen when one experiences and trusts in the loving and freely-given forgiveness of God.

In the effort to understand, to cope with the strangeness of the times, these friends had reverted to the most ordinary, most human, most routine thing for them – to go fishing. And isn't that what we all have to do at some stage in our lives, when we can't make much sense of the 'macro' scene, the huge hurts or anxieties? At such moments we often take refuge in the familiar, the mundane, the comfortingly human, until some small sense of peace comes. It comes somehow through the human action itself and only then can we begin to accept what we would rather not, to trust the confusion and to unravel enough of the mystery of pain and loss to make it possible to move forward. Into this scene of confusion comes Jesus, arriving quietly after the friends had kept casting their nets, continuing to fish even when the fishing itself had failed them. But they were together, and it was a routine they knew, and what else was there for them to do anyway? When the light is just beginning to change, a stranger calls to them from the shore with a simple human suggestion, 'Try the other side.'

The story is so familiar; we know the outcome is a huge trawl of fish. Just when the light really dawns, when the penny really drops, Peter recognises Jesus, the friend he has let down so badly that he contributed to his death. As usual, gorgeous, impetuous Peter jumps into the water and heads for the shore. He is coming home! What follows is one of the most beautiful and simple passages in the scriptures. There is no long theological discussion. There is no 'unpacking' of what had happened. There is no attempt to account for actions, to explain, excuse or justify. There is instead a meal, a fire burning and a simple breakfast of fried fish for these exhausted and bewildered men – food to be shared, and acceptance. Anyone passing by would have witnessed a very normal, routine scene of fishermen eating some of their night's catch before returning home – nothing remarkable. Yet it was in that everyday happening that they encountered the risen Jesus, where they began to understand. Jesus came to be alongside them on the shore. He engaged them in dialogue.

What is remarkable is that it is at the heart of these 'normal', 'routine', human happenings of our lives that we, too, begin to understand the meaning of the mystery, of the Word-become-human. Hearing this gospel again on the Third Sunday after Easter, I began to reflect on the nature of church, as we experi-

ence it 2000 years on, and to question whether our way of being
with each other as the body of Christ comes anywhere near the
simple, direct vision of Jesus, of being alongside people, wherever they are, and talking with them about things that matter.

What this gospel story reveals, too, is that it has something to
do with trust – basic, human, loving trust. That may sound obvious, even facile, but for me it all hinges on the questions on the
sea-shore, 'Do you love me?'; 'You know I love you.' This seems
to be a deeply intimate exchange between two vulnerable people needing to say out loud, and needing to hear, what each
knows deep in their heart. Isn't it so beautiful, and so reassuring
that the Son of God, risen and glorified, seems to need this very
human and direct encounter with the big-hearted Peter? There is
the whole world in their exchanges, for there is total acceptance,
the one of the other. In Jesus there is no condemnation, just forgiveness and opportunity for Peter's healing, three times, and
the greatest affirmation of Peter's humanity. It is as if Jesus is
saying, 'Yes it's you, Peter, with all your failings, all your weakness, you who've let me down in the past, it's you I trust. I know
you really love me, but I need to hear you say it. You see it is you
who must carry on in the way I showed you; you are the one
now who will have to look after my "little ones". And, Peter,
there's no one better. You are only human, and that's the only
way to be, the only way it can be. Come on now, let's eat.'

And, as often happens, it was over a shared meal with a
trusted friend, listening to honest reactions about difficulties in
sharing responsibility, in letting go of roles, about fears and anxieties, and about this gospel, too, that things began to fall into
place. Any attempt to build community can only ever happen
when there is deep trust in each other's goodness and giftedness, when there is real acceptance of difference and when there
is the capacity to forgive and overlook failings. Just as this is so
for any group, it became increasingly clear that 'church' is only
ever really incarnated in each age when the same degree of loving and trust happens. It doesn't happen just because of authority
of office, nor through schemes, plans and programmes, nor because we set the right structures in place, (though all of those
things must be there in some way). It only happens in the trusting exchanges between vulnerable people who, like Peter, will
sometimes get it badly wrong. But what was never 'wrong' with
Peter, which Jesus recognised, was the size of that human heart!

Peter's disposition, his stance on life, was to be open, impetuous, to risk, to follow, to dream! We never hear of him in the gospels ordering others around, nor did he seek the best place at table. His 'place' among the disciples must have been of a different order, his leadership following a different pattern.

How far away from that lovely intimate moment of trust, resulting in Peter's, and the church's mission, does the institution of Rome seem to so many! And is it too fanciful, I wonder, to imagine that two friends, sharing a meal, trying to let the gospel shed light on their daily struggles, is another way of theologising? Or do we always have to leave it to the professionals? Have we lost trust in our own human wisdom, our capacity to listen to the Word of God in our hearts? Those questions on the shore, and the answers, are they not the crux of the matter still for us today? Despite its protestations to the contrary, has the 'official' church lost the art of walking alongside people? Has it forgotten how to listen? Has it lost touch with its humanity?

> There is no question of seeing two distinct kinds of activity in Jesus, the first being his human actions and the second being a passive waiting for God to act in response to his petitions. The healing brought about by Jesus was not an intervention 'from outside' by God in response to the request of Jesus ... The deep meaning of the incarnation is that all of the healing, liberation and life-giving which God brought about through Jesus came through his human activity ... We are privileged to share both in the life and activity of Jesus. What he did is what we are called to do, in varying degrees. As we become more like Jesus we become more fully human. Conversely, as we become more fully human we become more like Jesus, sharing more and more in the creative and healing energy which was so characteristic of him. And as we become more like him we become more authentic images of God. Our mission is a continuation of his mission. It is to be a living revelation to others and to ourselves, of the hidden mystery of unlimited goodness, boundless life and inexhaustible energy which we call God.[3]

The argument here concerns the central theme running throughout this book, that the church needs to recover the radical nature of a truly incarnational theology, for pastoral practice based on such a theology would look vastly different. It is only when, in all our human endeavours, we embrace each other humbly, acknowledging our own sinfulness and weakness, and from that place reach out in compassion, that the grace of God will flow freely to refresh the spirit and bring new life. If we imagine that there is a realm outside our human interactions where we can miraculously engineer or manufacture a community spirit, then we are doomed to failure. If we think we can gather for worship on a Sunday without having concern for each other throughout the week, then the sacrifice we offer will be empty. If the local Christian community is vibrant, however, attendance at Mass will take care of itself. We cannot 'fix' the sad reality of the faithful departing, or stem the stream of those who vote with their feet, by jazzing up the hymns or changing the parish priest. The church will be full on Sunday when neighbours' hearts, broken and mending, are full of love for one another: only then will they reach, together, for ritual and sacrament to put meaning, shape and expression into the deep and mysterious struggles of the spirit. A return to the Latin Mass, and to hard-line threatening will not see the return of 'lapsed' Catholics to the pews. A dash of trendy preaching and trendy liturgy will not cause a rush to weekly worship in any lasting way.

It is only when parishioners are struggling to make sense of their own lives, recognise their neighbours' efforts to do the same, and reach out to each other in compassion, that the heart of a community begins to beat strongly and draws others to it. Then the community has something to celebrate and the Sunday eucharist becomes a two-way dynamic. On the one hand it gathers the lived experiences of all its people's joys and pain, and places them on the table in the form of bread and wine; on the other hand the bread is broken and the wine poured for the life of the world, urging and empowering each one to go forth from the table to forgive, reconcile and bring compassion.

Recently I had the privilege of travelling in the USA to meet with Christians of different denominations who, like many of us here, are struggling to stay on board a church that seems so out of touch with the real concerns of our times. In Downtown San Francisco, on a very rainy, first Sunday of Advent, it was a remarkable experience to be part of a worshipping community whose liturgy was exciting and vibrant, but whose outreach to the most vulnerable and most marginalised of that city was even more alive. Picture the scene outside Glide Memorial Methodist Church half an hour before the service was due to begin – people of all ages and races, poor, homeless people, drug users, peo-

ple with Aids, alcoholics – a bedraggled crowd thronging the
narrow sidewalk to get in. I'd been warned to go early but had
hardly expected such crowds. I edged my way in with them.
Inside stewards were guiding people to various parts of the
rambling, old building, according to their need for clothing,
food, advice or, as in my case, Sunday worship.

I was stunned to discover how the church, which held over
three hundred people, was almost bursting at the seams – with
half an hour still to go! Ten minutes before the official start-time
the gospel-style worship began, led by a band and a gospel choir
of almost a hundred. After some exuberant hymns of praise,
with much clapping and swaying, we were invited to hold
hands. What at first I had thought was just a gimmicky gesture
became a deeply moving experience. World Aids day was being
celebrated, and on a huge screen we had already watched the
roll-call of all those in that community who had died of Aids the
previous year. As we held hands the Rev Cecil Williams prayed
fervently, beseeching us to hold onto each other, because there
were people among us dying of Aids; people among us who had
lost loved ones; people among us full of fear; people among us
full of joy. The prayer continued, 'Hold on to each other, sisters
and brothers. We need to hold each other in our pain. Hold on to
each other, sisters and brothers. We need to hold on to those
who are strong today. Hold on to each other, sisters and brothers. We need to share each other's joy.'

And as we prayed the grip on both my hands tightened, just
as I found myself returning the hold. No longer was this a liturgical nicety, for holding hands had indeed become a way of
holding each other up. In that one, simple, but powerfully real
gesture, the life of the community was expressed. This was a
church whose Sunday worship was lived out in the drug reha-
bilitation programmes, the food and clothing it offered, in the
Aids counselling, the bereavement support, the parenting programmes, the day-shelter and many other services which
touched the lives of that city's most vulnerable people, not one
day a year, not one day a week, but every day. The people who
had not come to worship, but came seeking help, most surely experienced church, the healing, compassionate touch of Jesus.
The lively singing and dancing of the worship seemed even
more joyful because it carried the integrity of a community
deeply immersed in the world.

Living Stones

The church must be thought of first and foremost as the local church. Each Christian must have the impression that his or her local church has everything necessary to be, and to be called, church ... Human problems are similar the world over, but their local variations make it necessary to deal with them differently in each place. Only local churches are really effective in making Christ present to the world according to the needs and conditions of each place.[4]

The vibrant community in downtown San Francisco was certainly powerfully in touch with the lives of people round about, and offers a witness that many other local communities are realising more and more as the only way to be church. An experience of one parish travelling this same road, though in a completely different setting, and still with great distances to travel, convinces me that it is the only route for the church.

In 1998 the new church was opened in our parish of St Benedict in Garforth, Yorkshire. For four years we had been without a building after our previous church had been condemned as unsafe for worship and was demolished. For some parishioners our 'exile' in the school hall was too much and they went elsewhere for their Sunday worship. For the majority who remained, a gradual process began to reveal itself, whereby what had appeared as a devastating crisis became an immense opportunity for growing. For whilst we had to make do and stretch imagination, creativity and patience to overcome the many inconveniences, we were also forced into much more intimate surroundings, and were forced to help each other practically. During all the discussions and plans for a new church building, what suddenly became the real focus for people was the vision of church as the Body of Christ, and what that meant for us as a local community. As much effort went into developing our parish Mission Statement, and our New Covenant with the Poor, as went into planning the new building. Now that we are getting used to our beautiful new church, which reflects in so many of its features the hopes and prayer of our community, it is encouraging that the desire to grow in compassion is even more urgent, and I believe it is that which is drawing people to us. A beautiful summary of our hopes and dreams is captured in a poem written by the parish priest, before we started building.

Living Stones
We thank you, Lord, for calling us
to co-create with you,
a house of light and beauty,
a visible sacrament
of our heart-held faith.

May our holy work
be a poem of praise
crafted for your glory
by our inner child of joy.

And as our old church is dismantled
reduced to bare and empty space
may our hard inner stones melt down
to build a sanctuary for our souls.

May its walls of truth be built upon
the truthful minds
of our love-community.

May its singing roof of hope take shape
from all the brave beginnings
of our fragile days.

May its wondrous windows draw the light
even as our hearts, transparent,
draw each other.

May the blueprint for the altar be
already sculpted
in our service of compassion.

And when the world's bread and wine are raised
'Fruit of the earth and work of human hands'
may all the loves and lives of all the world
be celebrated as God's beloved body.

And may the ambo, the wood-work for the Word,
be hewn from every word of healing
we have spoken.

Nor will the room of reconciliation
hold much grace
unless it's formed
from each forgiving moment
in our parish.

May every drop of baptismal water
spring from wells of welcome
already flowing free
in our community.

And in our garden new,
embracing church and school,
may young and old
see dreams grow greener,
the seeds of which are set already
in the furrows of our souls.

And so we ask you God,
our Lord of sowing and reaping,
prepare our grateful hearts
as we prepare our mother earth
to build on
with *Living Stones* ...

During the first few weeks in the new church, our small community has lived and grown through the powerfully moving experiences of four funerals and a wedding. All of these unique celebrations naturally concerned life changes of mammoth proportions for the individuals and families involved. However, what is really intriguing and heartening is that they brought the community together in shared joy and pain in a most unusual way, a way which surprised and delighted all concerned. It had something to do with the fact that all five events were lived and celebrated as community events, rather than individual rituals at which the community was represented. The beautiful liturgies that emerged were possible only because they were the expression of shared experience at the heart of the community.

All four people who had died had lived and worked, struggled and celebrated, served and received from the community, each in his or her own unique way. They had each lived faithfully, but differently, offering their gifts for the greater good. Each death was felt as a great loss to the community, as if a part of itself had died, as indeed it had. There was a real sense in which the family of the parish journeyed alongside not only in prayer, but in offering thoughtful practical help, comfort, companionship and time – the human needs. Just as the sacrament of the sick was celebrated by anointing with oil, so parishioners visited homes to relieve physical pain by gentle massage of swollen feet and hands.

The Bread of Life was shared at each eucharist, just as parishioners prepared extra food to deliver to families too involved in caring to spend time cooking. These tiny, seemingly ordinary, practical acts of kindness were often a light in dark moments. In turn the families of those who were dying seemed to be able to allow their fear, vulnerability and pain to be shared in such a way that the mutual caring and trusting brought many unforeseen graces to the community. Because these threshold moments had been shared, the liturgical celebrations that followed expressed in a uniquely personal way, the degree to which families had felt cared for and supported.

Only One Love

This same dynamic was mirrored in the first wedding in the new church, which was a deeply communal celebration and experience of great joy. Here, too, the nuptial Mass was a culmination and an expression of the way in which Sonja and John had each shared their lives with the local and wider communities. All aspects of the celebration – food, flowers, transport, entertainment – were generously offered by the community, for it was the community which celebrated too. The liturgy that captured the moment of promise and hope for the couple, transmitted that promise and hope to us all.

None of this living liturgy comes without cost in terms of letting go of role, privilege, expectation – all the emotions involved in any human attempt to grow. And of course there will be mistakes along the way, as we own our human frailty. Throughout his ministry here, our present pastor has sought to witness to the invincible power of love. Because he owns his own vulnerability, struggles, sins and resistance – his humanity – as the sphere in which God can operate to bring transformation and healing, more of us are encouraged to do the same, and so the whirlpool of compassion ripples ever outward. This is appearing more and more to be the only authentic way of being church in this place at this time.

There is an ever deepening appreciation that the realm of our everyday concerns is the realm of God. It is why the institutional church often feels so distant, and so far removed from the conversation between Peter and Jesus. It is easy to consider what I have described as some kind of exception, but Cardinal Basil Hume's reflections, reported in *Briefing*, focuses on the revelatory nature of the experience of human love, in life situations as commonplace as those above:

I wish now to speak about experience. There are certain experiences which seem to me to point to something beyond the immediate. I take as an example the experience of loving. When a young person falls in love, and for the first time, that person may glimpse the high and low points of loving, the ecstasy and the agonies. It is a precious moment, for the mind and heart of the lover can be raised to see in the beloved an icon of the loveableness which God is. Human loving can lead us to the realisation of the intensity of God's love for each one of us.[5]

In a very moving article about the tragic death of her twenty-eight year old friend in a road accident, Susan Gannon affirms what the Cardinal is saying, and what is being argued in these pages, but in this case from the experience of suffering:

... Out of this experience of grief and loss, out of the mess of mind and soul, out of splinters of hope, I write. In doing so I hope to share with you something of how my spirituality speaks to this experience, or rather how this experience speaks to my spirituality ... Finding God in human experience begins with human experience itself. How we interpret and respond in the light of our faith, forms the authentic heart of our spirituality. The relationships, events, choices on all levels of our daily life are all we have to uncover the stuff God is made of, what we are made of and for. In my own faltering way, I have tried to be faithful to being attentive to my own life experience, trying to let it speak to me of a God who is within and beyond it, calling me and my community to the fullness of life. [6]

Such a truly incarnational view of church demands a radically different approach to all formation work, and to training for ministry, both the ordained priestly ministry and the priestly ministry of all God's people. That is why we keep emphasising that there exists an undeniable thirst for spiritual refreshment, a hunger for the discovery of the deeper meaning in all of life's trials and triumphs. The mystic within each one of us is struggling to be born. This fact has huge implications for our ecclesiastical leaders. What we desire from the church of our times is a recognition and blessing of any endeavour to truly love one another, no matter how messy this can sometimes become, and an appreciation of our often intense need of and search for meaning in our crowded, driven lives. Fr Kevin Kelly, in a resource paper for the National Conference of Priests, 1996, cited earlier, writes of how this is experienced within his parish:

> Life in our neighbourhood in inner-city Liverpool is hard for most people. The negative face of multiple deprivation over many generations are all too obvious. That is why pastoral practice has to take people where they are. Only in this way can it help them believe they are loved by God precisely 'where they are'. The main thrust of pastoral ministry here is to help people feel that everything they experience as good in their lives is accepted, affirmed and celebrated in God's presence. We are not in the business of judgement and condemnation. Where our people are at is different from a middle-class parish. Though not regular church-goers, in no way can most of them be labelled 'non-practising Catholics'. They 'practise' their faith and see themselves as the church. Hence the message they hear in liturgy should not be a disheartening 'no' condemning them where they are presently at in their lives. Rather it needs to be a resounding 'yes', accepting them where they are at but also encouraging them to believe that they are capable of even greater things.[7]

Occasionally in the past, at special times like Midnight Mass or First Eucharist celebrations, I have heard a tirade from the pulpit about infrequent attendance at the sacraments. Indeed only last summer, when on holiday in Ireland, on the evening of the dreadful Omagh bombing, the message from the pulpit at the beginning of Mass was a diatribe against holidaymakers like myself who had not 'kept holy' the feast of the Assumption by attending Mass earlier in the day, whilst expecting to 'get away with' only attending the Vigil Mass on the Saturday! Little wonder that an incredulous group of visitors to that place congregated on the steps afterwards to try to get a perspective on the level of concern about Mass attendance when we heard for the first time only in the Bidding Prayers of the terrible Omagh bombing atrocity and loss of life!

What a contrast there is when 'strangers', who don't come to Mass regularly, are greeted with genuine warmth and delight that they are there at all, not just by the priest but by the community too. No expectations or demands are put upon such people, but more the sense is conveyed to them that the community is blessed on every occasion when they can be present. There is nothing surer than to trust in the surprising blessings and graces that will follow from a consistently loving approach. When seeds of acceptance and love are sown there will be an abundant harvest, even if this happens in the secret places within human hearts, or years into the future. It demands of a community that it let go of all efforts to increase numbers, but instead deepen its own commitment to live according to the example of Jesus.

There is a popular saying that goes, 'When the church loses its heart, it loses joy. When it loses joy, it loses the people.' What needs to be reflected in all our adult formation programmes, in all our sacramental catechesis and celebration, in every fibre of every aspect of the church's ministry, is joy, but it will be an empty joy unless it comes from a compassionate heart. What needs to be proclaimed is a gospel of hope, but it will be a false hope unless it is founded on the doctrines of a truly incarnational theology. What needs to be revealed in the way the church relates to the world is the human face of God. What needs to be endlessly celebrated is the resurrection affirmation of human worth, where the church:

> ... invites humanity not to become something else, but to be more authentically what it already is. The whole of creation contains, as it were, the plan for its own perfection. The rediscovery of this Catholic humanist spirit was the most enduring legacy of the Second Vatican Council, which moved the Catholic Church from a stance of confrontation and withdrawal, as though it were a fortress drawn up against the errors of the modern world from which the faithful had to be protected, to one of co-operation and fellow-travelling, affirming the Psalmist's principle that all that is, is good. No other text of the council has quite the resonance, more than thirty years later, of the opening verbal trumpet-cry of the *Constitution on the Church in the Modern World, Gaudium et Spes*: 'The joys and the hopes, the griefs and the anxieties of the people of our time, especially those who are poor, or who are in any way afflicted, these too are the joys and hopes, the griefs and anxieties of the followers of Christ.' This is more than solidarity; this is – and the baptismal metaphor is not inappropriate – total immersion. It is the charter of the Easter people.[8]

Baptism Revisited

Our charter as an Easter people, therefore, is to understand sacraments in this light, as an explicit sign and manifestation of what is already holy about life itself. When parents present their child for baptism, that child is already, by his or her human nature, an epiphany of the divine. To understand baptism, one must first recognise that God loves each human being and has bestowed the gift of God's own self on each person, freely, from the moment of conception – 'Before I formed you in the womb I knew you.' This gift of God's own self is a challenge to become immersed totally in our humanity, for God is not only the bestowal of love, but the thrust towards fulfilment, towards becoming fully human. This is what the incarnation revealed, that in Jesus we see the human face of God, divinity within humanity, the glory which is our destiny.

The sacrament itself makes manifest the indwelling love of God, and through declaring itself in word and sign, fully realises this grace. This does not remove the freedom to accept, or not, the challenge of God's love, for the acceptance of baptism is the journey of the whole of Christian life. There is, of course, within our human condition an incompleteness, the capacity to choose darkness and sin, to deceive ourselves and to deny our true calling. This we have already referred to as 'original sin'. What is important now is to regain an understanding of the graces and challenges of baptism at work each day of our lives in all that we are about. Baptism can be seen as the gospel sacrament, the visible sign that brings about the transformed, healed, resurrection-life. When a baby is baptised, it is the visible sign that this Christian life has begun in another person, and the whole community is enriched by this new member who will grow to share the blessings, bear the sorrows and help the love within the community to deepen.

Baptism, for all its ceremony, is not a 'churchy' thing. It is a life-pledge ... and it therefore has a life-enactment. Going under the water and coming up again ... is a sign of new life emerging from death ... Daily throughout our lives we confront our pledge – and encounter Christ's power to die to the old corrupted way of human living, a way that is ego-centric, dishonest and blind ... But every day, perhaps it is possible for me, whether I do it or not, to see, repent of and try to overcome some small degree of my selfishness, my indifference, dishonesty and blindness. If I do it at all, in however a minute way, I do it through the power of my baptism. I do it because baptism has forever given me the power to open myself to a new life of truth, self-surrender and love.[9]

To take this view of baptism is a far cry from what many of us were brought up with, and it places so much more emphasis on the dynamic of divine grace at work in all the little attempts to live lives of service. I am sure, too, it would colour our response to parents seeking the baptism of their infant if we concentrated less on proof and conditions of regular practice, but more on the grace, love and support within the community, ready in its human kindness and forgiveness, to nurture and protect this new manifestation of God's glory. It also makes much more sense for baptism to be a community celebration, not only because the community is able to celebrate its own enrichment with the welcome of the latest member, but also because it gives individuals an opportunity to hear again the marvellous words spoken about each one of them, often so long ago.

The celebration of the Easter Vigil, with all its cosmic connections, realises the need to die again and again and yet again to all that is negative and fearful in our life, and to rejoice in the triumph of the cross. It is equally certain that if the institutional church acted upon the dignity and responsibilities conferred by baptism – the sharing in the priestly, prophetic and pastoral ministry of Christ – collaborative ministry in parishes would be the norm. What is at stake throughout this brief exploration of baptism is to grasp hold of the fact that it is the sacrament of life itself, constantly urging us to open to the fullness of our graced humanity.

The institutional churches today are not responding effectively as the early Christians did to the spiritual hunger of their times … On the one hand, there is a pressing need felt by many people of our time to 'escape' for a time from our oppressive and materialistic society into a deeply personal religious experience where they can have peace of spirit. On the other hand, there is an equally urgent need, experienced by the same or different people, to find an alternative system of meaning and values which challenges the dominant system in the public sphere of economics, politics and culture. Christianity has the potential to meet these needs. But it can do so only if it meets four conditions. First, it must be animated by a living faith; a purely institutional church will not meet the personal religious needs of our time. Second, it must be embodied in a way that provides effective public challenge to the dominant economic, social, political and cultural systems of today's world. This does not mean that it should offer a fully worked out blueprint for an alternative society; but it must propose fundamental beliefs and values as criteria for judging what would constitute a more humane world. Third, it should provide inspiration and energy for those who take on the challenge of constructing such an alternative, domination-free world. Fourth, the church must present its beliefs and values in an idiom which is appropriate to modern culture; this means it must express itself in thought-patterns and modes of experience which are meaningful to the 'searchers' of our world.[10]

Is the church that most of us experience through its sacramental and communal life providing this kind of nurture and challenge that will enable its members to live out their priestly and prophetic roles? Is it using symbols and language that carry meaning for people of today? Archbishop Rembert Weakland considers that the church needs to take up again the attitude of enthusiasm and hope which were characteristic of the Second Vatican Council, and to look for different ways of reaching people's lives.

> There is a need for a new God-language that our people can understand. Here I would call for a renewal of our mystical and contemplative traditions that have been so much a part of our past. One would not see that renewal as a contradictory to the liturgical renewal; rather the two go hand in hand. The sense of the sacred and the transcendent must be very much part of our liturgy and not something divorced from our daily life. In this way we can show the world that we are a sign of something which is more meaningful and more complete than just the daily tragedies that all of us must face.[11]

The Round Table
A humble image often carries hidden power. In our new church one the things visitors immediately notice, amongst the many striking features, is the beautiful, round wooden table, which stands on the same floor level as all the seating. In its simple elegance it stands there as a powerful sign of what the eucharist is

proclaiming. At this table, all are welcome, and there are no places that are higher than anyone else. It is a gathering place, the 'meaning-place' for all the cycles of our life, for the full circle of community living that week – whether this be the celebration of a ruby wedding, the closure of the local factory, the floods in Bangladesh, children returning to school after the summer holiday, in fact every single detail, mundane and boring, that fills our days and nights. With the bread and wine, all is offered, blessed, broken and shared so that we can remember and celebrate last week's experiences and be given the courage and strength to offer ourselves in the week ahead. God is truly praised and thanked each Sunday when we realise there are no sides to this table, and no one would be sent away empty, because it is the Lord's table. All who come to this table are ready or are struggling to forgive, but this is only possible because forgiveness has already been celebrated in healing moments during the week.

It is a place of challenge, for this is the table on which we commemorate the mystery of the cross, that it is in the heart of our pain and struggle that new life is born. At this table we are reminded that the fruits of this earth, the bread and wine, are for all people everywhere, that 'Christ is the bread seeking hunger,' as St Augustine wrote. Ours are the hearts and hands that have to feed the hungry as we have been fed. The table is round, and like the host, a symbol of the earth, the universe, and upon this table the whole of creation is celebrated. In song and dance, in word and sign, in silence and conversation, all is gathered and offered and draws people to the table only to the extent that what happens at this table is happening in our lives. There is a lovely poem which captures much of what I'm writing, and seems to have been created with our table in mind:

Concerning the why and how and what of ministry
one image keeps surfacing;
– a table that is round.

It will take some sawing
to be roundtabled;
some redefining
and redesigning ...

It would mean no diaising and throning,
for but one king was there,

and he was a footwasher,
at table no less ...

And what of narrowlong table ministers
when they confront
a roundtable people
after years of working up the table
to finally sit at its head
only to discover
that the table has turned round?

Continued rarefied air
will only isolate
for there are no people there
only roles ...

And ALL are invited
to wholeness and food.
Roundtabling means
no preferred seating
no first and last
no better and no corners
for 'the least of these.'

It means room for the Spirit
and gifts
and disturbing peace for all.

And it is we in the present
who are mixing and kneading
the dough for the future.
We can no longer prepare for the past.[12]

The eucharistic table is an intimate table. It invites us to draw close to a God who became a human body in its totality. We gather around this table with our deepest longings, our secret desires, our most exquisite intimacies, our moments of passion and ecstasy – with the totality of our humanity. We are bodily, sensual creatures and in that very bodiliness and sensuality God is made manifest too. Some theologians image the world itself as God's body. Wherever in the universe there is new life, ecstasy, fulfilment, God experiences these pleasures and rejoices with each creature in its joy. Why, then, does the church today deny so much that is so beautiful; why the suspicion of the loveliness of natural things, the wonder of our world and of our bodies, the greenness of all that the poets love and honour? Are not these among the first things to be celebrated in the eucharist? Why are we so afraid of our physical feelings, of our soul-emotions, of our gut-reactions, the things that bring tears of pain, pleasure and memory, the intense longings that lightened and darkened the thoughts and face of Jesus? For many people, overtones of passion or desire in God's love for creatures is somehow threatening. This is especially true in thinking of God as lover, and yet the *Song of Songs* uses the most erotic language, as do many of the mystics. Gertrude of Helfta writes in intensely intimate images:

> You are the delicate taste of intimate sweetness,
> Oh most delicate caresser,
> Gentlest passion,
> Most ardent lover.[13]

Bernard of Clairvaux mirrors the *Song of Songs* when he describes the incarnation as a divine kiss, God's mouth kissing the mouth of humanity. 'Happy kiss … in which God is united with his creatures.' Such were the metaphors that sprang to the lips of these holy people, and yet so many Catholics have been conditioned to think of their most ardent passions as somehow questionable. Could we instead rejoice that something uniquely precious to God is repeatedly incarnated every time the act of love is appropriately celebrated? What a pity that the lovely words of the couple, 'With my body I thee worship' have been dropped from the form of marriage. And just as in the becoming flesh of divine love in Jesus Christ there was transfiguration, loneliness and vulnerability unto death, so too in the loving embrace there are echoes of ecstasy, the 'little death', and, strangely, intimations of a deeper longing. How can our church revitalise itself by becoming, not the judge or the examiner of these essential dimensions of humanity, but their defender, purifier and champion? Maureen Kelly, writing in *The Furrow*, captures the essential truth that nothing is outside the arena of the holy and all is to be gathered and celebrated, as a different face of the supreme Lover.

> The liturgy becomes a privileged moment where the deepest meaning which is often hidden in the depths of life is brought to the level of consciousness and made explicit. The liturgy and sacraments are moments for professing, deepen-

ing, appropriating, personalising and celebrating what is always and everywhere happening, but seldom recognised. Seen in this way, liturgy is the Christian community's consciousness of grace. Celebrating the eucharist then adds nothing to the world, but celebrates what is really happening in the world ... Jesus' cross is not raised again, but its presence at the heart of the world is put into words.[14]

Ecclesia Semper Reformanda

We are beginning to get the picture of a radically different emphasis, where engagement in the world becomes the locus of experience of God. This in turn will lead to a reclamation of the significant part each baptised person has to play in the life of the church, and the new patterns of catechesis and leadership that must emerge. Theologian Edward Schillebeeckx's *The Church with a Human Face* attempts to trace the fundamental shifts, as well as the threads of continuity, in the church's developing concept of ministry since the first Christian millennium. It is fascinating to read his analysis of the types of ministry and models of leadership in the church of the first followers of Jesus, which guards against any form of dualism. It is misguided to imagine that divine revelation can be separated from the reality of ministry experienced by people within the church. What we experience communicates to us the reality within it, which is why *Lost Soul?* is so concerned that we rediscover the church of Jesus, and make that our model.

> There is no 'surplus revelation' behind or above the socio-historical forms of ministry ... We are always concerned with the one and the same reality: the form which has grown up through history and which can be explained sociologically or historically is precisely what the believer experiences and expresses in the language of faith as a specific manifestation of grace: a successful, less successful or improper response of the believing community to God's grace.[15]

Schillebeeckx argues powerfully that God-becoming-human in Jesus gives rise among men and women to a new relationship with God, and the visible sign of this new relationship is a new way of relating among men and women. This pattern of relationship between people reflects the presence and action of God, which Jesus himself calls 'the kingdom', and generates a community of peace which 'brings liberation and opens up communication.' The king-

dom exists as a social community where sinners, poor, the outcast, children – all the people Jesus sought out and with whom
he ate – have a place.

Between the second and the fourth century there was a huge
shift, and during that period a mystique began around the role
of 'consecrating priest', in contrast to the reality of the first
Christians where ministry and leadership was based on the variety of charisms of all those who were 'baptised in the Spirit'.
Gradually the process of discerning gifts and leadership roles
became more specialised:

> In the course of the centuries this gradual centralisation of
> ministry at the expense of the baptism of the Spirit was to
> produce all sorts of side-effects. From it arose the pattern of
> a) teaching (which is done by church hierarchy), b) explain-
> ing (which is done by theologians), c) listening to the teach-
> ing of the church as explained by the theologians (which is
> done by the believers, called laity) ... Vatican II has already
> contributed in some degree to the break-up of this ideologi-
> cal scheme.[16]

Although it was the intention of Vatican II to begin to dismantle
this clerical, patriarchal style of leadership, clearly the vision has
not yet come to fruition. Indeed many would admit to a certain
polarisation of attitudes, where there is little dialogue. What is
needed, according to Archbishop Weakland, is for the church to
regain a humble approach and be mindful of the call of Pope
John XXIII that the church is in constant need of reform – *ecclesia
semper reformanda*. Discussing the vulnerable state of the church
in Ireland at this time, Oliver Maloney considers that listening to
the Spirit '... requires patient and attentive listening to people's
hopes and aspirations, their fears and feelings of vulnerability.
To paraphrase Yeats, we must tread softly because we may indeed be treading on their dreams.'[17]

He identifies three areas of grave concern, where the Vatican
is in danger of imitating secular society in its systematic rejection of community life this century by

> ... the favouring of the institutional above the personal, au-
> thoritarianism and the suppression of dialogue ... The main-
> tenance of an institution becomes an end in itself, not a
> means to the achievement of the original purpose ... On re-
> cent evidence, there is less than the appropriate measure of
> respect in Rome for the individual characteristics and

importance of the various local and national churches. This does not serve community ...

Authoritarianism frequently follows from an excessive emphasis on institutional considerations ... Order becomes the dominant value; obedience the primary virtue. In recent years these traits characterise much of the Vatican's dealings with local church, theologians and laity ...

Whenever debate is suppressed the communitarian spirit is put at risk. Within the church the most notable example of this is the attempt to suppress open debate on the issue of the ordination of women ... Truth is a possession of the whole church, not simply the leadership ... Why do I pay such attention to these obstacles to community? I do so because there is a great danger that those who hold power in the church will repeat the error of the people of Israel, who identified the Kingdom of Israel with the Kingdom of God.[18]

Family Model

We know from our experience of church today that much of what Schillebeeckx describes as a 'centralisation of ministry' influences how the church operates. Equally, most lay people would not immediately identify themselves as being baptised in the Spirit with unique charism and ministry to offer. Many would still describe a hierarchical, pyramid model of church as the one most of us experience. For many, like Oliver Maloney, their image of church will be affected by what they have witnessed in recent times. The experience we have of church today is not always a manifestation of the church of Jesus, which leads one to wonder what sign the church is communicating to the world. When people are asked to think particularly about the church as community, again their understanding will most surely be fashioned by their experience. Many people today are reflecting on their vision of and hopes for the church. Gill Davis, a parish catechist and primary-school teacher, looked to her own experience of family life as a basic model. 'What image,' she asked, 'in our lives today can help us reclaim Jesus' vision?'

'There are many images,' Gill wrote, 'from everyday life that one could draw upon to be the seedbed of our growing church, all of which would highlight different aspects of being church, but for me the image of the church as 'family' is the one that has the potential to encapsulate and energise the message of the

gospel for our world today. Many may think that this is too simplistic a model for something as complex as a universal church,
which needs structure and order, but structures and orders are
only as important as the principles they uphold.'

'The question we now have to ask ourselves is, do we want it
to be a caring and ever-evolving community of love whose only
aim would be to bring to birth and nurture the divine potential
in one another? Because if it is, then we should stop at nothing to
help bring it about. Throughout my life I have always known
that I would be welcomed, held and loved by my family
whether I call once a week or once a month. I know that I will
never be excluded because of something I have said or done or a
mistake I have made. I know that the unity of my family does
not rest upon rules and regulations but the love we share.'

'With a deep faith in this love I know that all things can be
turned to good. I know that within my family there is a place for
everybody – the noisy toddler, the restless teenager, the hassled
parents, the distant relatives and the relaxed grandparents.
Above all, I know that my family loves me and accepts me just
the way I am.'

How many people could read this passage again and with
absolute sincerity replace the words 'my family' for 'my
church'? While Gill well knows there is more to church than the
notion of family, yet without this dimension, in all its beautiful
mystery, the doctrine of church as the Body of Christ, the *Corpus
Christi*, makes no earthly sense.

There are undoubtedly many dysfunctional elements in the
life of the church, many tensions, opposing viewpoints, even
deep divisions. Rather than avoiding these, or worse, pretend-
ing that they don't exist and retreating into the false security of
familiar patterns, the key is to acknowledge and encounter such
conflicts and then to forge new images. Put starkly, the most
urgent need at this time is for the church to re-imagine and re-
create itself in order to regain its soul. The stories of the people,
what is happening to them, and what we do with the happenings, are the places we mine for spirituality.

Sacrament of Failure

The way of Jesus is the way of paradox. If we were to focus on
the company Jesus kept, the people with whom he seemed most
at ease, we would surely find the poor, the outcast, the sinner. In

our current, success-orientated society such people would be deemed to have failed in some way. These people are hardly the most valued members of society, but instead are frequently the recipients of disdain and disapproval. And yet, if Jesus were walking our streets today, we would probably find that it was with these very people that he would be sharing the good news.

Jesus was particularly concerned about those who were outcast or disadvantaged in his world. The religious belief of his time gave little encouragement to such people. It was assumed that God shared the prejudices of the privileged categories of society. So those who were poor, or sick, or disturbed in mind – as well as those who engaged in such despised work as herding pigs – were given to believe that they were in some way cursed by God; certainly, neither their religious leaders nor their culture or belief-system gave them any reason to believe that God cared for them. Jesus went out of his way to meet and value such people. But he went further: as Albert Nolan points out, Jesus was so moved by compassion for the plight of the outcasts that he made a deliberate choice to join them, to become an outcast himself.[19]

Do we find the church alongside the outcast of our day, showing the same human compassion of Jesus? There are indeed many caring individuals, as well as church-sponsored projects, working with homeless people, with drug and alcohol abusers, etc., but in the main the institutional church seems more in tune with maintaining a comfortable, fairly affluent lifestyle. Jesus understood that his liberating mission would leave him very vulnerable, that it would bring him face to face with the powers of domination in his time, in a conflict of truths that would cost him his life. The church of today, national and international justice and peace work not withstanding, the teaching institution, in the eyes of many, seems very far removed from that level of commitment to the wounded and vulnerable, at a more personal and domestic level. Perhaps it needs to learn that it is in the unexpected places, amongst the marginalised, that we will find prophets of hope who will be able to touch us in such a way that we become transformed.

If reality is to do with God and if God is to be encountered wherever we meet the Christ, then where shall we find him? ... May we not encounter Christ living out the love of God in our world, in places of weakness, failure, poverty? Might it not be that the heartbeat of the gospel, the living touch of reality is revealed to us from among the weak, the vulnerable and the failures of today's world? Those who are not able to live a life we call normal: the homeless and the confused; the alcoholic who fails to kick the addiction; the child with cancer whose body fails in its fight for life; the Down's Syndrome girl whose mind fails to work in ways we think appropriate; the divorced priest whose failed marriage ruins his career and brings him closer to God? ... In our searching for reality and for meaning it may be that we discover this gift, this precious sacrament of life is offered by God ... but that we receive it from the unwashed hands of the priesthood of the poor.[20]

A Humble, Contrite Church

Within the church itself, there are many who feel alienated and hurt by the harsh attitude of aspects of the church's official teaching. At a recent Diocesan Pastoral Meeting (1999), delegates were invited to listen in a spirit of humility to the hurt felt by a divorced person because of the attitude of many within the Catholic Church. Delegates also heard about the extremely painful situations in which many divorced people who remarry find themselves because of church laws. It was significant to read in the feedback from delegates that the *sensus fidelium* called for a change in the official approach to the divorced and remarried, for an amnesty for priests who have left, and for a recognition that the church was completely out of touch with people's lives on a wide-range of pressing issues. It was also felt that the church should radically increase the number of occasions when intercommunion is deemed appropriate. It seemed quite shocking that our leaders should persist in denying a place at our table for those sisters and brothers of ours, who, in their belief and practice regarding eucharistic participation, often put us Catholics to shame.

Reaction to the recent guidelines from the Bishops' Conferences of England and Wales, Ireland and Scotland, on receiving Holy Communion, *One Bread, One Body*, recently filled the Catholic press. Mixed though the reaction is, the overwhelming feeling seems to be one of deep sadness, extreme disappointment, and some anger, that at this crucial time in the history of Christianity, those in authority in these isles find it necessary to base their decisions regarding intercommunion on premises and principles (mostly from Canon Law) rather than on the spirit of the teaching of Jesus. We are advised about 'norms' and 'lawful practices' as the foundation of pastoral action, rather than being encouraged to discern the stirrings in people's hearts these days, as they recognise each other's integrity in wanting to, 'Do this in memory of me', as Jesus asked. We certainly do not notice in the synoptic gospels that Jesus defined norms and lawful practices before inviting all to the table, and in John we only see the foot-washer, a Servant-God kneeling at the feet of sinners.

When we hear the words of consecration, 'Take this, *all of you*, and eat it: this is my body ... Take this, *all of you*, and drink from it: this is the cup of my blood, the blood of the new and everlasting covenant. It will be shed *for you and for all* ...', why do we immediately want to introduce conditions and rules? How has this fearful and defensive mindset grown within the Catholic Church in such a way that it can stray so far from the heart of Jesus and be so out of touch with the intuitive wisdom of so many of his ordinary followers? How have we made the food of life, bread and wine, into such an exclusive menu that it is out of reach of so many? Where is the compassion and service of foot-washing in this document?

As Archbishop Weakland notes, 'Ecumenism, too, has not worked as people had thought it might. There seems to be no attempt on the part of the churches to come to a true hierarchy of truth. Often what seems to be most important to theologians takes on a whole different weight with regard to the faithful themselves.'[21] The call for a rethinking about intercommunion certainly seems to be one issue where theologians were out of tune with many lay-folk who would have had good reason to expect that by now Vatican II's *Decree on Ecumenism* would have borne more fruit. Sr Mary Cecily Boulding, a theologian who taught for many years at Ushaw College, argues that if the same measure of loyalty had been given to this Council that was given to the Council of Trent, things might have been different. She believes that there have been

> ... deliberate and active attempts to subvert it and reverse the paradigm it adopted. Fear, insecurity, confusion and bewilderment are understandable and to be forgiven ... but deliberate betrayal is intolerable, whether it comes from the church's bureaucratic departments in apparent attempts to

limit the meaning and phrases in the documents of Vatican II; from clerics who repudiate any notion of vocation for the laity because it diminishes the little empires they have built for themselves; from naïve seminarians who refuse to see the real point of vernacular in the liturgy, or from laity – young and old – who simply prefer the old ways, oblivious of how many starving human souls those old ways failed to nourish. Catholicity means loyalty to the church, as church, as a whole, not just to those aspects which are comfortable, personally helpful or attractive. Such selectivity echoes the original meaning of the word heresy: 'to pick and choose'.[22]

Pope John Paul, in his Jubilee Letter, urges that we need 'an increased sensitivity to all that the Spirit is saying to the church and the churches ... Despite appearances, humanity continues to await the revelation of the children of God, and lives by this hope, like a mother in labour, to use the image quoted so powerfully by St Paul in his Letter to the Romans.'[23] The church is constantly giving birth to a new understanding of itself in every age, and for those who are fearful of new images, there is a tendency to cling tenaciously to a former, more limited understanding. There is great danger for the church if it succumbs in this way.

As with the Israelites of old, as with every weary or frightened traveller, the church is constantly tempted throughout history to stop travelling, to settle for something that seems not only a rest, a respite, but even a sensible safety precaution, a secure haven which, while clearly imperfect and not the completeness of salvation, is at least secure; secure against some of the worldly temptations which can divert our love from God; secure against errors, mistaken theological concepts and interpretations of what God has revealed to us about himself; secure against doubts and uncertainties as to whether this really is the right way. But we can only know that if we keep moving.[24]

Throughout its history, the journey of the pilgrim church has been marked by periods of great bursts of energy, when the Spirit seems to have been moving powerfully, whilst at other times there is a sense that the church is dawdling or even, occasionally, in decline. When Pope John XXIII inaugurated the Second Vatican Council he hoped windows would be opened for the wind of the Spirit to blow freely through the church, bringing renewed hope.

Sadly this explosion of energy and spirit has not met with anything like the loyalty that greeted the work of Trent – perhaps because the paradigm shift was so great and so obvious. Up to the sixteenth century it was possible at least to preserve the fiction that the paradigm – the concept framework within which new ideas and practices were assimilated and brought into continuity with what had gone before – had not changed fundamentally. With Vatican II that fiction was shown up for what it was: a blinkered refusal to admit that the church has constantly changed throughout its history, is always changing, and must go on changing if it is not to die. It is Christ's body in this world now, not in some ideal realm or some past, forgotten age. It is made up of, and is the vehicle of salvation for, the men and women of today just as much as for those of yesterday, and indeed of tomorrow: as the English Bishops said recently, 'The notion of tradition implies being faithful to the future as well to the past. *(The Sign We Give)* 25

Now is not the time for standing still. The third millennium beckons the church to renew its vision for the future. And what are the signposts the church will follow as it journeys towards the future? It will be a journey the whole people of God make together, confident that from amongst the people, prophets will speak their truth, mystics will inspire, and the indwelling Spirit will fill God's people with new energy. The church will grow in self understanding as *Sacrament of Humanity* as it immerses itself more deeply into the world, embodying the compassion of Jesus, the foot-washer, and celebrating the graced nature of all of creation.

Leadership From Within

In January 1999 the Conference of Religious in England and Wales held their annual general meeting to consider their identity in the church and how they might work in partnership with others. These two major issues had arisen as a result of a process of consultation that had taken place during the previous year. Many questions were raised and, in the president's address, the following were quoted:

How many of us have been saddened in pastoral work by the suffering of people excluded from the sacraments?

How many of us are horrified at the way questioning, creative or dissenting voices are silenced?

How many of us are frustrated, along with others, at the lack of nourishment for faith in our parish liturgies?

It is a pity that the gifts of the baptised, especially women, are under-valued and under-used.

It is sad if collaboration and consultation are considered to be unnecessary and time-consuming.

We hear some members of our province saying, 'I wish that I could be a religious and not be a Catholic.'

How many of our members have, to some extent, written off the church?[1]

These fundamental questions are on the lips of many clergy and lay people too. Many of the concerns expressed are explored further in this chapter with the aim of generating a dialogue and of giving fresh hope for the way forward. This chapter is concerned especially with the questions raised on matters of authority, leadership and collaboration within the church. The questions being asked by many lay people today arise directly out of the kind of authority and leadership they have experienced.

Have authority and leadership within the church become distanced from ordinary parishioners' faith development? Why do many in authority seem determined to maintain the current all-male power structure, thereby losing the energy, creativity and wisdom of the lived experience of deeply committed women and men? What styles and models of leadership do we need if our church is to fulfil its mission for the world at the beginning of the third millennium? Is it possible to get anywhere near the kind of servant leadership exemplified by Jesus when the Lord of the universe became a footwasher? Is this vision the one that will inspire hope and bring new life to an ailing church? What, then, would the styles of an appropriate, acceptable and renewed leadership be like?

'Never doubt that a small group of people can change the world,' the noted anthropologist Margaret Mead wrote. 'Indeed that is all that ever has.' There was only one Ghandi and a meagre band of disciples, one Martin Luther King and a few personal advisers, one Thomas Merton and a handful of like-minded friends, but in every case the influence of these few far outranked their numbers. Quality, not quantity, marked their presence. Substance, not the size of the group, brought attention to their message and their message to the forefront of society.[2]

To identify the qualities of good leaders is a very subtle art. Each of the leaders mentioned by Joan Chittister could be said to have led from below. None of them were given an office of high authority, and yet they did have authority, and people certainly followed them in droves. One quality each of these people had was a passion, a heart that was on fire, and that is quite an irresistible quality. Another quality that all three manifested was immense commitment to that passion and, again, others are challenged by such conviction. Perhaps here we have the kernel of what real leadership is about, that it happens from within. In other words, good leaders are those who are able to be in touch with their own weaknesses and failings, their own shadow, so that their energy is directed outwards, not to build up self, but to raise up others.

Paradoxically, leadership could be said to be about diminishment – becoming less so that others may become more. Seen in this light, leadership is more an artform, a delicate craft, than a set of skills to be learned. It is not a case of denying that there are skills involved in leadership, rather that these are not the essence of what makes a good leader. The essence of the kind of leadership Joan Chittister is discussing is about integration. All three leaders in question had the courage to make that inner journey of self-knowing and self-acceptance which gave integrity to their passion and their commitment. It is a dynamic that has been explored by Parker J. Palmer, whose insight has much to offer as a model for leadership for the church since he is primarily concerned with the spirituality of leadership, and the need within the church for leaders willing to make the journey into the inner life. The main thrust of Palmer's argument is that if leaders are not aware of their own weaknesses and fears, much of their attempts to lead will be a projection of these fears in order to maintain their own position or to secure a way of operating with which they feel safe. Leadership then becomes authoritative and stifling rather than freeing and creative. Risk and innovation are avoided because of fear of failure and therefore many opportunities for real growing are lost.

It is no exaggeration to say that, for thousands of Catholics, the style of leadership expressed through the public teaching and exercise of authority within the church today is not experienced as freeing, but rather seems to be concerned with maintaining a system, expecting the faithful to be submissive. I have in mind, especially, documents such as *Ad Tuendam Fidem,* discussed earlier in this book, as well as attempts to condemn theologians and spiritual writers like Tissa Balassuriya and Anthony de Mello, people who have brought freshness and hope to so many through their gifted writing and preaching. One has to ask about what fear may prompt such modes of behaviour on the part of some in authority within the church.

Before Vatican II, many people regarded the church primarily as an institution with the authority to make judgements and set rules for living. At its most simplistic, the church was seen as a hierarchy, a kind of pyramid, with the Pope at the head, the curia in Rome there to implement his teaching, the bishops to pass this on to their own dioceses, and the priests to filter directives down to the people. This model, overlooking any role in decision-making or discernment on the part of the laity, still pertains in most leaders' minds today, but is unlikely to facilitate the church's mission for the world. It is a very safe, fixed view, where everybody has a place and knows it, and which perpetuates the male, celibate, clerical style of leadership that still dominates. At the same time it diminishes and denies so many gifts within lay women and men.

Vatican II's vision of the church as the whole people of God, a sacrament of Christ's presence in the world, recognising the call of each baptised person to make Christ's mission his or her own, regards the very nature of the church as a 'communion', with each person having equal dignity by virtue of birth and baptism. The principle of collegiality was acknowledged, whereby the Pope and bishops *together* exercise authority in terms of pastoral service towards God's people. The Spirit was recognised to be at work in all parts of the community, calling each baptised person to take their rightful place in the life of the church. Thus, the security of familiar, hierarchical roles of pre-Vatican II times began to be exchanged for a more egalitarian style of leadership, which has naturally caused great discomfort and distrust in some circles, and unrestrained delight in others. The last thirty years or so since the Council, therefore, have been characterised somewhat by confusion and a certain polarisation between those who want to return to the safety of the past, and others who, in their efforts to promote the role of laity, seem to advocate a political-style democracy. However, this principle of collegiality does not seem to be exercised now in quite the way many bishops hoped, and there are some within the church today who perhaps perceive the authority of the local church being undermined by Rome. Writing in *Céide*, Fr Don McLellan observes:

> ... at a crucial moment in time, when the church was called to engage the future with courage and hope, her leadership chose to retreat to the past ... The curia, which had been off-balanced by the surge of enthusiasm for reform in post-conciliar days, regained its stride. Slowly, methodically, it reasserted itself as the centre of power in the church. It began to replace bishops who were collegial and co-responsible with those who echoed (if silently) the Vatican call for centralised power at the expense of national conferences and local communities ... The spirit of episcopal collaboration, given new life at the time of the council, recognised that all the bishops together were co-responsible for shaping the direction of the church. For the most part, this understanding of conciliar leadership has been 'redefined'.[3]

The Catholic Church, therefore, now finds herself in a paradoxical situation where mixed messages are being given out, and where there is a reluctance to grasp the nettle of a radical shift in approaches to leadership. It is also an exciting situation, present-ing great opportunities for fresh initiatives and new models to emerge. This spirit was captured in a talk given to the Bishops of England and Wales in October 1998, by Fr Anthony Philpot, who said, 'Catholic clergy in Britain have a sense of crisis and a feeling of guilt. No wonder. We are the generation ... who have lived across the watershed from boom to decline. We have presided over what in statistical terms is a reversal in the church's fortunes.' He warns that we must not go back 'to tighten discipline' but that we must have 'faith in resurrection (because) ... The coming church, whose face we cannot fully discern, will be new. It will be a resurrected, sobered, mature church, hum-bler, realising that all is gift.'[4]

The Sign We Give

On the one hand, *Christifideles Laici* in 1988 went a long way to affirming that all members of the church share in the priestly, prophetic and servant-king mission of Jesus, and in England and Wales, the Bishops' Conference brought out the document *The Sign We Give*, insisting on the need to develop different ways of ministering together in parishes. Both documents recognised that each person has unique charisms and gifts which are needed if the church is to fulfil its mission for the world, and the vision of co-responsibility and collaborative ministry was proclaimed. At a local, parish level, the role of the priest was suddenly less obvious, and much heart-searching continues still to discern what is the precise nature of ordained, priestly ministry. *Pastores Dabo Vobis* in 1992 declared the priest's primary task as someone who enables communion: 'As a servant of communion, he builds up the unity of the church community in the harmony of diverse vocations, charisms and services.'[5]

In the midst of all this dialogue and honest questioning about trying to redraw the shapes of ministry, and breaking into any brave attempts to forge new models of collaborative leadership, there was a surprising backlash from Rome, in the form of the *Instruction on certain questions regarding the collaboration of the non-ordained faithful in the sacred ministry of priests*, issued in the summer of 1997. This document brought strong warnings about the dangers of 'non-ordained faithful' exceeding their roles and encroaching upon ministerial priesthood. It seemed to under-mine the thrust and recommendations of *The Sign We Give*. The only response of our bishops was to imply that this *Instruction* did not really apply to Britain, but was more addressed to certain situations within some parishes in Europe. Many 'non-ordained faithful' felt disappointed to find that the bishops of these isles did not passionately defend their own, insightful *The Sign We Give*, based as it is on such visionary Vatican II theology.

Not only do such statements diminish the dignity of the people of God, they also, perhaps, illustrate clearly the fearful, defensive mind-set out of which such authority operates. What seems to be feared above all is the dialogue, the trusting listening to the hearts of all the faithful, in the search for styles of leadership which match the needs of our times. For some, when laypeople share in the many responsibilities for ministering to God's people, it is as if the role of the ordained priest is somehow diminished. Clearly there is need for a significant shift in understanding what the role of the priest in a community involves; for recognising the kind of leadership that will be a sign in the world that God's reign is amongst us. What needs to come to birth is a way of imaging leadership that enables the full potential of all God's people, seeks its wisdom in the humblest of places, and knows when it can stand back so that others can stand forward.

> Unity, communion, valuing everyone in the parish community and regarding them as being on equal terms with you; commitment to the good of all ... There's the object and thrust of not only the priestly ministry but that of the whole parish community. The parish as a whole is being asked to take responsibility for its pastoral care. There's no pyramidal, authoritarian structure, with the priest at its apex. But as *The Sign We Give* makes bold to point out, there's a paradox in all of this. Without firm leadership from the priest leading strongly 'from the front', this communion in mission won't happen. That doesn't mean that the style of leadership has to be domineering or bombastic, but there is a need for a Moses figure to keep leading God's people to the promised land and chivvying them along when necessary.[6]

The hopes and vision of *The Sign We Give* are, indeed, noble, but the paradox is all too evident. Only where there is a Moses figure, where the priest encourages co-responsibility, can a collaborative approach happen. As someone who has been working for the last four years on the Diocesan *Vision 2000* Programme, to promote collaborative ministry in parishes, I have observed that, even when such collaboration has the endorsement of the local and national bishops, it stands or falls on whether the priest agrees to invite the team in and agrees to be open and learn alongside his parishioners. Indeed, those of us who have been part of this programme realise more and more that collaborative ministry requires *a way of thinking* as a basic foundational principle, rather than there being a set of conditions to fulfil. It is much more about realising that steering the barque of Peter into new waters requires the energies of all its crew, and not just a captain. Avery Dulles, writing twenty years ago, recognised then that there would be resistance to renewal and reform in the church in the aftermath of Vatican II, and called the church a *Society of Explorers*.

> The church ... depends on all the help its thoughtful members can provide in the task of discerning the real meaning of the gospel for our time. Faith, then, is not simply a matter of accepting a fixed body of doctrine. More fundamentally, it is a committed and trustful participation in an ongoing process. For progress to be achieved there must be discussion, and for there to be discussion, all must be assured of their 'lawful freedom of enquiry of thought, and of the freedom to express their minds humbly and courageously about those matters in which they enjoy competence'. Without such freedom ... the church would be deprived of that creative interaction which is the key to authentic renewal.[7]

Changes in a parish, for example the arrival of a new priest unfamiliar with or fearful of the practices and benefits of collaborative ministry, may, initially, give rise to serious difficulties. However, none of these are insurmountable given goodwill by the priests and all who have the interests of the church and the community at heart. So too difficulties may arise where priest and people are endeavouring to establish a different model of pastoral practice in a parish if other parishioners are nervous about embracing the new approach. Change rarely occurs without some problems arising, and within any parish there are bound to be parishioners who feel attempts at collaborative ministry somehow undermine traditionally held beliefs and diminish the role of the priest. Also, more than once we have heard anxious parishioners say that they would rather live with a controlling priest than a powerful clique of lay people. There must be many priests, too, whose theology and vision would commit them to working collaboratively, but who are severely limited by the lack of formation and readiness of parishioners to do the same. However, with patience and sensitivity such situations are usually resolved, and it is vital that real listening and dialogue takes place in order that the gifts and graces of all God's people are harvested for the church's mission to the world.

There is, of course, a hard-won wisdom in the legal and administrative requirements for identifying the places of ultimate responsibility, the locus of the buck-stop. Institutions need a structured system, a *modus operandi*, in decision-making and to ensure its ordered continuity. Without such strategies, even insight and vision would remain undefined. There is no quibble, then, about the necessity of agreed constitutions and modes of procedure to cover all eventualities, because human nature is notoriously unpredictable and ambiguous. What is at issue is the mentality of control that runs through many documents and practices concerning not just the major decisions regarding the well-being of the local church, but even the day-to-day changes and developments within a parish setting, particularly where financial aspects are concerned. Most diocesan norms and guidelines for parish pastoral councils and parish finance committees are examples in point.

Most parishes can find among their members a wealth and variety of professional qualifications in the field of buildings, finance and organisation. What a transformation takes place in a community when parishioners, with the knowledge and support of the community, are encouraged to pursue courses (paid for out of parish funds) for developing leadership talents, group management and communication skills for the benefit of others. And what a joy and relief for the poor parish priests when they see a new greening taking place across the desert parts of their parishes before their very eyes! It is worth noting, too, that wherever we stand on the issue, collaborative ministry will increasingly become a necessity rather than an option, as the number of available priests decline even more.

The shift towards co-responsibility and a new agenda for clerical and lay teamwork will bring much blood, sweat and tears. But these liquid realities are, at least, the signs of life. We are dealing with elemental forces here. Many observers of the stalled condition of the Catholic Church today would trace its roots to a loss of heart, of nerve and determined commitment. It is extraordinary how all of us are so fearful of speaking the truth, of becoming unpopular, of being the 'odd man out', of being rejected, often silently, by the upholders of the *status quo*. The questions raised in this book in general will continue to be raised for many a decade into the future.

Such questions, I would suggest, are at the heart of the matter and concern the fundamental understanding of the nature of leadership. They are at the heart of spirituality, for spirituality is not divorced from the practical issues of life, but rather it is the lens through which all lived experience is viewed. Spirituality is concerned with how we find meaning in our lived experience by recognising God's presence and energy within it all. What spirituality requires of those in authority in the church is to acknowledge that shared responsibility is the grace-filled response of God's people, that collaborative ministry is a reality to be lived, not an imaginary idea to opt for or not, and hopefully it is here to stay. Such a spiritual journey will require much letting-go of the trappings of role and function which are not of the essence of ministry. It is the journey into one's own heart, and it is a journey that is vital for all leaders, but most especially for leaders within the church. It is here that P.J. Palmer's wisdom is most helpful in alerting us to the pitfalls and dangers of remaining in ignorance about the deeply spiritual nature of leadership.

Leading Light

Palmer notes that a striking fact about two acknowledged great political leaders of our time, Nelson Mandela and Vaclav Havel, is the capacity both men had to maintain a vision and a commitment under immense repression. For years it seemed impossible that the two mighty ideologies of apartheid and communism would ever crumble, but from within the confines of these repressive regimes, rose people with extraordinary leadership qualities. Addressing the United States Congress, and speaking of the wisdom learned from suffering oppression, Havel said, 'Consciousness precedes being. For this reason the salvation of the world lies nowhere else than in the human heart, in the human power to reflect, in human meekness and in human responsibility.'[8] Havel is making a most powerful statement about the deep sources of freedom and power, which have enabled people to bring about immense change for the good of so many.

In other words, the most important quality in this area is not political acumen or military strategy, but spirituality. And of course the Christian tradition, along with all the great religions, proclaims this too, that external reality (imprisonment, oppression) can never quench the spirit.

> The great insight of our spiritual traditions is that we co-create the world, that we live in and through a complex interaction of spirit and matter, a complex interaction of what is inside us and what is 'out there'. The insight of our spiritual traditions is not to deny the reality of the outer world, but to help us understand that we create that world, in part, by projecting our spirit on it – for better or worse ... The insight I want to draw from the spiritual traditions, and from Havel, is an insight from depth psychology. The word is 'projection'. We share responsibility for creating the external world by projecting either a spirit of light or a spirit of shadow on that which is 'other' than us. Either a spirit of hope or a spirit of despair. Either an inner spirit of confidence in wholeness and integration, or an inner terror about life being diseased and ultimately terminal. We have a choice about what we are going to project, and in that choice we help create the world that is.[9]

For Palmer, then, a leader is a person with the capacity to project on to other people either an enormous amount of light or an enormous amount of shadow, which means that leaders need to take special responsibility to be aware of their own inner consciousness. He further suggests that those who rise to leadership positions in our society, often do so by operating entirely in the external world, at the cost of internal awareness, and even come to see the inner, spiritual world as illusory, and that this, then, can be a very dangerous form of leadership. Leadership which embraces the spiritual journey, the need to go deeper into our own lives, to face our fears, enables us to 'find the most precious thing of all: the unified field, our complex and inexplicable caring for one another, the community we have underneath our brokenness, our life together ... Great leadership comes from people who have made the downward journey through violence and terror, who have touched the deep place where we are community with each other, and who can help take other people to that place.'[10] For leaders to cast light, they must know their shadow.

The deepest shadow many leaders carry is about their own self-worth, which is often well hidden in extrovert people, but causes an over-identification with role. The more such a leader identifies himself or herself with role or office, the more that may affirm their own self-worth, but it can, subtly and unnoticed, at the same time undermine the role of others. Within the church, as a tiny example, one can easily think of some priests who feel insecure if they are addressed routinely by their Christian name, whereas they would consider it natural to address parishioners in this way. The great gift of the spiritual journey is to know within one's heart that identity does not depend on roles or titles or degrees. The ultimate discovery, says Palmer, is that identity 'depends only on the simple fact that I am a child of God, valued and treasured for what I am'. The landscape around those who know themselves in that way is a landscape illuminated by a light, which encourages others to shine too.

As this book has demonstrated throughout, many people are operating out of a dualistic theology which sees this world as basically flawed. It is almost as if this world has to be overcome, to be fought and dealt with as if in a battleground, for some future heaven to be achieved. This kind of attitude to the world is characterised by a need to control and dominate, which results in a dictatorial approach to leadership. If, however, the spiritual gift of the inner journey is to realise that the universe is actually working for the good of all, that we are all interconnected and interdependent, then the style of leadership that emerges is one of consensus. Again, it is easy to see how one style may diminish other people, while another style is more committed to honouring, respecting and affirming them.

Palmer coins the phrase 'functional atheism' to describe the myth that those in leadership positions believe they are ultimately responsible for everything. 'It is a belief held even among those whose theology affirms a higher power than the human self, people who do not understand themselves as atheists, but whose behaviour belies their belief!'[11] This is manifested frequently in workaholic behaviour that can result in burn-out. It is also known in church circles as the 'Messiah syndrome', when leaders believe that if they don't do it, it won't be done, and then … the world might not be saved! I'm sure we have all witnessed elements of that sort of behaviour within our communities, and perhaps even within ourselves. The blessing received by those on the spiritual journey into the depths of their own heart, is to learn that we are co-creators with God, and that we only have our particular gift to offer. The rest we can trust to the many other co-creators, who each have their own unique role to play too. Leaders with that insight draw all around them into a circle of creative light.

Perhaps the most insightful words from Palmer for illustrating the state of leadership within the Catholic Church today, concern the shadow which he calls 'the denial of death'.[12] By this he means a real fear of failure, of any negative feedback, for such is experienced like a death, as if it is the end of everything. He describes the behaviour typical of leaders or institutions manifesting this kind of shadow, as a frantic endeavour to maintain projects, programmes, systems, or even the institution itself, when these have had but waning life in them for some time. Waste of energy and denial of reality drain the life force of any community. In contrast, those who know that death is natural, and that indeed death is not the end, realise that allowing something to die, enables something new to be born. It is the message of Easter, the message of Christian hope.

Servant Leader

What we need is a creative exploration of models of leadership within the church that understand the need for each person to do their 'inner work'. Pastor Ignotus, writing in *The Tablet*, having been in the unusual position of sitting in the pews for two consecutive weeks whilst on holiday, remarked that what the church needs now more than anything is 'leaders who could speak from their own hearts to the hearts of others'. The liturgy which he attended, in a beautifully planned church, with good musicians, readers commentators, eucharist ministers, lacked only one thing: 'The attitude of the priest himself. There seemed to be no real sense of communication between himself and the congregation. He was probably unconscious of the affected way he spoke and acted ... It was clear to me that the priest in question was suffering from what we might call ministry fatigue and was in need of a sabbatical. He was no longer able to talk from the heart or in a way that he could touch the hearts of others.'[13]

If we return to the gospels to consider the style of leadership exercised by Jesus, the most striking passage is the account of the washing of the disciples' feet. 'Do you understand,' Jesus

said, 'what I have done to you? You call me Master and Lord,
and rightly; so I am. If I, then, the Lord and Master, have washed
your feet, you should wash each other's feet. I have given you
an example so that you may copy what I have done to you.' (Jn
13: 15) This style of servant-leadership is not always immediately
recognisable in the authority structures of the present church.
Authority, viewed from this perspective, is not a question of
power or importance, but is there to serve all members of the
community, by helping them to realise their own unique contribution.

> The leaders do not have a monopoly of insights and gifts;
> their role, on the contrary, is to help all the community's
> members to exercise their own gifts for the good of the
> whole. A community can only become a harmonious whole,
> with 'one heart, one soul, one spirit', if all its members are
> exercising their gifts fully. If the model of relationship is
> worker to boss, or soldier to officer, then there is no under-
> standing of what community means ... There are different
> ways of exercising authority and command. There is the mil-
> itary model, the industrial model, and the community
> model. The general's goal is victory; the factory manager's
> goal is profit. The goal of the leader of a community is the
> growth of individuals in love and truth ... The essential for
> all people with authority is that they are servants before they
> are bosses.[14]

One of the most beautiful and telling titles for the pontiff is that
he is a *servant of the servants of God*. It seems strange, therefore,
that many people within the church feel that their voice is not
heard, that they are not valued, and that even their questioning
is stifled. Archbishop Rembert Weakland considers that:

> ... one of the new signs of our times is the whole crisis of au-
> thority both within the church and within society. Vatican II
> had raised high expectations for a whole new style of exercis-
> ing authority within the church. That style has simply not
> come about. And yet we as people see changes on the globe
> where we thought changes were absolutely impossible. But
> those changes only highlight the fact that the Catholic
> Church has not changed and remains somehow isolated. It
> leaves the church very defensive, then, in terms of its exer-
> cise of authority.[15]

How are we, then, to regain a style of leadership that mirrors
more the servant style of Jesus? Palmer's work, already referred

to, clearly indicates the need for all of us, but especially those in authority, to be rigorous in attending to our *inner work*. Jean Vanier, who has given his life to developing different styles of leadership and imaginative ways of living in community, is deeply convinced that the only option for Christian leaders is the option of Jesus, the footwasher.

> The people who carry responsibility best are those who re-
> ceive it as a mission from God and lean on his strength and
> the gifts of the Holy Spirit. They will feel poor and incapable,
> but they will always act humbly for the good of the commu-
> nity. They will have the community's confidence, for it will
> sense that they trust not in themselves and their own vision
> but in God. The community will sense that they have no need
> to prove anything, that they are not seeking anything for
> themselves ... It will sense they are willing to disappear
> when the moment comes.[16]

He also makes the vital point that leaders need not take them-selves too seriously, but should develop the art of carrying re-sponsibility lightly. 'The secret is to stay young, open and full of wonder.' Coming from years of living in L'Arche communities, Vanier is profoundly convinced that the whole ministry of lead-ership should be geared to the weakest members, those who have no voice. Leaders need to be the voice of those who cannot speak for themselves, and at the same time they need to be able to share their own weakness with the members of the community. What then emerges are leaders who 'engender confidence and hope.'

Community as Leader
The wisdom of Vatican II and the wisdom of *The Sign We Give* was to assert that all the qualities needed for good leadership within our local communities and within the church cannot pos-sibly be found in one person. Jesus gathered his disciples around him, and they in their turn enabled others to take up the role of leader. In *The Church with a Human Face: A New and Expanded Theology of Ministry*, Fr Edward Schillebeeckx com-pares the concept of ministry and leadership in the first Christian churches, with what we experience today. He de-scribes the shift from 'the charisma of many to a specialised charisma of just a few.'[17]

According to Paul and the whole of the New Testament, at

least within the Christian community of believers, relationships involving subjection are no longer to prevail. We find
this principle throughout the New Testament, and it was to
determine strongly the New Testament view of ministry.
This early Christian egalitarian ecclesiology in no way excludes leadership or authority; but in that case authority
must be one filled with the Spirit, from which no Christian,
man or woman, is excluded in principle on the basis of the
baptism of the Spirit.[18]

When one reads this description, one can sense the dignity and
value given to each person, filled as they are with the Spirit, and
as *The Sign We Give* says, 'The eschatological dimension of faith
calls us to be faithful to the future as well as to the past. Newness
is a constant part of the Spirit's gift and presence in the church,
and we need not fear it even if we must discern carefully what it
asks of us.'[19] A useful image of the intricate patterns made by
the veins of a leaf, forming a membrane of interconnections
which give both structure and nurture, provides a marvellous
analogy for the way successful collaborative ministry would operate. The same document also recognises that when people are
trying to share responsibility and leadership roles, there will be
conflict, and therefore a need for ways of dealing with this creatively. This process will demand a degree of 'emotional maturity'
that reinforces the necessity for priests and parishioners to be
aware of the movements of their own hearts. 'People who want
to work collaboratively need a strong sense of their own identity
and a desire for mutual trust and commitment. They must also
be willing to move beyond fixed roles and stereotypes, to explore new horizons, and to acknowledge their limitations and
areas of vulnerability.'[20] Fr Sean Ruth calls for the process of ,

> ... building close relationships, of simply making friends
> with people. This will involve skills of listening, breaking
> through isolation, our own and others', and creating safety
> for people to speak ... The only way the work of the church
> can be effectively progressed is if we see the central role of
> leadership as being the training of new leaders. We have to
> see ourselves, at all levels, as in the business of leading lead-
> ers who, in turn, will lead other leaders, and so on. This is
> probably one of the least understood and certainly least prac-
> tised aspects of the leadership role. The role of the parish
> priest, for example, then becomes, among other things, the

turning of lay people in the parish into leaders of the
parish.[21]

Cardinal Hume has reflected deeply on the development of the
church's understanding of leadership and ministry. His commitment to a collaborative style of ministry is because it more
truly reflects the image of the church as *communion*. The
Cardinal recognises that pastoral practices need a radical re-
appraisal, but the whole basis for that must be trust.

> No longer is it appropriate for the priestly ministry to be ex-
> ercised in splendid isolation and with a semblance of sancti-
> fied autocracy ... Trusting each other, we have to listen to
> each other as possessing in some measure the Spirit of God.
> ... Since Christ has entrusted his church to all of us, we are in
> turn called to deepen our own trust in his Spirit and in each
> other. This must lead us to a church which listens, which
> learns, which is prepared to work in a spirit of collaboration
> without manipulation and discrimination ... The church is
> not an institution dedicated to the pursuit and exercise of
> power. Ministry by its very definition is concerned with ser-
> vice. Collaborative ministry then is the fruit of that *metanoia*
> which involves death to assertiveness and letting-go of self
> interest. Collaboration and interdependence are essential if
> we are ever to transcend practices, habits of thought and
> ways of exercising ministry which owe more to dualism than
> to *communio*.[22]

The Cardinal wrote these powerful words in 1988. Are we any
closer to the vision he upholds so magnificently, or is there a
fearful retreating to former 'safer' positions? Whilst there is undoubtedly still much confusion and paradox, there is still reason
to hope. A final word from Archbishop Weakland adds a necessary perspective. He says, 'It was the Holy Spirit that brought
about and brought to conclusion Vatican Council II and gave so
many new insights and so many sources of renewed inspiration.
That same Holy Spirit is with us today in our generation, in our
day. And that same Holy Spirit will continue to guide us in a
truly creative and expansive way. A global church that is concerned about every individual and every aspect of this planet
awaits us. The Spirit pulls us on to an even greater involvement
if we have the courage to say yes.'[23]

There are many who are saying 'yes' daily in a variety of tiny
and more risky ways, sowing the seeds for a future harvest.

There is no one pattern or formula to this collaborative style of leadership, but there are distinctive characteristics. Paul Wilkes, an American Catholic author, surveyed the parishes he visited in a coast-to-coast journey, and came up with a clarifying image that serves as a kind of parable, which he called 'Sailing Boat or Rowing Boat Parishes'.

What sailing boat parishes have in common is that they don't believe that Catholic life entirely depends on us. They have this feeling that if they put up their sails, the wind (the Holy Spirit) will do a good deal of their work for them. Their course may not be predictable at times, in fact, it may be in the opposite direction to the one in which they think they should be heading ... On the other hand, the rowing boat parishes too often have been places that insist on human power to propel them. Heavy lifting and great exertion are advised, practised and extolled as the real way to live a Catholic life today.

The sailing-boat pastors are all pretty smart men but, they will admit, not that smart. They can be contradicted, told they are wrong. They are open to the *vox populi*, the *sensus fidelium*. There was an openness to the human condition in the sailing-boat parishes, the desire to be creative in solutions to the myriad problems that are the stuff of many of our lives today – bad marriages, ungrateful children, loss of jobs, millennial *ennui*, sizeable moral flaws. The rowing-boat parishes stressed formal 'church' answers as preconditions to full membership – the sacrament of reconciliation for sinners, the marriage tribunal and annulment for those in invalid marriages, membership of parish boards as a sign of commitment. It is not that sailing-boat parishes did not advocate these. It just wasn't where they started ...

In sailing-boat parishes, the faith stories of individuals as well as the faith stories of the priests and staff members are important. Through parish retreat-days and days of recollection, sailing-boat parishes encourage people to tell how their faith works, what they do to nurture it, or how they struggle to get it back. The gritty details of life – of a life of faith – are teachable moments that encourage others. For rowing-boat parishes, such personal stories are out of place, and not proper tools for teaching and witnessing. Only stories of centuries' standing are appropriate. Rules and regulations need to be promulgated, fingers need to be wagged. They don't seem to realise that new lives of saints are being written and lived each day by their own people as they take ancient truths into the modern world ...

Once committed to one of these sailing-boat parishes, amazing things happen in people's lives. Individuals who have never done anything more than slip in and out of the shortest Sunday Mass, find themselves teaching classes, going on retreats, working in a homeless shelter, saying a prayer over dinner with their families. It is desire, not guilt, that is the prime motivator. They want to be part of something like this; they know they need a spiritual home that offers comfort and yet continually prods them to do and be better ...

People want a 'faith community' which, in reality for most of us, will be a parish. And those parishes can be welcoming or forbidding, the parish priest a bridge or a barrier. We can put our muscle to the oar, or use our energy to hoist the sail and stand by the rudder.[24]

In Paul Wilkes 'sailing-boat' parishes, there seems to be an immense trust. Priests and people are ready to risk sailing into the uncharted waters of discerning a different way of being church, confident that it is the journeying together that counts. Much closer to home, in the diocese of Leeds during the last six years, many priests and people have also been embarking on a voyage of discovery. With its twin aims of, 'Rediscovering yourself and your parish', the Vision 2000 programme, designed to promote collaborative ministry, provides an opportunity to explore a new way of being human, of being Christian and of being church. The first aim is to enable parishioners and priests to deepen their own personal spirituality and self-awareness as God's people, as made in God's image, as the body of Christ, and as the heart of the church. The second aim is to facilitate the emergence of a renewed type of parish, where responsibility is shared between priest and people in collaborative ministry, through a recognition of the many roles that constitute a vibrant Christian community.

Participants benefit not only from current theology, discussions, and the sharing of good practice, but they are also invited to envision the church that they feel is closest to the mind and heart of Jesus, through creative workshops. It is amazing to witness the power of the imagination in giving birth to models of the church that fire people's enthusiasm and give them new heart. An example of such a session was when each group presented their vision in a unique way. The first group told a story of a woman arriving on top of a hill and looking down into a dark valley. Since she was carrying a burning torch, her immediate impulse was to want to share her light with the people down below. Courageously she ventured down the hillside and offered her light to the first man she met, who passed it on to his neighbour. Very soon the ripple of light spread through the village until the whole valley was lit up. This story created for that group an image of what can happen when we fire each other to use our gifts, and it was fitting that this could be incorporated into a closing ritual by lighting each other's candles.

A second group had made a giant jig-saw, where all the pieces were necessary, whilst a third group had availed themselves of a trolley of musical instruments that were in the classroom they were using, to create a well co-ordinated musical performance, which demonstrated the need for a variety of individual gifts, but that these have to be used in harmony with each other. The last group were inspired to compose a poem expressing the potential within each of us to play our part in revealing God's reign of compassion in our world. Entitled *Painting the Possible*, it seemed to capture all our hopes and dreams for the church of today:

On the canvas of our imaginations we coloured in
a valley of movement lit by a delighted sun.
Everything was in harmony, healing and touching
and calling into the circle.

In the valley everything was light and free and
wonderfully connected with pulsing divine energy
like the red life that runs from its heart-centre
bringing power and compassion
to each and every cell
of each and every body.

It is a valley of dancing between darkness and light
where stumbling blocks become stepping stones
and the road less travelled is crowded.
And everyone feels something beautiful is
just around the corner.
This reverent valley has many shrines – to the healthy

and wounded child within us;
to the holy image sculpted into our hearts
that will not release us;
to the healing dreams that people
our nights.

We painted the valley with the purple
of compassion; the green
of hope; the blue
of courage; the silver
of responsibility; and the elusive shades
of trust and letting go.

This painting of the possible
this picture of the valley
this portrait of the church
is textured by the hearts that reveal
to each other the rainbow colours
they never knew
they had.

There has been much critiquing of and modification to the programme, based on the evaluations of participants, but the most encouraging signs of hope are the different models of collaboration that are being bravely tried in many of our parishes, as well as the overwhelming conviction that ministering together is the only way forward. As an encouragement to all those who are engaged in similar journeys together, I offer these words of hope, shared by some of the earliest 'collaborators', in their evaluations of the programme.

'Vision 2000 revealed the amazing possibilities within ourselves and our parishes.' *(Parishioner)*

'The contribution of women on the team showed the talent that had been lying dormant for so long.' *(Parish Sister)*

'Something new and beautiful is struggling to be born.' *(Parish Priest)*

'I felt inspired with enthusiasm about what could be achieved.' *(Parishioner)*

'We all felt equal and respected. It is a wonderfully nourishing thing to participate in days like these.' *(Parishioner)*

'The granary doors are being opened up for the people to bake their own bread.' *(Parish Priest)*

Worldly Wisdom

Before leaving this section it can only help, I hope, to connect briefly with the current more secular developments about the leadership and authority debate in a wider context. There is, we have seen, a winter of discontent among our parishioners and many diocesan priests when it comes to discussing the bureaucracy of the ecclesiastial institution, whether at parish, diocesan or international level. They bemoan the way they are treated by their superiors, whether these happen to be Vatican Curial officers, bishops, or priests in parishes, with their incessant demands for uniformity, money, control, statistics and other sundry information. They feel misunderstood, unappreciated and inefficient. Their complaints, they say, fall on deaf ears. This state of affairs cuts deep. It is one of the main reasons for the well-documented low morale and disenchantment among today's Catholics.

It is interesting to note that the breakdown in trust is not confined to the Catholic Church or even to the churches in general. When interviewed by Paul Vallely about the BBC 1 Holy Week programme, *The Word on the Street* (April 1999), the Bishop of Liverpool declared that while there is a huge gap between the church and the community, it is only one of the institutions from which people feel alienated. 'There is, among our people,' he said, 'a serious disillusion with politicians, and an extreme cynicism ... That too is a spiritual crisis.'

There is, indeed, a worldwide crisis going on and it is deepening daily. No part of the world is untouched, no organisation will survive unless it engages in fundamental change. It is an economic, technological, environmental and spiritual crisis and it demands response and action of a different order from any past adjustments. There are little signs of this crisis being acknowledged or the ensuing response being worked at. In *New Leadership for Women and Men: Building an Inclusive Organisation* (1996), Michael Simmons reflects:

> Many of the people now in formal leadership positions, whether in government, in public service or in the private sector, are unable or are not prepared to grasp the scale of the crisis and its effects. Apparently they prefer solutions that offer short-term gain, while leaving the bigger problems to future leaders. Many deny that there is a crisis at all.

There is a risk of approaching 'the hard institution versus the compassionate community' debate as though they were extreme ends of the spectrum. Such dualism is futile. It is not a question of opting for one or the other, because they both need each other. The challenge is to find a way of creating a compassionate institution, of building an inclusive organisation and, thus, of transforming current practice in many dioceses. Achieving this aim requires that everyone is involved in planning the future direction of the diocese or parish and contributes to their continual improvement both pastorally and economically.

But, as many have experienced, lay/clerical and gender conditioning prevent many leaders from removing the barriers to the full involvement of all of the laity, most religious and ordinary clerics. Transformation means reaching beyond equality to an organisation where boundaries and limitations are not placed on anyone with a genuine interest in the welfare of the church. It needs a new kind of leadership, capable of harnessing the intelligence, creativity and initiative of people at all levels, especially of those who have been traditionally excluded. As Parker Palmer points out, it is often leaders' reluctance to face their own shadow that makes this exercise so difficult.

What is noteworthy here is that such approaches to the principles of Catholic leadership are far from new. The principle of 'subsidiarity', for example, a purely human concept, belongs to the basic understanding of the new canon law (1983). Long before that, Pius XI wrote in *Quadragesimo Anno*: 'Just as it is gravely wrong to take from individuals what they can accomplish by their own initiative and industry and give it to the community, so also is it an injustice, and at the same time a grave evil and disturbance of right order, to assign to a greater or higher association what lesser and subordinate organisations can do. For every social activity ought of its very nature to furnish help to the members of the body social, and never destroy or absorb them.'

In a *Tablet* article (March 1999), Cardinal Franz Konig points out that, even though there are many examples of good pluralism in the responsible government of the Catholic Church in the past, today, however, we have an inflated centralism. He reminds us of a Papal address in 1946 where Pius XII repeats his predecessor's classic definition of the principle of subsidiarity and applies it to both society and the life of the church within its hierarchical structure. In the interests of episcopal collegiality, diocesan and parochial collaboration, and general ecumenism, the Cardinal insists that 'we have to return to the decentralised form of the church's command structure as practised in earlier centuries. That, for the world church, is the dictate of today.'

Building successful organisations requires that we put people at the heart of everything we do. When people are excluded they feel marginalised, their morale suffers and they either get angry or give up. The new notion of the 'inclusive organisation' is about welcoming people with all their diversity of backgrounds and abilities because they add a value to performance that those who 'fit' the existing profile of people in the organisation are unable to offer. They are not always 'safe' in any orthodox sense, but they bring excitement and energy and a new competence onto the heart of the business/pastoral procedures and developments. In the opinion of Michael Simmons, a consultant in total systems change and development, all discriminatory practices and prejudices towards any individual or group of people, using the excuse of 'tradition', their gender, disability or any other aspect of their identity, is the biggest single reason for the waste of human potential in most enterprises and in society as a whole.

It seems to me that the institutional dimension of our church needs immediate and immense appraisal. Because the Catholic Church is big business by any standards, but tends to alienate so many by its often awkward, sometimes dismissive, behaviour towards its members, it has much to learn from its more enlightened 'secular' counterparts. One of these lessons is about the care and attention to be given to the feelings arising from the hurtful experiences of all the group's members. Until leaders take these realities seriously, it will be impossible to release the full and harmonious potential of the organisation or community.

I remember reading, many years ago, *The Human Side of Human Beings* (1971), a classic for leaders, written by Harvey Jackins. Most of today's top consultants in the leadership and management of business organisation would locate, with Jackins, one of the foundations of their approaches in the enlisting of the human potential of all members. Among the 'given' assumptions they make about human beings are the fact that they are inherently intelligent, inherently zestful, inherently cooperative, completely powerful, eager to learn and are natural leaders. Also that, once they are heard and understood, they recover quickly from past bad experiences. Most priests and bishops are not trained managers. I believe that a widespread and deep-seated examination of 'good management' across a number of developing areas in our society would benefit all in the church and eliminate many causes of friction.

Michael Simmons' popular book (above) is written totally for the hard world of business. It is about transforming and humanising leadership, about creating and sharing vision, about understanding men's gender conditioning and about how subtle oppression and exclusion damages and undermines the leadership potential of women and men. It is a wise and compassionate book, like so many others published during the last few years on humane managerial leadership, and offers guidance on how to achieve critical analysis rather than personal criticism, how to be firm without being hurtful, how to reach your goals in a collaborative way.

The Primacy Of Green

> The future of the Catholic Church (in America) in my view, will depend above all on its capacity to assume a religious responsibility for the fate of the earth. For ecclesial authorities to be so negligent, indifferent, or unaware of the imperilled status of the planet in all its living and non-living components can be considered a monumental failure. In order of magnitude, this goes far beyond any other failure for which the church may be responsible.[1]

This hard-hitting statement from the renowned cultural historian, Fr Thomas Berry, now in his late eighties, may come as a shock to many church-goers, and to those in positions of authority within the church, who think that the church's problems are much more to do with declining vocations and falling numbers at Mass. The wanton depletion of the planet's resources during the last two hundred years of industrialisation, and during the last fifty years in particular, together with the pollution of the sacred elements of life – air, water and the earth itself – don't seem to register high on the agenda for the mainstream churches. Routine worship in parishes rarely reflects concern for the ecological state of our planet, nor even for local environmental issues.

If we are concerned about these issues at all, they are seen more as fringe activities for groups like 'Greenpeace' or 'Friends of the Earth' – certainly not one of the main the concerns of religion. It is as if our human consciousness has been so blunted that we no longer feel any sense of belonging to the created world, but see ourselves more as superior to, in control of, and not interconnected with the planet which sustains all life. Whilst many prayers, hymns and liturgies are full of praise for the beauties of creation and full of thanks for the bounties we receive from the fruitful abundance of the earth, most of these arise from a dualistic understanding of creation, which somehow places humanity apart from and above created things. It is as if the world was created as a complete entity, once and for all, simply and solely to provide for every human need. In stark contrast, what underlies Fr Berry's dramatic statement is a creation-centred theology and spirituality that integrates the richness of the Christian creation tradition with the insights of modern science. Together these provide the foundation for us humans to understand and experience ourselves as an integral part of the magnificent ongoing process of creation, expressed anew in unimaginable ways each minute of each new day, as the universe continues to expand ever outward in time and space. What is required for our time is just such a radical shift in our anthropocentric understanding of the story of our origins which is, in reality, the story of the universe itself.

What is needed is a more authentic, non-dualistic theology of creation which accepts the universe itself as the primary source of revelation, which sees creation as the first incarnation of God's love. We need to move away from a mechanistic view of a universe of fixed laws, and begin to reflect on the universe as a numinous reality. We need to understand the development of the universe from the first fireball of energy over fifteen billion years ago, as a revelatory event which continues today. Only when we begin to experience ourselves as an intricate strand in the web of creation, when we feel part of the delicate and fragile balance of life on planet earth, when we sense that the universe is still unfolding its mysteries, will we be in a place to love, honour, protect, and, as the First Peoples of North America say, to 'tread softly on the earth'.

A brief look at some of the facts will make it easy to appreciate why Fr Thomas Berry expressed such a passionate plea for the church to wake up and do something. Conservative estimates say we are cutting down rain forests at the rate of roughly one football field every second. Such forests, having taken several hundred million years to evolve, of course help provide the oxygen we need to breathe. Each year over 18 billion tons of topsoil are lost, as well as good farmland being ruined by modern, intensive and chemically-aided agricultural practices, aimed at maximising short-term profit. An estimated 82 billion tons of toxic waste are poured into the rivers and oceans of the planet, not to mention the gases emanating from factories, and the pollution caused by the massive increase in the use of cars. All of this when the World Health Organisation estimates that 65 to 80 per cent of all illnesses are environmentally caused or aggravated.

Genetic engineering to produce the most desirable yield in plant and animal husbandry, has meant that the natural genepool has been altered irrevocably. Biologists now calculate that every year sees the extinction of 20,000 plant and animal species – one species every thirty minutes!

These facts are hard to bear. Even more difficult to contemplate is the damage already done to earth, water and atmosphere by the nuclear explosions that have taken place since the first successful test at the Trinity site in New Mexico (I wonder how we, as Christians, feel about this name?), and of the incredible loss of life and resultant mutations following the dropping of the first atomic bombs on Hiroshima and Nagasaki. One might have imagined that the human psyche or the collective conscience would have learned a salutary lesson after these atrocities, but history has demonstrated that even after the ending of the 'Cold War', ever more powerful weapons of mass destruction have been developed and tested, with the argument that it is in defence of the freedom and safety of people in the civilised democracies of the West.

That so much of this militarism is secret only adds to the lack of concern on the part of Christians citizens. One might ask why the voice of the church is not crying out against the waste of billions and billions of dollars now being spent on developing ways of controlling outer space with weapons of mass destruction. This, together with the fact that the world's best scientific brains are being lured into such research, when so few resources are put into ways of making peace and of providing clean water, food and basic health care for the world's poorest people, surely demands a prophetic voice to name truth. Even when the development of nuclear technology is for peaceful purposes, like the generation of energy, there is no guaranteed 'safe' removal or treatment of the nuclear waste that is the by-product of such processes.

The source of the problem

Fr Sean McDonagh, who has spent the last twenty years grappling with ecological matters, asks the hard question: 'How is a disciple of Jesus to respond to the rampant destruction and poisoning of the natural world which, if the current rate continues or increases, will threaten all life on earth?' How we have arrived at the situation in which we find ourselves today, and why the devastation of the planet continues unabated, are matters of the deepest spiritual nature. It is important to consider how a misguided interpretation of the Genesis creation account has had such disastrous consequences in the last four hundred years. A short reflection from one of the indigenous people in the United States might serve as a useful starting point.

Nothing the Great Mystery placed in the land of the Indian pleased the white man, and nothing escaped his transforming hand. Wherever forests have not been mowed down, wherever the animal is recessed in their quiet protection, wherever the earth is not bereft of four-footed life – that to him is an 'unbroken wilderness'. But for the Lakota there was no wilderness, because nature was not dangerous but hospitable, not forbidding but friendly. Lakota philosophy was healthy – free from fear and dogmatism. And here I find the great distinction between the faith of the Indian and the white man. Indian faith sought the harmony of man with his surroundings; the other sought dominance of surroundings.

In sharing, in loving all and everything, one people naturally found a due portion of the thing they sought, while, in fearing, the other found need of conquest. For one man the world was full of beauty; for the other it was a place of sin and ugliness to be endured until he went to another world, there to become a creature of wings, half-man and half-bird. For one man directed his Mystery to change the world He had made; forever this man pleaded with Him to chastise his wicked ones; and forever he implored his God to send His light to earth. Small wonder this man could not understand the other.

But the Lakota was wise. He knew that man's heart, away from nature, becomes hard, he knew that lack of respect for growing, living things soon led to lack of respect for humans too. So, he kept his children close to nature's softening influence.[2]

This insightful passage, written by an elder of the Oglala Sioux nation at the beginning of this century, towards the end of his long life, is a damning indictment of the 'white man's' understanding of creation. The key words in this passage for our purposes are 'harmony' and 'dominance'. For 'white-man' we can certainly read 'men and women in the Northern hemisphere at the end of the twentieth century'. There is no doubt that our planet is in crisis. In our belief that we could dominate creation and plunder the planet's resources at will, we have wreaked havoc with the delicate eco-systems of the fragile, living organism we call 'earth'. The mindset, the faith-story, the myth, that has underpinned this domination has certainly been a most damaging form of dualism.

Until the late Middle Ages, Western civilisations based their worldview, laws and political systems on the Genesis account. A benign creator ordered the universe, with the earth at its centre, and human beings, the pinnacle of creation, having stewardship over it. There was a certain harmony and balance between the accepted cosmology and the social order. With the Copernican revolution, when scientists could demonstrate that the earth spins on its own axis and travels around the sun, there came a radical challenge to orthodox theology. When Galileo was put on trial in 1633, and forced to retract the truth of what he had observed, it convinced scientists that church authorities would oppose their scientific research.

From that period there began a separation of the two paths of theology and science. 'Consequently, the theology of creation was generally ignored and almost all theological enquiry was confined to the process of redemption and salvation, the personality of Jesus, the interior spiritual disciplines needed to guide the individual soul along the path of salvation, and the internal constitution and juridical status of the ecclesial community.'[3]

The creative forces of Descartes, Bacon and Newton had an unparalleled effect on scientific, rational thinking, and the age of Enlightenment was born. The firmly held belief in the scientific and philosophical world, that the universe could be explained by laws and formulae arrived at through mathematical and physical experimentation and observation, removed any sense of mystery. No longer was nature seen to be sacred, with its own inherent value, but it was compared to a machine whose complex workings were only gradually being understood. The earth was no longer the realm of the divine, but rather a commodity whose workings, once understood, could be used or transformed at any cost. Indeed, with Newton, the idea of a mechanistic universe took hold, and no longer was there any vision of the universe as a living community of independent species.

This mechanical view of the universe proved enormously attractive to western man during the eighteenth, nineteenth and twentieth centuries. It provided a framework of perception and stimulus for inventors to develop new, more powerful and, in this view, more efficient, technologies to transform and process the Earth. With the Industrial Revolution the power and scale of these technologies increased enormously. Today, the chemical, nuclear and engineering industries seem to have a power of their own and are scarring the Earth, poisoning water, air, and soil, killing off life-forms and threatening to let loose a fireball which will engulf the planet and destroy every living being.[4]

We are just waking up to the consequences of living with such a cosmology, the predominant one being the rape of the planet, but also devastating are the ways in which the human soul has been cut adrift from its deepest source of identity and healing. The human imagination, separated from nature, is denied access to beauty, to that which calls forth the poet, the artist, the mystic in each soul. And in the end, to echo the sentiments of Simone Weil, 'It is beauty that will save the world.' Not only have our imaginations been set adrift, but we have also lost our 'story'.

Undoubtedly the biggest price we have had to pay for all the accomplishments of reason and technology has been the loss of a myth to live by. I mean 'myth' of course in the sense of a large truth which gives meaning to life. Christianity does contain such a myth. Despite all our deviations from the original insight, our religion is rooted in the ancient Hebrew view which saw creation as good, and the human person created in the image of the creator. What this means is that you and I are indispensable for the completion of God's creation … We have indeed used our creative powers to the utmost, but we have used them as much to destroy as to create … Preoccupied with using our reason to control and manipulate the outer world, we have neglected another myth which lies at the very core of Christianity, namely the myth of the incarnation. This myth, rooted in the reality and meaning of Jesus … declares that it is the venture of becoming fully human which is the greatest act of creation in which we can engage.[5]

The New Cosmology
Thomas Berry, Brian Swimme, John Haught, Rupert Sheldrake, Dermot Lane, Rosemary Ruether, Sally Mc Fague and many

other contemporary theologians and scientists would argue that it is only by making a 'paradigm shift', by developing a radically different understanding of the universe story, that there is any hope for the survival of our planet as we know it. The insights from modern physics concerning the origins and dynamics of the universe are of a different order from those of the scientists of the Enlightenment, in that the more scientific frontiers are breached, the more the realm of mystery is encountered.

From its coming into existence in the burst of primordial energy over fifteen billion years ago, the universe has been expanding, irreversibly, in time and space, becoming ever more complex and differentiated. Thomas Berry identifies the three basic characteristics of the universe as differentiation, interiority, and communion. By this he wants to show that the development of the universe has been from lesser to greater difference, each living or non-living form being a unique expression of creation, complete in itself, whilst at the same time all things exist in a community, or communion.

> What we have now, through our modern story of the universe, is new sense of a universe, one that had a precise beginning and has gone through a sequence of differentiating transformations leading from lesser to greater complexity and greater modes of consciousness. These two need, in some manner, to be related, an ascending universe of consciousness and the rise of the spiritual community. The universe is the most basic expression of community. The universe is ultimately sacred community.[6]

In its very nature and dynamics, Berry considers the universe to be an expression of the Divine, a revelatory experience, that the universe itself is primary sacred community. This confirms that all things came into being from a single origin, all come from the same source. In this very real sense we are born into the community of plants and animals that make up planet earth. The universe is still in the creative process of becoming, and humans are the first level of creation to become conscious, 'that being in whom the universe reflects on and celebrates itself and its numinous origins.' It is frequently claimed that the consciousness of humanity was changed forever once it saw a picture of the earth from space. For those astronauts privileged to have such a view, all would say it was a deeply mystical experience.

We have already referred to James Lovelock's rediscovery of

the 'Gaia hypothesis'. Rosemary Ruether, the eco-feminist theologian, uses this 'Gaia' concept, earth as mother goddess, a living sacred earth, whilst in *Models of God*, Sally McFague images the earth as God's body, seeing this as a primary metaphor for the way we relate to creation. If we could live in this planet open to such images and mindful of belonging to a community of different life-forms, our way of living within the delicate balances of the different eco-systems would be dramatically changed.

If the church was listening to the prophets of our time, if it was alert to the symbols that awaken the imagination, then preaching and teaching, liturgy and worship, practical witness in community life, would all be a clarion call to the world that the universe is indeed the revelation of the Divine. Only then will we demonstrate that we really do believe that the Cosmic Christ is 'reconciling all things in himself', and is indeed 'making all things new.'

Eco-theology, Eco-spirituality

Ideally the church in the next millennium would espouse the insights of Teilhard de Chardin who, nearly fifty years ago, was so instrumental in showing that the Christian story was identical to the universe story, and that if we really understood this, then our theological studies would help to renew our spiritual relationship with the universe.

It would proclaim loudly a creation tradition of original blessing and goodness, and a spirituality of self esteem, recognising that what God wants for all of creation is the abundant life. Its symbols and rituals would be designed to nurture and heal the planet, and foster a growing awareness of the human role within that process.

The challenge from liberation theology some twenty years ago, from a reading of the gospel through the eyes of poor and oppressed people in Central and Latin America, was to encourage the church to make a 'preferential option for the poor'. This demands that Christians develop a global consciousness. People in the rich one-third of the world need to recognise the connection between their own lifestyle and the issues of hunger and poverty. It is not just a question of responding to emergencies, nor just giving aid, but more to look at the structures which cause this tragic uneven distribution of global resources to come about. Crucial, here, is how we understand our connectedness, the role of transnational corporations, and the huge problem of the debt burden which countries in the first world have put on the poorer two thirds. Far from improving in the last twenty years, UN statistics indicate that the situation is becoming worse, with 1.2 billion people in Sub-Saharan Africa, Latin America and South East Asia living in extreme poverty. 'In 1960, the richest 20 per cent of the world's population had incomes 30 times greater than the poorest 20 per cent. By 1990 the richest 20 per cent were getting 60 times more than the poorest 20 per cent.'[7]

The demands made by our consumerist, affluent lifestyle have a direct effect on the lives of the world's poorest people. Our belief in the gospel of development presupposed an infinite supply of resources. What needs to be proclaimed by the church, in contrast, is a gospel of sustainability, recognising the limited resources of the planet and the clear indictment both in Hebrew and Christian scriptures that the fruits of the earth are for the good of all. Not only does our present lifestyle in the first world result in such staggering injustice to the world's poor, but our short-sightedness in wanting immediate gratification of our needs has devastating consequences for the planet and for ourselves. Dr Edward Echlin, a theologian and writer on ecology, is very clear about the role Christians have in exploding the development myth.

> People in consumer cultures are reluctant to acknowledge that our lifestyles or aspirations are earth destructive and that, despite our glittering technology, we have lost control of our lives, our planet, our future. We know that modern market societies are not sustainable – but addicted to consumerism. We indulge in massive reality avoidance. We repress the realisation that people are not above the rest of the soil community, but interdependent within it. Avoidance of the lucidly vivid reality of our own unsustainable behaviour, our fictitious fantasy that we are carefree masters of other beings debilitates modern humanity and prevents us from reintegrating with the rest of God's creation. We are not living as we are meant to be – creatures under God within a wonderfully diverse community with responsibility to love, nurture and share the planet with God's other creatures ... The challenge for Christians in public life today is literally to heal God's earth and secure a sustainable future. It means educating ourselves and our contemporaries to the frailty and interdependence of all creation on this planet.[8]

Dr Echlin would even advocate changing the name of the 'Catholic Fund for Overseas Development' to the 'Catholic Fund for Local and Overseas Sustainability', to emphasise clearly the road we must travel.

The Catholic Church has been slow to respond to the need to shape thought and change patterns of behaviour, but in 1990 the document, *Peace with God the Creator, Peace with all Creation,* was devoted entirely to the environmental problems we face today. This document built upon the 'Justice and Peace and the Integrity of Creation' programme, instituted in 1983 by the World Council of Churches. It would be salutary to learn how many Catholics know of its existence, or how many homilies have referred to it. In his encyclical letter for the new millennium, the Pope urges that we recover the theological principles of the Jubilee, outlined in Leviticus.

> If in his Providence God had given the earth to humanity, that meant he had given it to everyone. Therefore the riches of creation were to be considered as a common good of the whole of humanity. Those who possessed these goods as personal property were really only stewards, ministers charged with working in the name of God, who remains the sole owner in the full sense, since it is God's will that created goods should serve everyone in a just way. The jubilee year was meant to restore this social justice.' (*TMA* para 13)[9]

The principles of Jubilee were concerned with the cancellation of debt, freedom from slavery, and restoration of land. It is painfully clear that these are vital issues in today's world, where the Jubilee 2000 campaign is bringing to the attention of the world the plight of the poorest countries, burdened as they are with a debt in the region of two trillion dollars to repay. Slavery in the form of women and children, migrant and home workers, in many countries of Asia and Latin America, working for a pittance in dreadful conditions, is still far too common. The misappropriation of land is still prevalent in countries like the Philippines and El Salvador, where ownership is in the hands of very few exceedingly rich and powerful families, who use the land for producing cash crops rather than food. Or, as with the Ogoni people in Nigeria, the land is 'bought' by transnational oil companies, people are forced to move and leave traditional tribal ways of living, whilst their land and environment are polluted beyond repair. We would do well to recover the principles of

biblical stewardship, including the practice of letting the earth
lie fallow and rest every seventh year. Prophetic attempts at per-
maculture – reclaiming a more balanced way of farming that
recognises the need to rotate crops, and understands the dangers of chemical fertilisers – emphasises the need for balance
and harmony, as opposed to the usual intensive farming practices. Fr Frank Nally identifies graphically the agenda for
Christians today:

> For the new millennium we dream of sustainable develop-
> ment that respects the environment. We will not trade pollu-
> tion for profit. We will not ignore the links between our in-
> dustrial irresponsibility, our use of fossil fuels, and climate
> change. We will not pretend that multi-national control over
> food by genetic manipulation, rather than structural change,
> will feed the world. We will not be naïve enough to think that
> profit-making has given way to the partnership of big busi-
> ness, government and civil society. We will demand regula-
> tion and bans and moratoriums where necessary. When all
> the trees are gone it will be too late. When the rivers are pois-
> oned and the seas dead, it will be too late.
>
> And we must not only dream of justice but do justice. We
> will stop the chain saws and the bulldozers and the hawk
> planes. We will stop the earth's skin being ripped apart and
> her insides scraped out and bled of all her oil and precious
> minerals – even when there is a glut in the market. We need
> our mountains, trees, rivers, animal and bird life for what
> they contribute to the interrelated web of life.
>
> We will again see all created things as sacred. We will recog-
> nise the interdependence of the natural world: from human
> beings to the worms that make the soil fertile, to the trees that
> provide oxygen, filter our air, retain water and hold the soil
> in place. We will no longer be bully of the planet and we will
> realise that we have gone too far in our plunder.[10]

The role of the church has to be in raising awareness of the real
issues and in shaping people's thoughts to be prepared to enter
the next phase of the universe's history, which Thomas Berry
calls the 'Ecozoic' era. By this he means an age in which humans
are conscious that they live in community with the whole earth
and inaugurate a new era of mutually-enhancing human-earth
relationships. How this might be achieved is a matter of energising the human spirit and awakening the power of the imagina-

tion. This will involve a process of conversion and, for the Christian, a deepening awareness that any change of heart must involve conversion at the ecological level too. Rosemary Radford Ruether offers challenging thoughts on this issue:

The Western dream of infinitely expanding power and wealth defies the actual finitude of ourselves and the world and conceals the exploitative use of other people's resources. It must be replaced with a new culture of acceptance and finitude and limits. But not in the sense of a 'static-state' society which simply fixates the present poverty and inequality. We must change, not as endless growth, but as 'conversion'. Conversion means that we rediscover the finitude of the earth as a balance of elements, which together harmonise to support life for all parts of the community.

Conversion means the interconnectedness of all parts of the community of creation so that no part can long flourish if the other parts are being injured or destroyed ... Conversion suggests that, although there is no one utopian system of humanity that lies back in a paradise of the past, there are certain ingredients of a just and liveable society. These include the human scale of habitats and communities; an ability of people to participate in decisions that govern their lives; work in which everyone is able to integrate intelligence and creativity with manual labour; a certain just sharing of the profits and benefits of production; a balance of leisure and work, rural and urban environments. Most of us sense what the elements of this humanised life are like, and are constantly trying to get back to it.'[11]

Liturgy, Sacraments, Ritual
As we have seen already, there is an orthodox and fundamental dimension of the Christian faith, which the Pope calls creation theology, that does not separate humanity from the environment, that holds a picture of all creation as one, all of a piece from God. Original sin, scripturally referred to as 'the sin of the world', is the constant drive toward self-destruction, the denial of our part in the restoration and completion of what yet remains to be accomplished in the work of Jesus Christ, until God be all in all. To sin is to refuse to take responsibility for nurturing, loving and befriending the world-body in all its aspects:

Sin is the refusal to realise one's radical interdependence

with all that lives: it is the desire to set oneself apart from all others as not needing them or being needed by them. Sin is the refusal to be the eyes, the consciousness, of the cosmos ... The beauty of the world and its ability to sustain the vast multitude of species it supports, is not there for the taking. The world is a body that must be carefully tended, that must be nurtured, protected, guided, loved and befriended both as valuable in itself – for like us, it is an expression of God – and as necessary to the continuation of life. We meet the world as a Thou, as the body of God where God is present to us always, in all times and in all places. In the metaphor of the world as the body of God, the resurrection becomes a worldly, present, inclusive reality, for this body is offered to all: 'This is my body.'[12]

Over the centuries a kind of litmus-test for orthodoxy has developed within the development of Christianity – a five-point check-list towards truth. In the first place, the bible, obviously, is a prime source for guidance and discernment. Both the Hebrew and Christian scriptures can be read, studied and prayed in the context of the sacredness of the whole of creation and its solidarity with humanity in its origin, in the implications of the Fall (whichever interpretation is accepted) and in its final restoration and completion at the end of time. Then, when true to its own tradition, the Catholic understanding of creation and incarnation is rich, holistic and full of original joy and blessing. It is one of the signs of the times that theologians are again exploring within the bottomless 'deposit of faith', exciting veins of forgotten theologies, traditional doctrines, early rituals and scriptural interpretations, to find revelations that have more to say about creation as blessing, the environment as *imago Dei*, ecological sin and cosmic redemption, than we were ever told about in our old catechisms, at Mass, at school, or in the seminary.

Also, in recent decades, this growing interest among church leaders in saving the world is a most welcome development. In his Jubilee Letter, *Tertio Millennio Adviente*, the Pope writes: '... by taking flesh the Word renews the cosmic order of creation, uniting all things in himself, things in heaven and things on earth ... Jesus Christ is the new beginning of everything. In him all things come into their own; they are taken up and given back to the Creator ... All creation is in reality a manifestation of God's glory.' Many other letters, messages and official documents from Vatican sources witness to their renewed interest and even sense of urgency about the precarious state of our planet.[13]

One of the strong pleas in this book is to bring these concerns from the margins of ecclesiastical consciousness into the heart of our Christian lives. As with numerous issues in the history of the churches, it is the artists, the mystics, the writers, the prophets, the poets and the physicists of truth who keep the vision in focus and who refuse to succumb to the enormous pressures of a spiritless and myopic culture where governments, big businesses and a ruthless media can manipulate and persuade a gullible public and an often-gullible church towards extinction. 'In extinction,' wrote Jonathan Schell, 'a darkness falls over the world, not because the lights have gone out, but because the eyes that behold the light have been closed.'[14]

It is perhaps through its worship, a central source and focus of truth, that the church has the greatest opportunity to form hearts and minds. Symbol and ritual speak to the deepest dimensions of the human soul in ways that the spoken word often cannot. There are fundamental questions which the church as an institution, and each local community must ask. First, how can our prayer and worship reflect our concern for justice, peace and the integrity of creation? And second, how can our rituals and our sacraments encourage a new way of interacting with fellow human beings, and also with the natural world?

Fr Sean McDonagh, addressing a conference on 'Reconciliation with the Earth', in Lancaster University, June 1997, suggested some pointers from his own and others' missionary experience. He says the church could be more conscious of the natural rhythms of the earth and the cosmos by celebrating these in ritual and ceremony. We can benefit much from the Celtic tradition, with its deep awareness of the beginning of seasons, the winter and summer solstices, as well as the times for sowing and harvesting. The Celtic sense of presence, celebrating the sacredness of water, air and earth, provides us with a wealth of prayer, songs and ritual, which has only begun to be tapped in recent years. (See *Reclaiming Ritual*, below.)

McDonagh also suggests that the church might have a Feast of Creation, as the Orthodox church does, and also celebrate what Thomas Berry calls 'cosmological moments of grace', like the emergence of the flowers, trees or first animals. In these

ways Christians would be re-connected with the story of creation. In our sacraments there are many opportunities for symbols to transform experience, and for the symbols themselves to
be the carriers of a new consciousness.

> In a world where water is being polluted and wasted, the
> sacrament of baptism highlights the connection between liv-
> ing water and the power of the Spirit who incorporates those
> who are baptised into the Body of Christ. The parameters of
> this community into which the child is to be baptised must
> also be expanded to include the wider community of human-
> ity and all creation.[15]

If we understand ourselves as being part of a wider earth community, then we would strive to find ways of expressing this in
our baptism ceremony. An example of this is a rite used by a
Columban priest in the Philippines, who has enhanced the present ritual by inviting parents and sponsors to bring the child
outside, where prayers and symbols for welcoming into the natural world are used, such as, 'Rejoice you creatures of the soil,
for we have a new companion in our community. Celebrate
her/his presence among us because she/he has promised to
nurture God's living world.'[16]

Before baptism, adults in the African Independent Churches
in Zimbabwe confess ecological sins and commit themselves to
continue Christ's healing ministry by healing the earth in their
locality. This same church also has liturgies for planting trees,
where there has been massive deforestation, as well as acts of
reconciliation for polluting water and soil. The sacrament of reconciliation in the West is a powerful vehicle for challenging a
community to face the structural sins with which we are all involved. An examination of conscience could focus not just on
sins of a personal nature, but include questions about the use of
energy, wasteful use of resources, involvement in pollution and
other similar issues.

The eucharist provides a wonderful opportunity for focusing
on the communion of all life, and the need for the bread of the
world to be shared justly and compassionately. It also has the
potential to awaken people to the cosmic dimensions of the incarnate Word. Nowhere have I seen this more dramatically and
beautifully expressed than in the following passage:

> In the dynamic presence of the bread and wine on the table
> we have symbolised just about everything that can be predi-

cated of humanity, the Earth and everything on and in it, the universe and the cosmos itself – the past, present and future of all creation. These rich and simple elements gather up the intense agony and ecstasy of the world, its darkness and light, its failures and mistakes, its strivings and hopes, its indomitable creativity.

And then the eternal words of disclosure are spoken: 'This is my Body.' They sound around this Earth and they echo round the stars. They were whispered by our loving Mother when the terrible beauty of the fiery atoms shattered the infinite darkness of space with unimaginable flame, heat and light. And God has waited for her creation to unfold in the power of her own love and, in that unfolding, the cosmos became self-reflecting in the consciousness of humanity. And it is this human awareness that repeats again the words first heard in its infancy many years before, when God spoke her creative words into the void, 'This is my Body.' It is God-become-atom, become-galaxies, become-stars, become-universes, become-Earth, become-human that speaks the words to her own body in a human voice, 'This is my Body.' It is a remembering, a reminding and a confirming that the divine and the human, the sacred and the secular, the holy and the profane are all God's one body by virtue of creation, first in time but revealed to us later in the incarnation.[17]

In his more recent book, *Passion for the Earth*, Fr McDonagh urges the Christian churches to use the sacrament of reconciliation to foster an awareness,

> ... of the moral implications of injustice and environmental destruction. Through the experience of appropriate prayers and symbols incorporated into a rite of penance, individuals and the community as a whole could seek God's forgiveness for what they were doing to the local and global environment. The collective examination of conscience might spotlight how individuals and the society as a whole use energy; whether they try to live simply; whether they waste resources; and finally, whether they purchase and use dangerous chemicals.[18]

For most of us these connections are rarely made in the routine celebration of these two sacraments. The more common practice is to focus on relationships between ourselves and God, and ourselves and other human beings. Seldom is there any real attempt to focus attention on our connectedness with the planet, and the responsibility we have for its care and preservation. The whole point of using liturgy and ritual in these creative ways is to bring about a transformation in how we live as individuals and as local church community. Paula Gonzalez, writing about an eco-prophetic parish, sees the following opportunities:

> For Christians the so-called environmental crisis may well be a blessing in disguise. It calls each of us to be converted from consumerism to what I sometimes call the 'six Cs': connectedness, collaboration, creativity, community, commitment and celebration. The environmental situation we face calls us to an embodied faith, just as our parishes are a potentially potent social locus wherein we can be schooled in a new consciousness of our status as children of God and the cosmos.[19]

Finally, there are pastoral initiatives and strategies. Parish communities provide the natural base for families to support each other in making choices for appropriate, sustainable living. There are many practical possibilities: to live more simply, to buy fairly-traded goods, to engage in re-use and recycle schemes, to take an active part in groups which campaign on environmental issues, to make such issues part of local and national politics, to use public transport and consider car-pooling, to minimise the use of fossil fuels and maximise the use of solar power and to use appropriate small-scale technology wherever possible. To attempt any or all of these on one's own requires tremendous courage and conviction. How marvellous it would be if parish communities' understanding of creation theology was witnessed in the prophetic stance parishioners were encouraging each other to take. Let us end, as we began, with words from the eminently wise and prophetic Thomas Berry.

> Presently the church has a unique opportunity to place its vast authority, its energies, its educational resources, its spiritual disciplines in a creative context, one that can assist in renewing the earth as a bio-spiritual planet ... Only by assuming its religious responsibilities for the fate of the earth can the church regain any effective status in the human community or in the earth process.[20]

A Church with No Walls

It is autumn. The leaves of a beech tree in the garden are a deep golden copper, blown in unison by autumn gales. The leaves are more vividly and variably beautiful now than in spring and summer days. Time and the seasons have burnished and polished them and they swirl and sing strongly together in shades of crimson, streaming with rain and wind. The maturity of autumn brings a beauty that contains within it the different splendours of new birth, the exuberance of spring and the fullness and flowering of summer and early autumn. The leaves grow lovely before they fall and die. The beauty of the tree is caused by the round of the seasons and is hidden from the eye. The tree's roots lie deep in the earth and take life and nourishment microscopically from the soil and the moisture so that root fibre and soil are almost indistinguishable in their closeness. The tree's branches and leaves take life from the moving air, the warmth of the sun, the coolness of rain in a constant fine and balancing synergy, an interdependent chemistry. The tree is ever open to the air of heaven, its roots ever naked in the soil of earth. It seeks no defence against soil or sky, for these bring it life and are the causes of its beauty. It stands vulnerable and dependent for its life on the quality of the soil, the air, on the provision of sun and rain. There can be no barriers between the tree and its environment. It is inextricably earth and sky and is lifted up between them in glory. It would be understandable but misguided of a gardener to fence the tree in, to place walls around the tree in attempts to shield it from gales or drought or pollution or heat – for the tree will surely die and its precarious beauty fade, its song silenced. There are no walls for trees. Moreover if the tree was walled in, who would see its beauty, who would hear its song?

It is autumn. The church stands in the autumn of an age which is fading and in which there are both signs of winter but also many signs of a new springtime.[1] The search is on for new images, new songs, from within which a newly energised and renewed church will be able to answer the questions being asked of it. The church depends for its life not just from God in heaven but from the vibrant and diverse life of the world in which it has been planted, since this too comes from God. The word *synergy* means the co-operative action of two agents to enhance life. The church is most beautiful when, like the tree of the cross, it stands naked between earth and sky, open to the synergetic life force of both. Only if it is prepared to accept life from both will it become beautiful. Its beauty will come from service to its task – to work for the kingdom of God. If there are walls or barriers in the church, which restrict or prevent the twofold flow of its life, then these will have to come down. From the life of the church and from Christian living will come the answers to the questions the church now faces.

The Question of the Religious Other

There are two interconnected, urgent, inescapable and radical questions facing the church. How can the church respond to the suffering poor? How can the church respond to the person of another faith?[2] The church has for long understood that 'action on behalf of justice and peace is a constitutive element in the preaching of the gospel.'[3] How the church can continue to define and implement this 'option for the poor' is the subject of another chapter. Here we want to explore the second but related question: how should the church relate to the 'Religious Other' – to non-Catholic Christians and, more widely, to members of the other world religions? How the church answers this question will determine the extent to which it can truly become a global, universal, world church (a world religion). It will determine how effectively it can fulfil its mission to announce the good news of the reign of God. It will radically re-shape the church's self-understanding of its life and ministries so that they can work collaboratively to fulfil that mission.

The church must declare that, as it does in the case of its work for justice: 'the work of dialogue with the world religions is a constitutive element in its life and mission of evangelisation and proclamation'. It will then have entered a new phase in the story of its service of the kingdom of God. It will have served the peoples of the world best, 'no matter the appearances'.[4] It will have taken down the walls. It will have entered into a 'correlational dialogue' (Paul Knitter's term) with the world religions, not just as teacher and speaker of truth, but as listener and learner of truths which the Spirit of God has sown in those faiths long before the human dialogue started. The church will learn and grow in beauty from the Spirit of the one God that breathes through the great world religions. The church will be caught up into that eternal dialogue of song and dance, begun first in the community of the Trinity. It continued in time and space with the whole of creation. It was refined in the Spirit as it breathed to every human being ever created and was distilled in the words revealed by the Spirit to every religion of the world. It coalesces in whatever is true, good and beautiful in the present great world religions. The church was born to be part of the dance and song of this dialogue. It is beginning to recognise that the other dancers are dancing and singing to the same divine tune.

The question is urgent because there is a feeling of crisis in the air. Crisis in terms of a Spirit-sent time of challenge and decision. A Spirit-intended *kairos* or moment of truth, grace and opportunity for the whole nature, purpose and mission of the church. The Spirit of God is issuing a challenge to the church to act anew in the service of the kingdom. There is a feeling that the church stands on the cusp of a new epoch that will constitute a new springtime for it. We all need to remember that leaves die when they are at their most beautiful.

The sense of urgency arises also from the expectations of the great mass of people who are not religious but whose spirit cries out to the world religions for nourishment. There is a great spiritual hunger. In this country there is much talk of 'regeneration' – economic, social and ecological. There is also a realisation that regeneration will not be achieved without attention to the regeneration of the human spirit. A secular political and social initiative has issued a challenge to the leaders of the great faiths, whose members are often living in areas of the greatest poverty and multiple deprivation in this country.[5]

It is a stark challenge. 'If your religion has nothing to offer by way of love and human liberation of spirit, mind and body from conditions which destroy humanity, then your religion, with all its beliefs and practices is worse than useless.' All the citizens of the world can legitimately expect the faiths of the world to work together in a dialogue of life to improve the quality of life for all.[6] No terminus is placed on what is meant by life. It certainly does not exclude what Christians mean by the kingdom of God 'on earth as it is in heaven.' It is embraced by the saying of Jesus: 'I have come that you may have life, life to the full.' (Jn 10:10) There is also a growing realisation that 'without peace between the religions, there will be no peace between the nations.'[7]

Peter and Paul heard the call of the nations and the early church left the walls of a Jewish church to meet the challenge of the then known world. A similar challenge now faces the church. It is called by the peoples of the world to leave the still secure but autumnal splendours of its Euro-centric structures and enter into a real dialogue, with no barriers or walls, with the other world religions. The best ways forward will be in the dialogues of life and action, where the church joins with others to improve the quality of life of the poor and the suffering – as Jesus did. This is the connection between the two great questions that the world is asking the church. There is an enormous potential to be realised. It is as if the church is asleep, its song muted. The glory of its autumn leaves is fading into winter. It must gather itself for the spring.

The question is inescapable, if only because we are commanded to love our neighbours and our neighbours are increasingly experienced to be Muslims, Hindus and Sikhs, Jews and Buddhists, Jains and Rastafarians. We increasingly experience, in our own streets, cities and towns, what some call the globalisation of the planet. Europe is becoming rapidly a multi-cultural and multi-faith society. There are Danish Moroccans who are Muslim, Dutch Indians who are Hindu, German Turks who are Muslim, English Punjabis who are Sikhs, Norwegian Indians who are Muslims and Hindus. Many Christians are finding, through daily contact with devout Muslims, Hindus and Sikhs that the old explanations for religious diversity (e.g. these are 'anonymous Christians'[8]) no longer ring true. Experience tells them so.

Improved communications and speedier travel have brought the opportunities for more contact and conversation. They have not necessarily brought an end to prejudice, ignorance or hostility. Our world may be a global village for some, mainly the rich, but it is a village without human solidarity.[9] Still, for the first time, the potential exists for creating a multi-faith society at the service of the deepest aspirations of the human community. This

calls for dialogue between the church and the 'religious other'
on a global level. No religion or tradition or belief can now escape the imperative to engage in dialogue with the other.

This question for the church is also a radical one. It is as radical, in its implications for the church's self-understanding of its
mission and the subsequent reshaping of its ministries, as the
one that ended the first epoch of the church's history. Then the
option was to remain behind the walls of a Jewish church. The
walls would have become barriers to the movement of the Spirit.
But the Spirit of God will not allow the church to stay behind
walls if these negate the church's purpose. It is remarkable that
the person who caused the radical, tectonic shift in the church
from its Jewish confinement to its great expansion into much of
the then known world (as our European perspective would
quaintly have it) was a member of another faith. 'There was in
Caesarea a man named Cornelius ... a religious and God-fearing
man together with his whole household. He gave generously to
the people and constantly prayed to God.' If we want the same
impact today: 'There is in Bradford, a man named Ishtiaq or
Mushtaq ... a religious and God-fearing man with his whole
family'. The book of Acts (chap 10) goes on to describe how
Peter dreams of a great sheet being lowered by its four corners
to earth. It contains every kind of creature. Peter is bidden to
take and eat. 'What God has made clean, you must not call un-
clean.' (10:15) Peter is still puzzling when messengers from
Cornelius arrive at his door. Peter goes with them to Cornelius'
gentile home, so violating Jewish law. Peter and Cornelius begin
a dialogue in which both listen and both learn. It is in this sense a
truly 'correlational dialogue.'[10]

Peter declares: 'Truly I realise that God does not show par-
tiality but in all nations he listens to everyone who fears God
and does good.' Peter and Cornelius – the first Pope in dialogue
with 'the religious Other', each caught up into that previous dialogue between the Spirit of God and humanity, each learning
and listening to the other's truth. Peter learning from Cornelius.
Today the image is of the Pope sitting at the foot of the Muslim
'other' and coming to a greater understanding of God. There are
then, urgent, inescapable and radical questions surrounding the
church's dialogue with the other – the 'religious other'. Are
there old images of the church, taken from the early days of its
dialogue with the Spirit of God, that we can use to frame our an-

swers? Are there new ones drawn from the soil of contemporary
life, also suffused with the Spirit, which can supplement these?

Powerful Songs and Images
On the radio recently (autumn 1998) an Anglican Bishop spoke
eloquently and with love about the church as 'the sign of God's
irreversible, eternal love for all humanity.' Yes! It raises a question for us: do we celebrate the church in sufficient story, poem
and song – in terms that 'make love' for us? The 'Saw Doctors'
are an Irish pop group. One song of theirs is worth quoting.

When the troubles of the whole wide world come knocking
on your door.
And there's problems of a different kind that you've never
had before.
When you've played against a gale force wind and it changes
at half time
And you find your strength deserting you and there's empti-
ness inside.
There's people that will harm you and you've done to them
no wrong,
    It's time to sing, it's time to sing,
    To sing a powerful song.
    When the spirits they need a-rising
    To be happy, proud and strong,
    It's time to sing, it's time to sing,
    To sing a powerful song.

We do need to remind ourselves in these autumn days that not
only is it time to sing a powerful song but that our powerful
song is the song of the church. It is a powerful song because it is
the song of God in irreversible loving dialogue with human
kind. The other world religions are likewise powerful songs because they, too, are the irreversible dialogues of God with
human kind.

St Paul sang a song about the beauty of the church. We know
it as the 'Letter of St Paul to the Ephesians.' In it he tries to express the inexpressible relationship between the church and
God which he knows to be true. He writes from prison in Rome.
The troubles of the whole wide world had come knocking at his
door. He is awash with the vision of his revelation. 'Even when
in chains I am an ambassador of God!' It is by re-acquainting
ourselves with the scope and breadth of images such as Paul's

that we will be able to answer best the question of how the church should relate with the 'religious other'.

Paul's vision is vast in its scope and terrifying in its awful beauty. Paul talks about world salvation and the place of the Christian community. 'God chose us in Christ before the creation of the world.' (1:3) Paul sets his vision of the church against the magnificent backdrop of the whole of God's creation. Christ is the head of the church. 'He washed her and made her holy by baptism in the Word. As he wanted a radiant church without stain or wrinkle or any blemish, but holy and blameless, he had to prepare and present her to himself.' (5:26, 27) This prose poem of mixed references to marriage and the church provides us with a remarkably vivid imagery with which to meditate about the church and interfaith dialogue. We are often tempted to view the church as 'stained (by scandals), wrinkled (by out-moded, out of date and aged structures and attitudes) and blemished (by time serving, bitterness, dis-spiritedness, lack of confidence, laziness, cynicism, etc)' and so she is – even as we are. The faults of the church are grave. There is a feeling that the church faces a crisis of immense proportions.

But so might the church have looked to Paul from his cell. The church was in crisis. It was newly emerging from what some characterise as its first phase of development as a Jewish church, into a church for the gentiles. It was vulnerable and a prey to the power of the Roman Empire. It was riven by dissension. There were those who, out of love for the church, wished to hedge it about and who opposed its expansion into Europe and the uncertain, multifaith world of the gentile, non-Jewish, peoples. From love of the church they wished to protect it from the soil and air of God's prior creation. But St Paul argues that this is to misunderstand the role of the church. The church has a mission. It is the same as Paul's – to announce to the pagan nations the immeasurable riches of Christ. (3:8) And so he chooses to describe, in the most vivid and extraordinary terms, how Christ has 'washed his church' like a husband in love with his new wife who wants to 'prepare and present her to himself' – radiant, holy and blameless. Paul turns for his image to the domestic intimacy of a married couple in love where the new husband bathes his wife. In his eyes, this physical bathing will betoken how he sees her with the eyes of love – beyond compare, lovely in every way. This is how Paul sees the church.

Muslims, Hindus, Sikhs and all those who seek dialogue with the church, do not want to find us frightened or depressed or weak. They will benefit the most from Christians who are in love with their church and who can sing its powerful song clearly and who can bring old and new images to the telling of its story. These songs and stories and images have been created out of the correlational dialogue between the Spirit of God and human kind. They have come from the dialogue between the first Christian leaders, Peter and Paul, with the 'religious other' – Cornelius and the gentiles of Europe who called to Paul. Peter, Paul and countless others sang the powerful song and entered into that dialogue of faith with Europe which resulted in the church of today.

Where can we find the strains of that old but powerful song today in the church? Are we taking up the challenge of how we will relate to the 'religious other'?

Development of the Songs of Dialogue

Nowhere are the signs of the church's ability to sing its powerful song more apparent than in the speed of the development of its dialogue with the world religions. The church has begun to take down the walls of its European fortress in a movement of emergent globalisation, even if there are those who, out of love for the church, would wish to see this, that or the other redoubt of the walls defended. The first burst of expansion took the church out from its Jewish origins into the multi-faith world of the wider Roman Empire. This movement rested on the example of Jesus. Story after story in the gospels shows Jesus in 'correlational dialogue' with people of other faiths. Interestingly enough, Jesus in his lifetime never spoke to a single Christian! It seems certain that Jesus learnt as much from these dialogues with the 'religious other' as from his Jewish roots. The Spirit surprises Jesus in what Romans, Syro-Phoenicians, Samaritans and others have to say to him. The movement was sustained by Peter and Paul in the ways they developed images of the church which sprang from their dialogue with the other plural world of the gentiles, represented by Cornelius. These early days of proclamation and mission were inextricably also days of truly correlational dialogue.

We return to the question: Is it possible for the great world faiths to sing their powerful songs in unison for the benefit of the rest of humanity and especially for those who suffer?

The Second Vatican Council

Hinge and pivot, the second Vatican Council brought 2000 bishops to Rome and they opened doors which we still need to push against to ensure they do not close again. One of these doors is marked 'Other Faiths'. There are good Catholics whose love of the church has been threatened immensely by the Council opening of doors and they are seeking to close this one again. They believe that the only mission of the church is to bring the 'religious other' to knock in supplication at the closed door of the wall of the church to seek entry into the fullness of truth and of salvation. If, however, the door is kept open and we go out through it, then this will mark the church's successful entry into the third millennium and a renewal of its mission as dialogue with the other faiths to the benefit of the whole of humanity.

In the Second Vatican Council *Declaration on the Relationship of the Church to Non-Christian Religions* (*Nostra Aetate*, 1965), the church began to sing its old and powerful song in a new key. The declaration marked a turning point in the Catholic theology of religions. It sees the church's task in a new light: 'to foster unity and love among nations', because it believes that all peoples have a common origin in God the creator of all and God is their final goal. God's saving designs extend to all men and women. Can we hear strains of that song sung by Paul in his cell? 'The Catholic Church rejects nothing which is true and holy in these religions.' The church respects the ways of life and teachings of the other faiths. Christians are urged 'through dialogue and collaboration with the followers of other religions to acknowledge, preserve and promote the spiritual and moral goods found among these men, as well as the values in their society and culture.' The door is now ajar and we can hear the sounds of the song of dialogue. The church lays the ground for a global, potentially correlational dialogue with the other faiths. If Christians 'lovingly and prudently, in dialogue and collaboration, acknowledge, preserve and promote the spiritual and moral goods' of those of other faiths – it becomes obvious that no dialogue can start from a position which says, however lovingly, 'We possess, in all humility, the only truth and your choice is simple, either to resist or to be converted.' Nor can dialogue be real if it proposes that 'your truth is but a pale reflection of the fullness of the truth which we possess.' Real dialogue as it is emerging from contacts with the other means recognising that the Christian faith is a unique expression of God's design and work of salvation, but it is not the only one.

True dialogue is a two way process. Each partner must proclaim their truth, but must also listen to the truth of the other and not regard it as in some way a deficient expression of itself or a lesser route to its own preferred way to salvation. Dialogue calls for each partner to self-review and change, as a response to what it learns of itself from the other. The church has to learn how to learn from the other faiths.

Beyond the Council: Opening Wider the Doors
There is no option for the church but to open wide the doors of dialogue and collaboration. This has been made plain by the way that the church and the Vatican have developed further the Council's theology of religions. It is summed up in two key texts: the encyclical *Redemptoris Missio* (1990) and in *Dialogue and Proclamation* (1991), a document of guidance for interfaith work issued jointly by the Council for Interreligious Dialogue and the Congregation for the Evangelisation of Peoples. Both serve to remind us that the theology of dialogue is not complete and will only emerge from engaging in such dialogue.

Both these documents strengthen the seminal idea that the church is not the kingdom of God. The reign of God is something much vaster and broader than the church. More than that, the church is subordinate to the kingdom in that it exists to bring the kingdom about by being the servant of the kingdom. The prime mission of the church is to convert people to the kingdom and its justice and to convert them to itself only as a means of serving its prime mission. Asked why she was held in such regard in India, Mother Teresa replied, 'Because I converted no one. She helped them find God and be good Hindus, good Muslims, good Buddhists.[11] She undoubtedly converted them to the kingdom of God in so far as she pointed them to the elements in their faith that lead to God and his reign. The other faiths may also be 'agents of the kingdom', moved by the same Spirit which breathes through the church. Do we need to balance more, in our understanding of the mission of the church, the mission of Jesus, the Second Person of the Trinity, with the mission of the Spirit? What is the Spirit doing beyond the church, within other religions?

The document, *Dialogue and Proclamation*, goes further than

Vatican II and says that the religions play a 'providential role in the divine economy of salvation.' Christians may learn things about that kingdom from the other faiths, just as they will learn from Christians. This is because the kingdom is not defined fully by the reality of the church. The church is more fully appreciating that its mission is to reshape all human life towards the reign of God. It is realising that this mission is the purpose of all its members as they live out in collaborative ministries the calling of their baptism into the life of the mission of the Trinity. The mission of all Christians is not primarily to convert people to sit in its pews, though this can be legitimate. *Redemptoris Missio* talks about two forms of conversion and affirms the distinction between the church and the kingdom which they rest on: 'It is true that the church is not an end unto herself, since she is ordered towards the kingdom of God of which she is the seed, sign and instrument.' (*Redemptoris Missio*, 18)

The revolutionary character of the church's understanding of dialogue is taken further in the two documents. Both of them link mission and dialogue. Both state that dialogue constitutes an integral and essential part of the church's mission. 'Proclamation and dialogue are ... both viewed, each in its own place, as component elements and authentic forms of the one evangelising mission of the church.' (*Dialogue and Proclamation*, 2) The church is saying that dialogue with the other faiths is essential to its mission and cannot be replaced with something else. 'Interreligious dialogue possesses its own validity.' (*Dialogue and Proclamation*, 41) It is part of the mission of the church. 'The way Christians understand their religion and practice may be in need of clarification.'(*Dialogue and Proclamation*, 32) Dialogue is genuine if it challenges Christians to change. The Committee for Other Faiths of the Bishops' Conference of England and Wales felt that the document *Dialogue and Proclamation* was so important that they wanted it to be made available for all those who come into contact with peoples of other faiths. The summary, *Ways of Sharing Faith*, contains the basis for the forms that dialogue can take.[12] It identifies four of these:

* Dialogue of life: when people try to live in harmony, sharing their joys and sorrows, their problems and preoccupations;

* Dialogue of action: when people of different faiths work together for human development and liberation;

* Dialogue of theological exchange: when specialists seek to understand each others' religious heritage and appreciate each others' spiritual values;
* Dialogue of religious experience: when people, rooted in their own religious tradition, share their spiritual riches with people of other faiths.

Signs of a Springtime of Dialogue

The church, then, is already providing the framework for the work of 'dialogue-in-mission'. This is no small thing to say. It looks as though our leaders are being as bold, visionary and prophetic as their predecessors Peter and Paul. Like them, at a time of crisis for the church, they are pointing the way forward. In 1964 Pope Paul VI set up the Secretariat for non-Christians, now called the Council for Interreligious Dialogue. The Bishops' Conference of England and Wales established the Committee for Other Faiths in 1984. In that same year the present Pope, in an address to the Council for Interreligious Dialogue, said: 'Dialogue is fundamental for the church.' In 1986 he called all the leaders of the world's faiths to join him at Assisi to pray for world peace – dialogue in action.

In the years since the Vatican Council, an increasing number of Catholics have become involved in interfaith dialogue. Out of this dialogue of life they have reflected on their own faith and have learnt that 'she or he who only Christianity knows, knows not Christianity.' Many have been able to change and deepen the tune of the 'powerful song' of the church that they sing. They can no longer believe that their Muslim friend is excluded from revelation and from salvation. They can no longer even say that really their Muslim friend is an 'anonymous Christian', just as they would experience deep concern if their Muslim friend were to say that that he believed that the Christian is 'really a Muslim, would they but acknowledge it.' It is deeply insulting to suggest to a member of another faith that 'really they are Christians, if only they would admit it!' Some Christians have learnt, from the beauty and spirituality of Sikh, Hindu and Muslim, to re-assess and deepen their own Christian faith. They have learnt to realise that God, creator of all, is beyond the descriptions and insights of all faiths – is mystery. They have learnt that the Holy Spirit of the Christian Trinity has been at work in the world and in the faiths of men and women since the creation. They have experienced that many other members of the great faiths of the world are active co-partners and agents of the will, the justice, the love of the reign of God and the mystery of God's kingdom that is beyond all our imagining. In this sense they have come to believe that there are many true religions. Conversion is to enter into the dialogue of work with men and women of all faiths to build human justice, peace and the integrity of the creation.

What of Jesus Christ in all this? All Christians believe that Jesus is at the heart of dialogue – just as he is at the heart of the Divine Dialogue we call the Trinity. As he was at the well with the Samaritan woman, he is now listener, learner, delighting in the meeting of his Father's children as they come to know more about one another as sisters and brothers of the one Father and as, from that dialogue, they grow more and more into the community of the Divine. Like Jesus, Christians marvel that they often find more faith in the non-Christian than in many of their fellow Christians. Like Jesus, they experience people of other faiths as co-agents of the kingdom of God. Jesus is the friend and brother present in the circle of encounter. All Christians will honestly share their devotion, their relationship with Christ as Saviour and Lord. Some Christians are exploring what the implications for their belief in Jesus Christ are as a result of their dialogue with members of other faiths.

The truth of the Christian claims about Jesus Christ are better to emerge as a result of dialogue. The best way to proclaim the truth about Jesus Christ as the unique one who 'walked the kingdom', is by trying to present and live a life of faithfulness to his values and example. The rule for believing is to be found in the rule for praying and both should be found in this 'rule for following'.[13] Most Christians involved in dialogue accept that in Jesus we meet God fully. Some want to explore the notion that this does not mean that we have therefore grasped the fullness of God. Some agree that 'divinity, while truly available in Jesus, is to be found beyond Jesus' and 'to say that the whole of Jesus is divinised, does not mean to say that the whole of divinity is humanised.'(Knitter, p 37) They want to explore further the notion that proclaiming that what God has done in Jesus 'does not mean insisting that God has done it only in Jesus.' (Knitter, p 43) They want to explore the idea that Christians can affirm Jesus' uniqueness in that he brings a universal, decisive and indispensable, but not total word, and that this leaves open the possibility of other universal, decisive and indispensable manifestations of divine reality besides Jesus. (Knitter, p 79) Jesus is truly, but not solely, God's saving Word and Presence. Jesus is truly God's saving revelation. Some Christians want to explore further the notion that 'he does not have to be God's only saving revelation.' (Knitter, p 21)

It must be emphasised that there is no need for Christians to feel they must espouse these ideas about the position of Christ, if they are to engage in interfaith dialogue as supported by the church and its teachings. It remains true that there are some ways of speaking of Jesus which encourage dialogue and some which kill it stone dead. It would be tragic if the person of Christ, as presented by Christians, became not a way or a door to dialogue, but a hindrance. The adventure of interfaith dialogue, so persuasively advanced by the official church and explored by new generations of theologians, is beginning to be taken up by local churches. It is a risky and often a lonely pursuit. Misunderstandings and fears come from within the church also. The song being sung is too siren-like for those whose love for the church calls for caution.

Into the Third Millennium: Opening Wide the Doors of Dialogue
There are some remarkable and clear signs of spring in these autumn days. There are signs that the church has in some aspects already become the world church of a new diaspora. The work of CAFOD and other aid agencies is an illustration of how the church is learning to sing its powerful song as it makes an option for the poor across the whole world. This work is drawing in more and more ordinary Christians who are learning to act locally and think globally. If we want a model of what the church of the new millennium will look like as it begins to take up its song of the interreligious dialogue of action for liberation, here it is. The director of CAFOD talked recently of the fact that we have a global market but do not have a global family of brothers and sisters.[14] This will be created by action for justice. This can arise out of the dialogue of action between religions.

All religions are co-creators of the reign of the one God. This alone must be the criterion we can use to judge the church. The church is only church and is only true 'religion' to the extent to which it proclaims and builds and works for the accomplishments of the heart of God. Similarly this is the criterion we can use to judge the authenticity of other faiths. But to do that we have to tread carefully, prudently and with loving compassion. Sometimes we must hum the tune of our powerful song lest it drown out the harmonies being sung by others. Together those harmonies are parts in the infinite song of God

The task of the local church in dialogue with the other faiths will be, within the framework provided by the magisterium and the new theologies of dialogue, to enter into the correlational dialogue of life, action and experience. Out of this will come new theological insights and this life of the following of Jesus will in turn prompt the magisterium to bring both new and old truths from the treasury of the church's self-understanding. Local churches will create the world church if they 'act locally and think globally' in terms of dialogue. The Pontifical Council for Interreligious Dialogue is encouraging local action. Each year, for instance, it sends out greetings and messages to Hindus and Muslims on the occasions of the great festivals of Divali and Eid al-Fitr. The Bishops' Conference of England and Wales Committee on Other Faiths has produced some nineteen leaflets that introduce different faiths and contain guidance on important aspects of interfaith relations.[15] The local diocese may have an Interfaith Group that offers advice to the bishop and people of the diocese on interfaith affairs. Individual Christians are working in the connected dialogues of 'life, action and experience' with those of other faiths. They can feel supported by the church but still too often experience the wounds of isolation and misunderstanding.

Sometimes dialogue is risky and can be opposed by those in the church whose task it is to maintain the church's sense of tradition and faithfulness, but who do this sometimes at the expense of openness. Still there are signs in the local church that interreligious dialogue will be part of the new 'powerful song' of the church.

The church will learn from Berlin, Russia, South Africa and Northern Ireland and wherever the walls are torn down by people seeking justice, that its own European walls must come down so that the world's peoples can hear the powerful song and recognise it as a part of the mighty one they have been singing for all this time. 'In the next millennium the only Christians will be poor or friends of the poor.' (A South American Bishop) In the same way, in the next millennium the only Christians will be those in dialogue with those of other faiths.

A Church without Walls?

What will characterise this world church? Selecting some areas of the church's life, what will change look like? In nurturing the development of people for ministry in the church, both for lay and clerical roles, in preparing people for entry into the church, in initial and in-service programmes for all ministries, it should become increasingly impossible to study theology in ways which are confined to the study of Christianity or an under-standing of the Christian faith only. Because Christianity can only be defined in terms of its relationships – with God, with Jesus, with the whole of humanity. Christian theology which does not include study of interfaith dialogue and experiences of other faith practices, worship and traditions, we will appreciate, is unable to be truly described as 'Christian theology.' It is not possible to 'do theology' and then bolt on a bit of 'religious stud-ies' in which Christians take a peek at Hindu Dharma or at Islam. Nor is it sustainable for those wishing to exercise ministry in the church any longer to maintain a distinction between Christian formation or catechetics and religious studies.

This distinction is valid for those wishing to be students of religions. But Christians want to proclaim the kingdom by dia-logue, not to study those who do this. No-one should be able to teach theology or catechetics or programmes of formation or nurture to others (in seminary, school or parish) who has not in-cluded some experience of at least one tradition of the 'religious other' in their training or preparation. This should include ex-tended contact on the ground, in the street, in the communities of mosque, gurdwara, mandir, synagogue or temple and in the families of those of other faiths.

At local diocesan level, all pastoral agencies should develop a response to the question: 'How do we reflect the need to be a church whose mission is defined by the extent that we are a part-ner in local correlational dialogue with those of other faiths?' At the level of administration and finance, and in terms of generat-ing diocesan pastoral planning, the question becomes: 'How is the diocese serving and supporting the development of mission in terms of interfaith dialogue? Have we identified criteria, in collaboration with those of other faiths who are our neighbours, for assessing the decisions we take about pastoral planning, so that success is measured by the extent that these decisions en-courage dialogue and do not hinder it?' If such approaches had been adopted in the church of Europe just before the time of the Crusades, would the church have been dragged into such blasphemous a denial of its relations with our fellow sons and daughters of Abraham, the Muslims? If such criteria had been in use before Christian acts of anti-Semitism against those other sons and daughters of Abraham, the Jews, would the Christians have been so implicated in centuries of pogrom and holocaust?

We must beware of painting too rosy a picture of our fellow religionists. Truth demands that we speak out when they do not avoid bigotry or interfaith hatred and act on the instincts of ignorance and stereotyping. But what we can do is to seek to remove the beams in the eyes of our own traditions first so that Muslim suspicions, for instance, of Christian motives for seeking dialogue are more easily shown to be groundless. There are innumerable reasons for interfaith rivalry and hatred that too often can result in persecution and deepening human misery and sorrow. Correlational dialogue is an even more urgent necessity because of these all too frequent examples.

Are we sufficiently informed about other faiths to ensure that our coverage of them and of interfaith dialogue initiatives is accurate and furthers the mission of dialogue of the church? Have we learnt about and experienced the patterns of worship and family devotion of those of other faiths in homes, synagogues, mosques, mandirs and gurdwaras so that we can further the dialogue of religious experience, worship and prayer as advocated by *Dialogue and Proclamation*? How many of us who exercise some form of ministry in the church have been able to spend time sitting in the local mosque observing Friday prayers and letting the great sense of the presence of God which this brings, wash over and through our Christian sense of self and belonging? If we are to become truly the world church of the new millennium, many more of us should have some experience of the prayer and worship of our neighbours of other faiths.

At the level of personal spirituality and everyday experience, whether through initial or in-service training and resource support, how many priests feel equipped to take a lead in interfaith dialogue? How many could support lay people in their ministry by preaching and teaching about our other faith neighbours and the ways of authentic dialogue? How many have been given the opportunities to meet Muslims or Hindus at prayer, and in their own communities to talk about faith and dialogue? Do clergy and other lay ministers, at diocesan and deanery levels, learn the skills and attitudes of mission as dialogue? How often can a parish take up the lead provided by the Pontifical Commission for Interfaith Dialogue and include neighbours of other faiths in the prayers of the faithful at times of festival and offer greetings and the hand of friendship and solidarity? Have priests and people been able at all to experience something of the faith, beliefs and worship of their Muslim, Hindu and Sikh neighbours?

Perhaps most crucial of all are the questions which we can ask of agencies responsible for Christian formation. In their work of promoting understanding and appreciation of the faith, what model of that faith are they encouraging amongst adults and young people? Which song, story, which dance, are they teaching the next generations to live by? Increasingly there is a choice. Do we set out the old tunes on the shabby hymn sheets or are we gently but confidently proposing the 'powerful song' of the world church of the third millennium? How far is correlational dialogue a 'constitutive element' in our promotion of an understanding of the faith? In programmes for collaborative ministry, do we encourage people to see that baptism links us into that dialogic life of the Trinity and the prior work of the Holy Spirit which brings alive the mission of God with all men and women and to which God calls us as missionaries of dialogue?

Or, more practically, have we invited a Muslim, as a critical friend, to offer a critique of our programmes from the point of view of the 'religious other'? If Catholics do not understand that collaboration in ministry leads to mission, as a means to an end, then ministry in the church is moribund. If they do not include dialogue with the religious other in mission, then mission is pointless. We will continue to hug one another behind our lovely walls whilst the rest of the world goes by outside. The church will have become an irrelevance to the world and hence to the kingdom of God. We do not, by the way, believe that this will be the fate of the church – and neither did Jesus or Peter or Paul or a whole host of others!

In schools there are some signs that the church is opening the doors and encouraging its children to sing the new song of world awareness. In 1997 the Bishops' Conference of England and Wales produced a consultation paper, *Catholic Schools and Other Faiths*. This provides guidance for schools so that the spiritual and moral development of children of other faith backgrounds can be furthered in Catholic schools and so that Catholic children can begin to develop the skills of interfaith dialogue. There are moves to include consideration of other faiths more systematically in Catholic Religious Education. More needs to be done to ensure that pupils have the knowledge, understanding, skills and attitudes they need to be active creators of the church without walls. They need to be able to sing the powerful song and have the skills of listening to the powerful songs of the other faiths. They need to learn that devotion and commitment to Christ and the church, far from leading away from dialogue, actually includes a commitment to it.

How can interfaith dialogue be linked to the work of those agencies working for justice, those engaged in that other equally important dialogue, that with the 'suffering other'? A dedication to the 'option for the poor' as a constitutive element in the preaching of the gospel is the church's mission. It creates the will of God, the reign of God. 'There is a clear and strong sense that an effective, enduring, really transformative dialogue with the suffering of this world will have to include a dialogue with the world religions.'[16] The church must address the suffering of humanity and of the world. It can only do this if it also makes it the object of a correlational dialogue of action with the world religions. In this dialogue it is the future which is important. There needs to be less talk about our origins and rituals and what necessarily divides the faiths. The focus needs to be more on salvation, liberation for humanity and the earth and the hopes and prayers of the faiths for the future. 'When religious people together listen to the voices of the suffering and oppressed, when they attempt together to respond to those needs, they are able to trust one another and feel the truth and power in each other's strangeness.'[17]

Lastly, in this benign questioning of diocesan church structures, what of those agencies working for unity? Some dioceses have, as part of this work, a group advising on interfaith dialogue. Often the stress will be on Christian ecumenism. Even the most dedicated devotee of ecumenism recognises that progress here is laboured and the church's effective attitude a mixture of indifference and torpor. May this be because we have not been able to accept the fact that the richest environment is the one where many species flourish, particularly when they are the result of a process of natural, human and historical development?

What richness would be lost if all the Christian denominations were merged into one great multi-national, multi-denominational sameness – a great super-church. This is not the unity for which Christ prayed. We have domesticated his plea. In the light of his commitment to the building of the kingdom of God, his prayer was for human solidarity in seeking its coming. He prayed that the faith of all humanity would be dedicated to the salvation of the whole of humanity and of the whole world. This was and is the will of God. True unity will be achieved and the wish of Christ fulfilled when the great world faiths unite in a dialogue of action to save the world and its peoples from the effects of sin, injustice, poverty, greed, untruth and domination. Christian unity should be conceived in this way.

> When religions are strong their hearts are strong and their skins thin and transparent – they talk together about common tasks and challenges and work to achieve them. When religions are weak their hearts are weak and their skins thick and they build walls to sit behind and cogitate narrow self-imposed tasks which bring on-one any freedom.[18] *(Based on an idea from John Hull, Professor of Religious Education, Birmingham University).*

Work for Christian unity will never succeed because it is trying to succeed at the wrong task. Its sights are skewed. It must realign them and begin to hum the tunes of the songs of the new churches of the third millennium. There are those who are already singing the song of the unity of God. And they are finding that other religions are singing the same song – the freedom of humanity and of the planet.

Conclusions

It is almost winter. The leaves of the copper beech tree in the garden are all fallen. But the wind still sings its song through the bare branches, and if you listen carefully you can hear the song of the spring. It is so powerful that the dead leaves stir and rise with the breath of the wind. So it was over the waters in the beginning. So it was over the tomb on Easter eve. So it is now over the church. So it is over the world's religions and the peoples of the world. So it will be at the end of time. Then there will only be the Spirit of God breathing life and renewal into all things. The task of the church and of Christianity will have been completed. So will the task of the other faiths. And no one and no creed will be called 'other'.

Reclaiming Ritual

'Since we have seven sacraments and many other ceremonies, why,' a reader may ask, 'do you suggest that a recovery of ritual is a huge part of a renewed church?' The answer takes us down many and mysterious roads. One of these has to do with rediscovering the initial wisdom in the human/divine conception of some of these sacraments in the dawn of human consciousness, long before the Christian advent. But what began as a deep, archetypal and natural ritual, has, over the millennia, often become, automatic and lifeless. A recent study-day (February 1999) for priests and parishioners revealed a great uncertainty about the underlying theology for a number of sacraments and the bewildering variations in the practicalities of their celebration.

The Role of Ritual

Ritual takes many forms. At the simplest level there are those recurring personal rituals which we all use for getting up in the morning, going off to work, settling down to work, coming home, relaxing and going to bed. All such personal rituals enable us to come to terms with the reality of each day, imposing some kind of order on what otherwise might be chaos.

One of the first insights about ritual that needs to be understood is that, even though accessible to the senses in their expression, their roots are deep within the human psyche. This too is how the sacraments came into being. They grew out of the longings and habits of the human heart long before they found the fixed, imposed formulas to which we have become accustomed. (It is interesting that this process has also happened to the once-living and experience-based agreed wisdom of the early Christians, so much of which is now presented to us in the shape of detached doctrines.)

If we are to live our meaning, to sing our own song, tell our

219

own tale before we go to heaven, then we have to be prepared to
go on a journey into the interior, in search of the riches that lie
within each one of us. As all myths teach, it takes courage to
plunge into the unknown, and on the way we must expect a se-
ries of trials or 'passages of the soul'. This is the name of the
book I have relied on throughout this chapter. The author, James
Roose-Evans, describes ritual as such a passage or threshold,
rightly termed a 'rite of passage'.

> We pass over from one state of being into another (just as in
> death we pass over from time into eternity), experiencing a
> *metanoia* or complete change. There is, at such a moment, an
> unalterable shift of perception. We can never again be what
> we once were. It is a process brought about, not by intellectual
> debate, but by direct experience ... There are various routes
> to the world within. For some it may be by way of analysis;
> for some by way of meditation and prayer. Yet rituals, like
> symbols, cannot be invented. They must well up from within,
> as dreams do.[1]

The church is well aware that society can only be renewed by renewing individuals. The family, the 'domestic church', is seen as
the key unit in the wider community and, within that, the individual is the source of its life. The whole world of Christian spirituality is about the purification, redemption and celebration of
each one's soul within the circles of communities and cultures.
The spiritual classics chronicle and craft the journey of the soul,
the way we are drawn towards wholeness, the way we seek the
seed of our true and God-given essence, the way we labour to
reveal the hidden self that St Paul writes about – the self that is
unique to us, the person that we are meant to be. This work is
rarely accomplished alone. It is in this enterprise of contacting
one's inner spirit and resources that ritual, which usually presupposes the presence of others, plays such an important part
according to the journal-therapist Ira Progoff.

> We gradually discover that our life has been going some-
> where, however blind we have been to its direction, and
> however unhelpful to it we ourselves have been. We find
> that a connective thread has been forming beneath the sur-
> face of our lives, carrying the meaning that has been trying to
> establish itself in our existence. It is the inner continuity of
> our lives. As we recognise and identify with it, we see an
> inner myth that has been guiding our lives unknown to our-
> selves.[2]

It is foolish to dismiss this kind of reflection as superficial, or 'too deep', or airy-fairy New Age gobbeldy-gook. Such a dismissal usually springs from an insecure person's fear. The imagery and language of searching for the God-within is as old as Jesus, and indeed, as humanity itself. It is because the search is so difficult and so painful that most of us are tempted to avoid it by indifference or ridicule.

From where does the power of ritual come? There are those who bestow an awesome role for it, who see much of the current malaise within the mainstream churches and, indeed, within society as a whole, as a consequence of its absence. Today, in the West, there are scarcely any true rituals or rites of passage. Robert Bly, in his inspirational book *Iron John*, discusses one instance of the lack of such rituals – for the young. 'The recovery of some form of initiation,' he writes, 'is essential for the culture.'

Even before Arnold Van Gennep's *Rites of Passage*,[3] anthropologists have held the obvious view that all true rituals mark a transition from one mode of being to another, working a transformation within the individual or community, at a deep psychological, physical and spiritual level, resulting in an altered state of consciousness. Such major rituals, as we have seen, are sometimes known as rites of passage. Clearly the passage is not geographical but rather a journey of the heart, into the interior landscape of each individual, resulting in 'a sea-change into something rich and strange' as Shakespeare wrote in *The Tempest*.

Journeys and Boundaries

Those who travel into the mystery of their own lives, of their own deaths, of love and of God, will arrive at many crossroads and frontiers. Pilgrimages are rituals of a sort, to help us cope with the confusion and loss of direction that we so often feel. Whether it be to Mecca, the Holy Land, Benares, the Ganges, Lourdes, Walsingham, Croagh Patrick, there will always be pilgrims. Because there is so much happening within us at the many levels of our souls, people will always take to the road, head for the mountains, enter the desert. The great religions know that somewhere in the human psyche there is something essential to the development of the individual and collective spiritual life in the ritual of pilgrimage. The plea here is for the recovery of that awareness within our Christian churches.

Pilgrims, whatever their religious tradition, are engaged in a search for meaning and for spiritual advancement. There are those who go on a pilgrimage solely to get merit for themselves, and those who go not only for themselves by simultaneously wishing all beings to go with them ... The purpose of such a pilgrimage is surely to summon us away from the safe and familiar pattern of every day into a context of danger and demand.[4]

Paradoxically, it is the very difficulty and danger of the pilgrimage that makes it so necessary for the churches to bring the ritual centre-stage once again. Writing in *The Tablet*, Eamonn Duffy comments, 'In the raw experience of hunger, cold, lack of sleep, and elemental contact with earth, rock and water, unshielded by roof or shoe leather, we can find a sense of fragility and creatureliness which is vital to any true perception of God.' So many of our modern pilgrimages are comfortable and genteel. The bruising edge of limits and endurance are never reached.

Last summer it was as though the fury of the gods, of cold and wet, were unleashed upon us, as we battled our way to the top of Croagh Patrick. The temptation to join all those who had already turned in panic and were fleeing down the mountain against us, like ragged scraps of human fabric, was very enticing. We gritted our teeth and forgot about broken limbs, pleurisy and all temptations towards self-pity. We hoped, too, that our remarkable sanctity was fashioned in the crucible of self-denial rather than in the showcase of machismo!

Some years ago, while privileged to be the guests of some Native American Indians of the Lakota tribe, near Sacramento, we were finally accepted as participants in their famous Vision Quest. After several truly testing sessions in their Sweat Lodges, an experience that often felt like being shut up in a red-hot iron coffin, and after several days of full fasting, we were taken to some lonely mountains and each one was asked to select a grave-sized patch of ground for our 24 hour vision quest, out of sight and out of ear-shot of any other human being – totally alone. Having carefully and prayerfully, over the preceding weeks, prepared the 'scapulars' to be hung at the four compass-points of my tiny place of destiny, to protect my high sanctuary, I faced a long night of confrontation with my own frailty and mortality. These dark and deep shadows of my psyche were personified in the terror-filled encounter with the wild beasts who snarled and threatened, but did not cross over the threshold, the *limen*, the fragile thread of prayer that demarcated my *temenos*, my holy space.

It was all about determination, boundaries, seduction, surrender, raw fear and even rawer courage, evil spirits and angels, sweat, both hot and cold. I was being purified in my quest for the vision of my future, in my desire to discern the will of God. The famous American dancer, Martha Graham said, 'In my work I have always sought to reveal an image of man in his struggle for wholeness, for what one might call God's idea of him rather than man's idea of himself.' Now in my seventh decade of years I find within myself a desire towards wholeness, a kind of compulsion towards gathering the grain and shedding the chaff, towards selling all to buy the field with the treasure. I want my harvest to be true even though small. Peter Brook, the British theatre director, once asked an Indian actor his secret, and he replied: 'I try to bring together all that I have experienced in my life, so as to make what I am doing a witness for what I have felt and what I have understood.' It is when a community of individuals bring to the creation and enactment of a ritual such a total dedication that then the invisible becomes real.

'Proclaim the pilgrimage among men. They will come to thee on foot and mounted on every kind of camel, lean on account of journeys through deep and distant mountains.' Throughout the history of world religions, mountains appear as places of holiness, from the sacred mountains of India, to those of Japan and that of Jerusalem. The meeting of Moses with God on the summit of Mount Sinai is an archetypal pattern which constantly repeats itself: 'I will ascend and go to thy holy mountain ... I have come to Thy holy mountain ... Be true to the design which I showed thee on the mountain.'[5] I'm sure we have done no favours to the Christian religion in general, or to the Catholic tradition in particular, by dropping almost all the ritual elements of folk-faith – those sometimes quaint devotions such as novenas, processions and ceremonies whose origins were often shrouded in a vague Celtic/pagan origin, maybe even of a superstitious nature, but whose participants entered into the experience with some kind of exilic passion as their senses were touched by the scents, the lights, the mandala-shaped monstrance, the mysterious language of a priest almost invisible within his brocaded cope and gold-threaded humeral veil. The eucharist, sublime and beautiful, with its own fine dimensions of ritual, is so often in danger of

being degraded, neutralised and inappropriately domesticated
by unacceptably frequent and unthinking usage.

There is no spiritual breakthrough, no real ritual, in such
liturgies. Their power is broken and tamed, their energy spent
from over-use. Not much in the current celebrations of the
Catholic Church calls out, sacramentalises, even a semblance of
the blood and sweat of primitive religious ritual, of the experiences of Jesus in the desert of his temptations, in the agony of his
violent last supper, in the reality of human trauma. Where is the
ritual-door into the awful desert, into the enchanted garden?
How, in our church, do we recreate the rites of passage that
mark the mysterious moments in the journey of a soul?

Sacrament and Ritual

Understood in the light of an early theology and spirituality of
creation, the Catholic notion of sacraments has a tradition of fine
fullness and a sensitivity to all that can be said about good worship, liturgical and paraliturgical. But this sense has long since
disappeared. A terrible stripping of the ceremonies, rites and
symbols has happened, a stark minimalising of ritual and liturgical meaning. We have lost touch with the art of thinking in images, of the place of movement and dance in worship. Our
thinking is largely discursive, verbal and linear.

Central to our understanding of sacred ritual is the meaning
of worship, the adoration of a superior being ... All sacred
ritual, indeed all ritual, should give expression to the deepest
yearning within us, urging us towards something which always remains beyond us. But worship is more than a feeling.
To worship is to do, and a ritual is an act, but for worship to
be truly meaningful it must permeate our whole lives and
make them meaningful. 'In too many churches, public worship has become almost entirely cerebral and verbal,' writes
Bill Jardine Grisbrooke, 'and that, in an age which is particularly attracted to, and conditioned by, the visual, cannot but
be counter-productive, in terms of both spirituality and pop-
ularity.' As Victor Turner wrote, what the churches and indeed all the major faiths, need to realise is the necessity to
evolve new rituals as well as to rediscover the ancient rites.
John X. Herriott, in one of the last pieces he wrote for *The
Tablet*, spoke of the need for 'rites that reflect and express realities as they are experienced now, and the insight of our
own times, not a regression to past ages'.[6]

Because of a strange and relatively recent winter of distrust, the institutional church is currently suspicious of many aspects of creation and of the human psyche. Nevertheless, it is still faithful to its unique tradition of sacramentality. Even though minimalised, reified and functionalised by so many of us, priests and parishioners, in our repetitive daily and weekly routine of the sacred mysteries of our faith, the elemental basis, the rich symbolism and imagery are all still there. So, too, precariously, is the disappearing concept of sacred space.

> In all religions one finds a *temenos,* a sacred or purified space, separated from the profane world outside, into which the deity may be safely inducted. A place of worship should be like a mandala, that powerful symbol for isolating and enclosing space which is also a symbol of the womb in which the disciple or initiate is newly conceived and grows. Stepping across the threshold of a holy place we enter into another region where time and eternity, God and humans meet.[7]

Attractive as this insight into the significance of sacred space is, it is still coloured by the demon of dualism. The creation tradition within Christian revelation throws another clarifying light across habits of religion such as this one. What we tend to forget in our originally sinful seduction by dualism, is that the sacred space referred to above is sacred, not because it divides the holy from the profane, as is still the common understanding of the notion. It is sacred because it is the sacramental space where the unity of God and creation is reverently symbolised and celebrated. It is sacred because it witnesses to the collapse of all such divisions in the light of the incarnation. It is sacred because it ends the dualism that holds one reality as being more holy than another.

The sacred space of sanctuary, the sacred heart of Jesus, the blessedness of the Blessed Sacrament, the heavenliness of the Heavenly Banquet, the holiness of the holy Catholic Church, of holy ground and of holy water – all of these are testaments, affirmations, guarantees and confirmations of the most mystifying and difficult of all truths, that everything now is holy and always has been, that grace has no boundaries, that, in the end, only authentic life is left to be celebrated. We bow to the God already at home deep within us. The divine imagination of God's people, fired by the energy of the Holy Spirit, sustained by the truth of the infinite humanity of Jesus Christ, will soon begin to explore this truth.

The ritualising of an experience is essentially a creative act in which one takes the broken pieces of one's life and assembles them into a mosaic of meaning, creating, as Robert Frost once expressed it, 'one more stay against confusion'. But it only becomes a healing or integrating influence when we continue to meditate upon it, to experience such images in the depths of our being, for both wisdom and grace reach us by many different routes, but most of all in the silence of our own meditation.[8]

To what extent does the eucharistic food and drink permeate our soul as our breakfasts and suppers do our bodies? Does our experience of the sacrament of reconciliation nourish our personalities and attitudes for days on end, even as a moment of forgiveness with an alienated member of our own natural family would? Gill and Phil are very good friends of mine. The impact of a certain liberating piece of good news was shining in their faces for months. Perhaps many of us are in danger of being liturgically and sacramentally unaware, trapped into a lifeless habit of weekly, passionless repetition.

So many of those who visit our churches and other places of worship are alienated by what they find, wondering what relevance it has to their own lives. To what extent do these rituals reflect an interior reality? Too many clergy, in the United States and Britain, of all denominations, seem wholly unaware of what it is they are enacting. Although Christians of the Roman and Episcopalian and Anglican traditions are taught that the Mass or Eucharist is valid however it is celebrated, we do need to ponder the way in which these liturgies are celebrated.[9]

Over the past few decades, when celebrating the tenth Mass in one week, I have seriously questioned the real meaning and true value for myself and the participants of what often seems to be a routine and rushed ceremony. Of course it is a good thing that people should meet to pray, chat and help each other, but such engagement is not what the Mass is about. Why do I feel so ambiguous about such repetition? Does the problem lie with me? It is well known that when a man or woman of holiness and wholeness officiates, the ritual is always transformed, and the word becomes a living word, the bread becomes the living bread. In *The Heart of Religion*, P.D. Mehta wrote:

In the hands of the great ceremonialists these rituals produced psychological effects. Trained to meditate, the attention of the skilled celebrant was wholly concentrated upon the psycho-spiritual significance of the ritual. It was the power of concentrated thought of the celebrant and of the devout feelings of the participants which made the atmosphere of ceremony, exerted the influence for uplift and inner vision in the congregation, and made the ritual a veritable sacrament, a ceremonial magic. The actual presence and benediction of the invoked and worshipped deity was deeply felt. Such magic was essentially a communion with the divine and with nature.

One of the characteristics that make the Catholic Church unique is its understanding of the principle of sacrament. Our current practice has no coherence with that principle. Small wonder that so many people, young and old, find little relevance to their lives in the Sunday Mass. Recent surveys among the thousands of the disaffected spell it out in incontrovertible ways.[10] We just cannot argue any more with the repeated findings of those who keep asking the question 'Why are you all leaving?' People who are in search of truth, love, meaning and divinity are turning away in frustration, anger and sadness from our mainstream churches. The spirituality for which they hunger demands symbol and ritual. To regain its lost power and beauty, the Catholic Church needs to spend all its energy in recreating and revisioning its sacramental and ritualistic nature. We must become sacramentally literate once again. The Catholic Church, unaware of its buried treasure, needs only to dig into its tradition and reveal to people the relevance of its symbolic story to their life situations today. Sir Laurens van der Post has confessed:

Fewer and fewer of us can find religious awareness any more in churches and temples and religious establishments of our time. Much as we long for the churches to renew themselves and once more become, in contemporary idiom, an instrument of the pentecostal spirit, many of us now have to testify that, despite the examples of dedicated men devoted to their theological vocations, they have failed to give modern man a living experience of religion such as I and others have found in the desert and in the bush of Africa.[11]

Fear, Death and Letting Go
To fully understand the plea I'm making for reclaiming the trad-

ition of ritual for Catholic Christians, the value of the *experience*
of ritual must be addressed. It is not about avoiding boredom by
doing something different, or introducing variety to our liturgy,
or challenging people to be more creative, but about the inner,
unconscious change that happens through the actual experience
of good ritual. Our regular sacraments are in danger of losing
their depth through a mechanical and deadly repetition, through
endless explanation, information and catechesis, through a fear
of being emotional or spontaneous. Reduced to words, the
sacrament or ritual loses its main power and impact. A true ritual
will always take one beyond and deeper than words, to the very
source of words, for words are but symbols of a deeper reality.

The great strength of ritual, when it is performed with the
totality of our being, is that we gain insights on an intuitive
rather than an intellectual level. This is why ritual can effect
changes which analysis cannot always achieve. For instance, I
feel sure, these days, that the process of my grieving for my recently departed mother is not happening as, perhaps, it should.
But I'm also beginning to believe that my sad and disturbing
dreams during the last few weeks are helping and healing my
condition. The point I'm making is that it is precisely in the
aching experience of loss that troubles my nights, that my consciously absent, but necessary mourning happens. Likewise, it is
the experience of the ritual, as its full meaning is slowly absorbed into the essential soul, rather than a cerebral analysis of
its contents, which can prove transforming.

If the work of ritual is to both consciously and unconsciously
dismantle the stranglehold of our compulsive shadow, then
fear, that stalker of our days and our nights, will forever be
under siege. And as long as Christianity celebrates our transcendence over certain human conditions, we will always make sure
that fear and death are on the short-list. Many would hold that
ultimately they come together in the fear of dying. This fear is
compounded by all our fears. And is it not fear that finally has to
be exorcised by ritual?

Lock any of us in a darkened room, and left alone, completely
alone, even for a day, our hidden fears will come out from
under their stones: the fear of failure; the fear that love will
not last and that, in the end, we shall be rejected; the fear that
we lose our health, our job or fail to pay the mortgage, the
rent, the bills; the fear that we have taken on too much, been

too ambitious, too much the high flyer; the fear that we may
do something irrational which will ruin our lives or our careers; or the fear that some skeleton we had locked away will
come tumbling out of its cupboard; the irrational fear of
being found out, of being a sham, stemming perhaps from
some earlier inferiority. We think that we are in control of
our lives until suddenly something takes hold of us and
sends us sprawling; the unconscious trips up the conscious
self ... Many of these fears, and the list is endless, are project-
ions of our own shadow side, those aspects of our natures
which all too often we prefer to ignore and even will not
admit exist ... But what do all these fears have in common? Is
it not the fear of the unknown, typified by fear of the dark
when nothing can be identified or distinguished, when all
orientation is lost? It is the fear of not knowing our identity,
of having to let go of all that is most familiar and assuring.[12]

Those who die well, whatever that may mean, will have died
many times, in different ways, before the final exit. In fact, I
sometimes think there are often more significant, more ultimate
and more difficult deaths in many people's lives than their last
death to this world; more grim reaping throughout the journey
of life than the Grim Reaper's visit at its end. It may well be,
therefore, that instead of just one funeral ritual for dying, magnificent as the raw Christian Last Rites in church and cemetery
are, we need to create many rituals for those countless small
deaths which we experience on our way to physical death the
death of a love, of a relationship, of an ambition, a creative skill,
a heart-felt hope.

Also, in a strange kind of way, since each one of us is a company of many selves, a community of characters within our
inner soul, and these selves are often acting in contradiction of
each other, causing conflict and pain to our conscious selves, we
need to mark and honour the changing roles of these essential
voices. At the centre to which each of us has to return, is the
need to mourn the passing of each of our many selves. When Job
covered himself with ashes, it was his way of saying that the earlier, comfortable Job was dead, and that the living Job mourned
the dead Job. Only our individual *anam-chara* or spiritual director
or priest can help us recognise the need and the timing of such
grieving and help us to fashion the appropriate ritual.

Perhaps also we need rituals for ageing, as each decade leads into the next and so closer to our moment of departure. Instead, however, in today's cultural climate of ageism, we tend to do the opposite. The men bolster up their naturally wilting virility with the latest boosters, the women erase their lines and wrinkles with unnatural, surgical treatments. The more we try to hide our age, the more difficult we will find it to die. The lower our tolerance of life's challenge to risk, change and grow, the higher the walls of our denial of the immanence of death. One of the most difficult tasks for the dying is learning how to let go and just *be*, so that they, in the fullness of time, like a ripening apple from a tree, let go. All too often the elderly (rather than the young people) cling tenaciously to life and power. If we are to die well we have to start learning *now* how to let go of each moment. But it is not enough to know these things intellectually, we must learn them *experientially*. Hence, as we have seen, the constant need for ritual.

It is only because the fear of letting go, and of any form of dying, is such a huge issue for all of us, all of the time, that I emphasise its relevance to the role of relevant rituals in the way the church is present to our lives. Carl Jung described death as a 'fearful piece of brutality'. Maybe that is why Karl Rahner wrote somewhere about 'dying by instalments', about dying from the moment we're born. Recent Roman Catholic instructions to the clergy about preparing and caring for the dying and their families, reveal a new and welcome sensitivity to the occasions of grace inherent in such moments. As over-worked priests we can often miss the eternal significance of death as the harvesting of all the fruits of a person's life, let alone recognising the need to create and craft a home-made ritual to honour and celebrate the sowing and reaping in this particular person's seasons of life, and to guide them safely home.

What does the dying person most want and need so as to negotiate the uncharted waters to a further shore? From a lifetime's experience of such moments, James Roose-Evans tells us that it calls for gentle skills in counselling, being alert to the smallest hint, to discover this. It may be that the dying want to see certain people, to say goodbye, or to make reconciliation with those from whom they have been parted. Some may want to revisit certain places that have a resonance for them. Such journeys are always in the nature of a ritual-pilgrimage, and those who accompany them on such a journey will need to be sensitive to when it is time to talk and when to be silent. The dying person may want to sit out, well wrapped up, if only for a few minutes, under the stars, sensing the mightiness of the universe.

There is usually a desire to see things in order, to make a will, to plan their own funeral service. It is very important that people be gently invited to talk about such things, and planning one's own service is often a creative and ritualistic way of coming to terms with the reality of letting go, of saying goodbye, and of reviewing one's life. Some priests seem to have this gift; others don't. Some years ago, on his official visitation to our parish, St Benedict's, I brought Bishop David to see a dying parishioner. Within minutes I could sense an empathy, a fine rapport between David and Frederick. For the family and for me, it was a moment of grace.

A regular visitor (the priest?) might introduce a ritual of lighting a candle or a night-light for the duration of a visit, and just sit quietly gazing at its flame. The gentle movement of the flame, like a living presence, can have a very calming and healing effect. Sometimes the dying person may like to be helped to create a collage of snapshots, representing their journey through life. Often a handshake, an embrace, a kiss, can assume a ritualistic importance as well as the simple reassurance that someone cares.[13]

And for those who are left behind, is there a ritual for letting go of grief? We all know people who cannot achieve this breakthrough. It is such a difficult thing to do. In *The Tibetan Book of Living and Dying,* Rinpoche Sogyal describes grief as the hardest thing of which to let go. 'Grieve,' he says, 'but do not become absorbed in your grief.' How do the Christian churches facilitate, in ritual, this universal and personal challenge concerning the nature of our relationship with the departed?

In the Roman Catholic Church there are two very important feasts which are also celebrated by some Anglicans and Episcopalians: those of All Souls and of All Saints. Winter is a time of dying, when the daylight shrinks. It is not surprising therefore that in the eighth century, the church in the West should have created the Feast of All Saints at the onset of winter, grafting it upon a more ancient ceremony, the Druidical feast of Saman, Lord of Death. Darkness is something that our ancestors understood more vividly than do

we. They went to bed with the setting of the sun and they
rose with the dawn. Beeswax candles were costly and burned
more quickly than modern candles. One can imagine a
church deep in shadow on a winter's morning with only the
flickering of two candles reflected in the gilt and brocade of
the priest's vestments, and the blessed sacrament in its monstrance rising like the sun itself.

Darkness is frightening to a child and also, as we have seen,
to many adults. The approach of winter in the western hemisphere affects people, especially the elderly, psychosomatic-
ally. Darkness obliterates all known landmarks, removing all
sense of identity. The ancient Feast of All Saints marks the
edge of this darkness. It speaks to us of the massive power of
evil not only 'out there' but all about us and within us. And
so at the edge of the winter darkness the faithful would light
their candles of prayer, knowing that they were not alone but
encompassed about on every side by a mighty gathering of
saints, as is expressed in the Office for the Feast of All Saints.[14]

The Making of a Ritual

Apart from poor, irrelevant preaching, poor and lifeless liturgy
is the most commonly given reason for people's disaffection
with the weekend worship. Writing in *Liturgical Reform and
Liturgical Renewal* and referring to the Christian churches, Bill
Jardine Grisbrooke warned that 'the performance of the greatest
drama of all in the average church is of a standard which would
disgrace the worst of amateur theatrical companies. Most clergy
have no idea of the correct use of the body, of how to carry themselves, of how to walk and stand and sit, of how to perform gestures and so on.' At the other end from the sloppy and careless
set, are those who are so drilled that all spontaneity vanishes.
Rubricists rather than liturgists are often prone to insist that
everything must be done strictly to form and by the book, without any variation whatever.

In the making of ritual, less is often more successful than
more. Simplicity, appropriate repetition and presence have
great power. Ritual is a time when the inner balance and harmony
of a participant shines out. It was said of the fine modern dancer
Martha Graham that she could stand absolutely still and yet the
effect was like watching the Niagara Falls. Stillness, like a rest in
music, is so important. Likewise with sound and silence. The

English poet Ted Hughes observed in a radio interview with the playwright Tom Stoppard, 'What you hear in a person's voice is what is going on at the centre of gravity in his consciousness at that moment. When the mind is clear and the experience of that moment is actual and true, then a simple syllable can transmit volumes. A survivor needs only to sigh and it hits you like a hammer. A commentator could chat on for a month and you'd get nothing.'

Very often, it is only when parishioners, any group of women, or women and men and young people, are invited to meet regularly, to share their collective experiences and create a ritual for one reason or another, for any of the rich feasts or anniversaries throughout the liturgical year, that a fresh and dynamic ritual or para-liturgy emerges. 'It is when people are entrusted with creating their own rituals,' writes Roose-Evans, 'or even evolving variants from existing rituals, that such rituals become like lanterns, lit from within.' In *The Joy of Ritual*, Tom Driver points out that ritual grows as we grow. 'What we learn by doing ritual is not only the ritual and how it has been performed before. We discover how to do it next time ... Without creativity ritual dies ... A rite that has lost its power to transform becomes an empty show.'[15]

Robin Heerens Lysne describes the impact on her family of a ritual she crafted to mark the passage of the oldest grandchild from childhood to adolescence. When the extended family were gathered to celebrate three birthdays, both grandparents as well as grand-daughter, she invited them to take part in a ritual which enabled each family member to affirm and bless the thirteen-year-old child. The ritual involved passing round all the adults a beautifully hand-carved blue heron, a birthday gift to the child, each adult taking a turn to speak when holding the carving. (The heron had significance because of its association with their family name.) This initial ritual was so profoundly rich in meaning for all concerned that it became a long-lasting tradition in the family. Not only do rituals have an effect upon the individuals concerned, they also bring meaning to the wider context.

Creating rituals in our families could help us give a legacy to our children. Through honouring one another, we respect the changing individual within the context of the ever-changing world. By affirming life as it is expressed in each of us, one-by-one, we acknowledge the changes the culture has made as a whole ... From my point of view rituals were effective when those involved felt different about themselves, having internalised the transformation, acknowledgements, discoveries or releases that took place as a result of participating. Another way I've measured the effectiveness of ritual has been to ask if there was meaning for people ... although I could not presume that what held meaning for me would be meaningful to others, there seemed to be universal aspects of life that everyone needs to nourish their souls. Those aspects are namely to give and receive love, to be acknowledged, and to have meaning in life.[16]

One can only conclude that there is a great anxiety within our official experts when it comes to enlisting so much 'lay creativity'. Why is there a fear of encouraging individuals and families to refashion old ceremonies and devise new ones, thus bringing added flavour and freedom to the liturgy (from *leiturgos* which means 'the work of the people')? Two very moving examples of this happened here within the last few months, when two women expressed the need for some sort of ritual to mark miscarriage. The first situation concerned a woman who had suffered two miscarriages years earlier, but had not been able to grieve or mark these painful experiences appropriately. She decided that she would place two beautiful lilies before the altar, each bearing the simple message she wrote for the babies. The second instance involved a young mother whose first baby had miscarried and who requested a simple ceremony to celebrate and bury the tiny remains in the church grounds. There is grace and mystery when one trusts the movements of people's hearts in this way, for on both occasions several other parishioners reported how these simple rituals had profoundly moved them, and how through them, they had been able to deal with some of their own pain. It was a group of women, too, who created a beautiful Marian service honouring Mary and, through her, all women. Through the media of song, dance, story, and personal witness, the service managed to connect the deep faith and courage of Mary with women in our world today, who witness similar qualities of endurance, faith and hope. In a paraphrase of a reflection from Dom Sebastian Moore, OSB, in 1970, Roose-Evans writes:

As woman opens up, bewilderingly, to her depths, and

knows newly that they are hers, so must the church open up
and accept a freer, less systematic, and more variegated presence of spiritual power in its members. While many women
continue to work within their own religious traditions and to
effect change from within, many more have abandoned the
churches, and set up their own spirituality groups, shaking
off the centuries-old domination of men.[17]

In the evolution of ritual, there is another aspect to remember.
While sacraments, even when renewed and celebrated vibrantly
and meaningfully, remain for the most part prescribed and predictable, ritual has a built-in flexibility and spontaneity. 'The ritual process', observed the anthropologist Victor Turner, 'must
be able to transcend its frame.' In the performance of a ritual, the
process is liable to transform itself. The rules may frame the performance, like low banks will guide a river, but the flow of the
action and interaction within the frame may lead to unexpected
insights and even generate new symbols and meanings which
can then be incorporated into subsequent celebrations.

For this reason it is important, if there is to be experiment and
growth in new rituals or in the adaptation of old rituals, that
there be time for assessment and reassessment, for asking questions about the experience itself, about what it achieved, about
what was unclear, and so on. Like sacrament, ritual is guided by
the needs and desires of the whole community as much as by its
holy women and men. This must have been true in the evolution
of all the sacraments and in the genesis of the rituals of the so-
called primitive peoples. The whole world of Celtic rites and ritual,
for example, is such a rich seed-bed for exploring the way in which
ritual can become embedded in the essential life of a people.

From the blessing of the kindling first thing in the morning to
the smooring of the fire at night, the whole day was punctuated
with invocations and blessings – for journeys, work in the fields,
fishing, milking the cow, preparing a meal or weaving cloth –
the whole daily round. So imbued with ritual was the Celtic
culture that each morning people would make a circle, creating
a holy space, a *caim,* in order to wrap themselves with the protection of God. Alexander Carmichael quotes a typical invoca-
tion of this kind.

The compassing of God and his right hand
Be upon my form and upon my frame;
The compassing of the High King and the grace of the Trinity

Be upon me abiding ever eternally,
Be upon me abiding ever eternally.

May the compassing of the Three shield me in my means,
The compassing of the Three shield me this day,
The compassing of the Three shield me this night
From hate, from harm, from act, from ill,
From hate, from harm, from act, from ill.[18]

James Roose-Evans, our guide in this section, points out that it is important for any ritual to be open to the moment and, even within existing liturgies, this is possible. A sensitive awareness and compassion in the midst of a formal liturgy can make it a living reality. At such moments the ritual transcends its frame.

When an anxious grandmother came to receive communion, clutching the photograph of her tiny, premature grand-daughter, who was desperately clinging on to life in an incubator, how easy it was to take the photograph and ask the congregation to offer a moment of silent prayer for her. The agony of waiting, the precariousness of fragile life, and the anxiety of loss were no strangers to the members of our congregation, each identifying with the passion of Jesus in their own silent way. Suddenly it was a living eucharist. And when, months later, the still tiny Bethany graced us with her presence, she was greeted with genuine joy and delight. We already knew her. She already belonged. She had eastered her way out of her first calvary. And on Easter Sunday morning, when the sun came streaming through the beautiful, coloured creation-windows of our new church, who could resist the golden opportunity to celebrate the Son's rising at the rising of the sun, and Bethany's kicking feet and clapping hands incarnating both those dimensions of the perennial mystery?

The spontaneous creation of such spaces for noticing, naming and celebrating the easily over-looked reality of the present moment, adds a telling and authentic flavour and heart to the ritual. But it is only when the celebration is preceded by a long and thoughtful preparation by all concerned, that the necessary confidence and relaxed but vigilant presence will prevail. Only then can the ritual be negotiated with integrity and full commitment.

On Prisoners' Sunday, when our young children offered Christmas cards, lovingly made for prisoners of conscience, with the bread and wine, the impulse to read aloud one or two, created a moment when we could all sense the transcendent goodness of their heartfelt messages. Since liberation and justice are at the heart of the gospel and of the eucharist, who knows the powerful effect of the compassionate words of these children on those victims of greed and torture who would receive them one dark morning. In that brief and simple gesture, when, at the end of the liturgy of the Word the work of the children was brought to the table, we were all present to a disclosure moment, when the difference between being 'gospel consumers' and 'gospel creators', between being 'eucharist consumers' and 'eucharist creators' was simply but vividly brought home to us.[19]

Sometimes we get too fussy about the celebration of the sacraments. A fixation with rubrics can kill all spontaneity. Because we are dealing with mystery it is foolish to draw lines around it.

'Since the message of the gospel is liberation', writes Tom Driver, 'and since a sacrament celebrating that gospel is the performance of a freedom, a Christian sacrament tends to break through any particular form ... Christian sacraments celebrate something that is humanly absurd, something literally unbelievable and beyond all wordly expectation. The sacraments are about deliverance from oppression, including the grip of death. Made fresh by their rehearsal of spiritual power, the sacraments are neither ancient nor modern nor timeless, unless, as can sadly happen, their form comes to be valued more than their spirit.

Because they are celebrations of the breaking of bondage, Christian sacraments have repeatedly to break open their own forms. They cannot always repeat themselves. They must find, in particular situations, in quite immediate contexts, the means to laugh, cry, play, and shockingly truth-tell their way into the world-altering liberty of Christ's presence.[20]

End Word

Finally, dear reader, we have reached the last moment of this conversation about the urgency of the crisis in which we Catholics find ourselves. As I have already indicated, the contents of this book are exploratory and tentative, but hopeful and even playful. While there is deep concern, there is also deep trust in the Holy Spirit incarnated from the beginning in the human condition. Our suggestions for renewal are based on the graced energy and creativity of 'God's people', the *Corpus Christi*. When we talk about 'the spirituality of layfolk' it is something of this mystery of an enfleshed God that we hold on to. Richard Woods expresses one dimension of this whole profound, simple and unexplored insight, in the following words. He is referring to our heartfelt hopes for the imminent recreation of the church, based on a powerfully renewed sense of the spiritual.

A spirituality capable of embracing such wide extremes of human experience can only be one rooted in the depths of human nature itself, one which is not the expression of nor linked to any particular cultural form or value system, and one which expresses the age-old and deepest human longing for communion with the ultimate personal Source of all meaning and value. It must be a form of life that promises and effects human integrity and connection with what is truest, most real, best, most noble and most beautiful in the universe.

Neither closed by the past nor trapped by it, such a spirituality will therefore have to be creatively open to possibilities yet unfathomed by the human mind. Centred within an ever-expanding consciousness of the loving Presence that is always ahead of us, as well as with us, in us, and before us, only such a spirituality can propel us ever onwards, as it has from the beginning, towards becoming what the human family was created to be: the full image and likeness of that God. In the last analysis, such a spirituality is what Christian life was undoubtedly meant to be and has sought to become over the past two millennia. For Christian spirituality is 'only' human spirituality in its most universal, inclusive and progressive expression.

Here and now, of course, the synoptic vision of the paths we have taken so far should also humble us with the realisation that such a spirituality is still evolving, as it must, from its imperfect seed-like origins as it all-too-slowly and all-too-often painfully matures into fully responsible citizenship in the Realm of God.

We still have a long journey ahead.[21]

Notes

Introduction
1 Karl Rahner, 'Concern for the Church' in *Theological Investigations, Vol 20*, Darton, Longman and Todd 1981, pp 152, 153.
2 see Michael Brundell O. Carm., 'The Church of Tomorrow: Can Rahner's Vision Happen?' in *Spirituality*, Vol 2 No 5.
3 Pope John Paul II, *Tertio Millennio Adveniente*, CTS 1995.

1. Who set the Compass?
1 Philip Richter, *Gone but not Forgotten: Church leaving and returning*, Darton, Longman and Todd 1998.
2 Bishop Reinhold Stecher, *The Tablet*, Dec 20 1997.
3 Michael Winter, *The Tablet*, May 1997.
4 Bernard Tracy, Editorial in *Doctrine and Life* , 1998.
5 Archbishop John R Quinn, 'The Claims of the Primacy and the costly call to Unity' in *Briefing*, Aug 1996.
6 Avery Dulles, 'How to read the Pope' in *The Tablet*, July 1998.
7 Home News, *The Tablet*, Sept 19 1998.
8 Darra Molloy, 'Women, Church and Power' in *Céide*, Vol 1 No 3 Jan/Feb 1998.
9 Richard Rohr, 'Christianity and the Creation' in *Embracing Earth: Catholic Approaches to Ecology*, Albert La Chance and John Carroll, Orbis Books 1994, p 153.
10 Roderick Strange, 'Taking Risks for Christ' in *The Tablet*, Sept 27 1997. (See also Anthony Philpot, *Priesthood in Reality*, Kevin Mayhew 1998, and Daniel O'Leary, *New Hearts for New Models*, Columba Press 1997.)
11 Fabian Radcliffe, 'A Church for Adults' in *Priests and People*, Aug/Sept 1998.
12 'Clergy Stress Rates go under Microscope' in *Liverpool Catholic Pictorial*, Sept 20 1998.
13 'Survey reveals how Priests suffer stress' in *The Tablet*, Sept 19 1998.
14 'Priest quits ministry over Rome's stance on women priests' in *The Tablet*, Sept. 19 1998.
15 Bishop Willie Walsh, 'Strength in Weakness' in *The Furrow*, March 1995.
16 *Catholic Herald*, Sept 7 1998.

17 National Conference of Priests Resource Paper, 1996.
18 Kevin Hegarty, 'Faith of our Children' in *The Tablet*, March 14 1998.

2. *Resetting the Compass*
1 John Swindells, ed., *A Human Search: Bede Griffiths reflects on his life*, Burns and Oates, 1997.
2 Bishop David Konstant, 'Master Builders' in *Briefing*, March 1996.
3 Michael Morwood, *'Tomorrow's Catholic'*, Twenty Third Publications 1997, p 124.
4 ibid., p 102.
5 *Declaration on the Relationship of the Church to Non-Christian Religions*, Part One, Vat II.
6 *The Church in the Modern World*, Vat II, para 54.
7 Karl Rahner, *Theological Investigations, Vol IV*, p110.
8 Karl Rahner, 'Secular Life and the Sacraments' in *The Tablet*, Vol 225 No 6823, p 267.
9 Michael Morwood, op cit, p 82.
10 ibid., p 88.
11 *The Church in the Modern World*, Vat II, para 22.
12 Andrew Greeley, *The Great Mysteries*, Gill and Macmillan 1977, p 59.
13 George Maloney, *Inscape*, Dimension Books, p 72.
14 Daniel O'Leary and Theresa Sallnow, *Love and Meaning in Religious Education*, Oxford University Press 1982, p 22.
15 'Vacillation', *The Works of W. B. Yeats*, Wordsworth Poetry Library 1994, p 212.
16 H. Richard Niebhur, *The Responsible Self*, Harper and Row 1963, p 178.
17 Bede Griffiths, *Return to the Centre*, Collins 1976, pp 117, 118.
18 James Mackey, 'Grace' in *The Furrow*, Vol XXIV No 6, p 341.
19 Christopher Kiesling, 'Paradigms of Sacramentality' in *Worship*, Vol 44 No 7, p 426.
20 Gregory Baum, *Man Becoming*, Herder and Herder 1970, pp 75, 76.
21 Karl Rahner, 'Secular Life and the Sacraments', op cit.
22 Tad Guzie in William Reedy, ed., *Theological Challenges*, Sadlier Press pp 168, 169.
23 Karl Rahner, *Theological Investigations, Vol 5*, DLT 1988.
24 Jerome Murphy-O'Connor, *Becoming Human Together*, Veritas 1978, p 60.
25 Juan Segundo, *Evolution and Guilt*, Orbis Books 1974, see pp 51–103.
26 Cardinal Basil Hume, 'Need for Spiritual Vitality', in *Briefing*, Vol 27 issue 2, 1997.

3. *Finding True North*
1 Michael Doyle CSSP, 'The Changing Face of Mission', in *Spirituality*, March/April 1999, p 117, 118.
2 Richard Rohr, op cit, pp 151, 152.
3 Richard Rohr, op cit, p 153.

4 Richard Rohr, op cit, p 131.
5 Patrick Collins, 'Models of Evangelisation' in *Doctrine and Life*, Vol 48 No 1, 1998.
6 Richard Rohr, op cit, p 117.
7 Tad Guzie, op cit, p 168.
9 For a fuller account of all eight models see Daniel O'Leary, *New Hearts for New Models*, Columba Press 1997.
9 John O'Donohue, 'Address to the National Conference of Priests', *The Furrow*, July 1998.
10 Richard Rohr, op cit, p 155.
11 Richard Rohr, op cit, p 154.
12 Michael Morwood, op cit, p 125.
13 Karl Rahner, *The Practice of the Faith*, SCM Press 1985, p 22.
14 Karl Rahner, 'Concern for the Church' in *Theological Investigations*, Vol 20, p 150.
15 Aidan Nichols, *Epiphany: A Theological Introduction to Catholicism*, The Liturgical Press (A Michael Glazier Book) 1996, pp 466, 467.
16 I have dealt with this liberating revelation more fully in *Passion for the Possible*, Columba Press, 1998.
17 Aidan Nichols, *op cit*, p 468. Some of the theological principles about the uniqueness of Christ in this quotation are discussed more fully in *A Church With No Walls*, Part Two of this book.
18 ibid., pp 468, 469.
19 Michael Morwood, op cit, p 137.
20 Richard Woods, *Christian Spirituality*, Thomas More Publishing 1989, pp 356, 357.

4. A Wider Spirituality

1 Diarmuid Ó Murchú, *Reclaiming Spirituality*, Gill &Macmillan 1997, p ix.
2 Diarmuid Ó Murchú, op cit, p 30.
3 ibid., p 31.
4 ibid., p 33.
5 ibid., pp 33, 34.
6 Sean Fagan, Letter in *Religious Life Review*, p 362.
7 Diarmuid Ó Murchú, op cit, p 44.
8 Elizabeth Roberts and Elias Amidon, *Earth Prayers*, HarperSan-Francisco, 1991, p 200, 201.
9 Michael Dowd, *Earth Spirit: A Handbook for Nurturing an Ecological Christianity*, Twenty-Third Publications 1992, p 95.
10 Diarmuid Ó Murchú, op cit, p 47.
11 Albert Nolan, *Jesus Before Christianity*, Orbis 1987, See chapters 17 and 19.
12 Daniel O'Leary, *Passion for the Possible*, Columba Press 1998.
13 Diarmuid Ó Murchú, op cit, p 64.
14 Rosemary Ruether, *Women-Church: Theology and Practice of Feminist Liturgical Communities*, Harper and Row 1985, p 99.

15 Diarmuid Ó Murchú, op cit, p 68.

16 Thomas Berry, *The Dream of the Earth*, Sierra Club Books 1988, pp 134-135.

17 Diarmuid Ó Murchú, op cit, pp 96-97.

18 ibid., p 97.

19 see Daniel O Leary, op cit, pp 255-270.

20 Diarmuid Ó Murchú, op cit, p 100.

5. Ministry of Women

1 *This is the Laity*, Grail 1989, para 4, p 66.

2 Bishops' Conference of England and Wales, *The Sign We Give*, Matthew James Publishing 1995, p 23.

3 Penny Jamieson, *Living at the Edge: Sacrament and Solidarity in Leadership*, Mowbray 1997, p 144.

4 *Caretakers of Our Common House: Women's Development in Communities of Faith*, Nashville TN 1997, esp. chapters 6 and 7.

5 Sandra Schneiders, *Beyond Patching*, Paulist Press 1990, p 89.

6 Penny Jamieson, op cit, p 66.

7 ibid., p 66.

8. Anne Thurston, *Ministry, Clerics, and the Rest of Us*, The Columba Press 1998, p 62.

9 ibid., p 58.

10 Anne Primavesi and Jennifer Henderson, *Our God Has No Favourites*, Burns and Oates 1989, p 98.

11 *Rediscovering Mary: Insights from the Gospels*, Burns and Oates/Dove 1995, pp 13, 14.

12 Joan Chittister, 'The Message of Beijng: Challenge to the Church', *The Way Supplement*, Autumn 1998, p 9.

13 ibid., p 15.

14 ibid., p 16.

15 Bishops' Conference of England and Wales, op cit, p 13.

16 *This is the Laity*, op cit, para 4, p 66.

17 Kevin Kelly, *New Directions in Sexual Ethics: Moral Theology and the Challenge of Aids*, Geoffrey Chapman 1998, p 9.

18 ibid., p 14.

19 Sandra Schneiders, op cit, p 91.

20 Regina Bechtle, 'Embodying God's Life: Women and Spirituality', in *The Way Supplement*, Autumn 1998, p 34.

21 Sandra Schneiders, op. cit., p 87

22 ibid., p 88.

23 Stephen R. Covey, *The Seven Habits of Highly Effective People*, Simon and Schuster 1992, p 264.

24 Sandra Schneiders, op cit, p 103.

25 Elizabeth Roberts and Elias Amidon, *Life Prayers*, HarperSanFrancisco, 1996, p 8.

6. The Sacrament of Humanity

1 Tony Philpot, 'Preaching and Teaching', in *Priests and People*, Aug/Sept 1998.

2 Rembert Weakland, 'Church Reform: What Remains to be Done?' in *Doctrine and Life*, 1990, p 175.

3 Donal Dorr, *Divine Energy*, Gill and Macmillan 1996, p 83, 85. (For a full and challenging exploration of incarnational theology, and its implications for Christian life today, consult *Passion for the Possible*, Daniel J. O'Leary, Columba Press, 1998.)

4 James P. Mackey, *The Church: Its Credibility Today*, Bruce Publishing 1970, p 150.

5 Basil Hume, 'Address to Headteachers of Grant-Maintained Schools', in *Briefing*, June 1996.

6 Susan Gannon, 'Honest to God: Finding God in Human Experience', in *Spirituality*, Vol 1, 1995.

7 Kevin Kelly, National Conference of Priests Resource Paper, 1996.

8 Editorial, *The Tablet*, 11/18 April 1998.

9 John J. Ryan, *The Jesus People*, Sheed and Ward 1975, p 95.

10 Donal Dorr, op cit, pp 139, 140.

11 Rembert Weakland, op cit, pp 175, 176.

12 Matthew Fox, *A Spirituality Named Compassion*, HarperSanFrancisco, 1990 pp 66, 67.

13 Gilbert Markus, 'The Potency of God the Father', *Spirituality*, Vol 1, 1995, p 154.

14 Maureen Kelly, 'Towards A Renewed Liturgy', *The Furrow*, July 1998.

15 Edward Schillebeeckx, *The Church with A Human Face: A New and Expanded Theology of Ministry*, SCM Press 1989, p 6.

16 Ibid., p 122.

17 Oliver Maloney, 'Church, Community and the Presence of God', in *Céide*, March/April 1999, p 23.

18 ibid., pp 25, 26.

19 Donal Dorr, op cit, Gill and Macmillan 1996, p 62.

20 David Rhodes, *Faith in Dark Places*, Triangle SPCK 1996, pp 99, 100, 101.

21 Rembert Weakland, op cit, p 172.

22 Mary Cecily Boulding OP, 'Can the Church, the People of God, be Perfect?' in *Spirituality*, Nov/Dec 1998, p 378.

23 *Tertio Millennio Adveniente*, CTS 1994, para 23, pp 31, 32.

24 Mary Cecily Boulding OP, op cit, p 375.

25 ibid., p 378.

7. Leadership From Within

1 Presidential Address, National Conference of Religious in England and Wales, January, 1999.

2 Joan Chittister, *The Fire in these Ashes*, Gracewing 1995, p 71.

3 Don McLellan, 'New Age? Dark Age? Twenty Years of John Paul II', in *Céide*, Jan/ Feb 1999, p 14.

4 Anthony Philpot, *The Tablet*, 3 October 1998.

5 Bishops' Conference of England and Wales, op cit, p 23.

6 Fr Peter Jones, 'Collaborative Ministry in the Parish', in *Music and Liturgy*, Winter, 1997.

7 Avery Dulles, *The Resilient Church: The Necessity and Limits of Adaptation*, Gill and Macmillan 1977, p 112.

8 Parker J. Palmer, *Leading From Within: Reflections on Leadership and Spirituality*, Harper and Row 1992, p 2.

9 ibid., p 4.

10 ibid., p 6.

11 ibid., p 13.

12 ibid., p 14.

13 Pastor Ignotus, *The Tablet*, 30 Jan 1999, p 141. (In an earlier book, *New Hearts for New Models, A Spirituality of Priesthood Today*, Columba,1997, Daniel O'Leary argues powerfully for priests to make this journey into their own hearts, in order to find a fresh, richer way of being a priest amongst people.)

14 Jean Vanier, *Community and Growth*, Darton, Longman and Todd, 1980, pp 149, 151, 152.

15 Rembert Weakland, op cit, 1990.

16 Jean Vanier, op cit, p 153.

17 Edward Schillebeeckx, op cit, p 121.

18 ibid., p 39.

19 Bishops' Conference of England and Wales, op cit, p 29.

20 ibid., p 29.

21 Sean Ruth, 'Leadership in the Church', in *The Furrow*, June, 1997.

22 Cardinal Basil Hume, *Towards a Civilisation of Love*, Hodder and Stoughton 1988, pp 56, 57, 58.

23 Rembert Weakland, op cit, 1990, p 177.

24 Paul Wilkes, 'Sailing Boat or Rowing Boat Parishes', *The Tablet*, 30 Aug 1998.

8. The Primacy of Green

1 Albert La Chance and John Carroll, eds., *Embracing Earth: Catholic Approaches to Ecology*, Orbis 1994, p xii.

2 Kent Nerburn and Louise Mengelkoch, *Native American Wisdom*, New World Library, 1991, pp 47, 48.

3 Sean McDonagh, *To Care for the Earth*, Bear and Co 1987, p 63.

4 ibid., pp 72, 73; see chapter 4 in full.

5 Tad Guzie, *The Book of Sacramental Basics*, Paulist Press1981, p 119.

6 Thomas Berry and Thomas Clark, *Befriending the Earth*, Twenty-Third Publications 1992, p 13.

7 Human Development Report, United Nations Human Development Programme, 1992, (quoted in *Passion for the Earth*, Sean McDonagh, Geoffrey Chapman 1994, p 9.)

8 David Clark, ed., *Changing World, Unchanging Church? An Agenda for Christians in Public Life,* Mowbray 1997, pp 16, 17.

9 *Tertio Millennio Adveniente,* CTS 1994, para 13, p 20.

10 Frank Nally, 'All Things are Connected', in *Vocation for Justice,* Spring 1999, p 1.

11 Rosemary Radford Ruether, *To Change the World,* Crossroad 1983, pp 66, 67, 68.

12 Sally Mc Fague, *Models of God,* SCM Press 1987, p 77.

13 In *Passion for the Possible,* Columba Press 1998, Daniel O'Leary offers an introductory synthesis of these five sources of Christian Orthodoxy. He tries to balance an over-emphasised sin/redemption understanding of revelation with a creation-centred one. For further development see: Robert Murray, SJ, *The Cosmic Covenant,* Sheed and Ward, 1992; Ian Bradley, *God is Green: Christianity and the Environment,* Darton, Longman, Todd 1990; Sean Mc Donagh, *The Greening of the Church,* Chapman 1990; Edward P. Echlin, *Earth Spirituality,* John Hunt Publishing, 1999; Robert Murray, SJ, 'The Bible on God's World and Our Place in it', in *The Month,* Aug/Sept 1988; Pope John Paul II, *Peace With All of Creation* (Papal Message for World Peace Day), CTS 1990; Margaret Atkins, *Must Catholics Be Green?* CTS 1995. *Priests and People,* February 1995 and *The Month,* February, 1995 were both devoted to these issues.

14. Jonathan Schell, *The Fate of the Earth,* Avon Books 1982, p 128.

15 Sean McDonagh, *Passion for the Earth,* Geoffrey Chapman 1994, p 149.

16 ibid., p 149.

17 Daniel J. O'Leary, *Year of the Heart,* Paulist Press 1989, p 134-136.

18 Sean McDonagh, op cit, p 151.

19 Albert La Chance and John Carroll eds., op cit, p 215.

20 ibid., p xiii.

9 A Church with No Walls

1 We may, more accurately, only be able to speak of autumn in the church of the West. Elsewhere there may be signs of spring. But many of the autumnal characteristics of the church (organisational features of centralism, the imposition of a certain style of discipline and theology) do pervade the whole church worldwide and come from its Western centre.

2 The identification of these two questions as central and converging has been made by Paul Knitter in: *Jesus and the Other Names,* Oneworld Publications, Oxford 1996. Grateful acknowledgement is made here to Knitter since his argument forms the basis for much of what follows. The experience of interfaith dialogue from which his vision and argument springs 'rings true' for some Christians who have been involved in similar dialogue over the last twenty-five years.

3 The Synod of Bishops, Rome 1971. See: *Our Best Kept Secret,* CAFOD 1988, p 9.

4 Idries Shah, 'See the Themes for Solitary Contemplation, Sufi Literature' in *The Way of the Sufi*, Penguin Books 1974, p 241.

5 For example, a meeting for members of faith communities was called in Tower Hamlets in early summer 1998 to discuss how together they could make a contribution to social, economic and ecological regeneration. Local politicians set the agenda. The challenge was taken up by the religions of the area. What together could they contribute to 'regeneration'?

6 See the preface to the 1996 Agreed Syllabus for Bradford: *Faith in Our Future*, Interfaith Education Centre, Listerhills Road, Bradford BD7 1HD.

7 See Hans Küng, *Global Responsibility. In Search of a New World Ethic*, SCM Press 1991, and *A Global Ethic*, SCM Press 1993.

8 Karl Rahner's phrase. Described in Knitter (op cit, pp 7-8). Whilst Rahner moved the theology of interfaith dialogue on immensely, it is true to say that many Christians now find themselves unable to describe their Muslim or Hindu friends as 'anonymous Christians'. They are searching for a theology that recognises pluralism.

9 *Globalisation Without Solidarity*, Used by Cardinal Francis Arinze in 'Christians and Hindus: Together in Hope. A Message for Divali 1998' from the Pontifical Council for Interreligious Dialogue.

10 Knitter's phrase (op cit, passim)

11 *The Tablet*, 27 Sept 1998.

12 *Ways of Sharing Faith*, Committee of Other Faiths publication. Available from The Westminster Interfaith Programme. Heythrop College, Kensington Square, London W8 5I IN. Tel: 071 795 4211.

13 Knitter, op cit, p 66. Much of this section is indebted to chapters 4 and 5 in Knitter where he discusses what could be meant by the uniqueness of Jesus and how faithfulness to this tradition can be combined with correlational dialogue with other faiths.

14 Talk to the Bradford University Chaplaincy, November 17 1998.

15 All available from the address in note 12 above.

16 Knitter, op cit, p 16.

17 Knitter, op cit, p 14.

18 In *Nostra Aetate* of Vatican II and in *Dialogue and Proclamation* there are signs of a Catholic Church whose heart is strong and whose skin (its 'walls') is thin. At present there are, unfortunately, signs of a church whose heart is weak and whose skin is thickening. A symptom of this is the increasingly active work of the Congregation of the Faith in questioning the orthodoxy of theologians and popularisers involved in the work of interfaith dialogue. So Tissa Balasuriya and Anthony de Mello (1998) have had some of their writings declared 'incompatible with the Catholic faith'. (*Westminster Interfaith*, Issue 6, p 2, for an account of the judgement made on Anthony de Mello.) In 1998 many theologians were shocked to learn of a Vatican demand that a theologian of the Gregorian University in Rome, Father Jaques Dupuis, was being asked to reply to

an interrogative survey of his 1997 book, *Towards a Christian Theology of Religious Pluralism*. Father Dupuis is 'well known for his orthodoxy and uncompromising stance on Christ's uniqueness.' (Press report)

10. Reclaiming Ritual

1 James Roose-Evans, *Passages of the Soul*, Element Books 1994, pp xiii-xiv.

2 Ira Progoff, *A Journal Workshop*, Dialogue House 1975, p 100.

3 Arnold Van Gennep, *Rites of Passage*, University of Chicago Press 1908. Also, for an introduction to the world of ritual in a Catholic/Christian context, some knowledge of the work of Victor Turner is suggested, e.g. *From Ritual to Theatre*, Performing Arts Journal Publications 1982, and (with Edith Turner) *Image and pilgrimage in Christian culture*, Columbia University Press 1978.

4 James Roose-Evans, op cit, pp 23-24.

5 ibid., p 32.

6 ibid., pp 49-52.

7 ibid., pp-56.

8 ibid., p 58.

9 ibid., p 59.

10 Bill Cosgrove, 'Reflections on a recent Mass Attendance Survey' in *The Furrow*, December 1998.

11 Laurens Van der Post, *Testament to the Bushmen*, Viking Penguin 1984, quoted in *Passages of the Soul*, p 59.

12 James Roose-Evans, op cit, pp 61 62.

13 ibid., p 80.

14 ibid., pp 75-76.

15 Tom Driver, *The Magic of Ritual*, HarperCollins 1992, p 95.

16 Robin Heerens Lysne, *Dancing Up the Moon*, Conari Press 1995, pp 109-110.

17 James Roose-Evans, op cit, p 96.

18 Alexander Carmichael, *Carmina Gadelica*, Floris Books 1997, p 220.

19 Juan Segundo, *The Sacraments Today*, Orbis Books 1974. No one has written more profoundly or more lucidly about the ritual of the eucharist and human liberation than this author. For a thoughtful introduction to his work, see Tom Driver, op cit, pp 195 seq. Also, it is quite illuminating to browse again through some of the pioneering works on liturgy in the sixties and seventies. Under chapter headings such as 'Creativity and Spontaneity' and 'Clergy Managers and Lay Consumers', Charles Davis in *Liturgy and Doctrine*, Joseph Gelineau in *The Liturgy Today and Tomorrow*, Louis Bouyer in *The Liturgy Revived* and Bernard Häring in *The Sacraments in a Secular Age*, write with a richness, a freshness, a flexibility and a courage that is rarely in evidence today.

20 Tom Driver, op cit, pp 202-203.

21 Richard Woods, op cit, p 356.

Copyright Acknowledgements

The author and publisher gratefully acknowledge the permission of the following to use material which is in their copyright: The editors of the following journals for their generous permission to quote from articles: *Briefing, Céide, Doctrine and Life, The Furrow, Music and Liturgy, Priests and People, Religious Life Review, Spirituality, The Tablet, Vocation for Justice*. The Crossroad Publishing Co for *To Change the World* by Rosemary Radford Reuther; Gill and Macmillan Ltd for *Reclaiming Spirituality* by Diarmuid Ó Murchú and for *Divine Energy* by Donal Dorr; Hodder and Stoughton for *Towards a Civilisation of Love* by Cardinal Basil Hume; Mr Ollie Jennings, Manager, for the quotation on page 204 from a song by the Saw Doctors; The Liturgical Press for *Epiphany: A Theological Introduction to Catholicism* by Aidan Nichols; Paulist Press for *The Book of Sacramental Basics* by Tad Guzie; Twenty-Third Publications for *Befriending the Earth* by Thomas Berry and Thomas Clark. We have also sought permission from the following: Bear and Co for *To Care for the Earth* by Sean McDonagh; Bruce Publishing for *The Church: Its Credibility Today* by James P. Mackey; Collins Ltd for *Return to the Centre* by Bede Griffiths; Conari Press for *Dancing Up the Moon* by Robin Heerens Lysne; Darton, Longman and Todd for *Theological Investigations* by Karl Rahner; Doubleday Ltd for *The Resilient Church* by Avery Dulles; Element books for *Passages of the Soul* by James Roose-Evans; Floris Books for *Carmina Gadelica* by Alexander Carmichael; Geoffrey Chapman for *Passion for the Earth* by Sean McDonagh; Harper and Row for *The Responsible Self* by H. Richard Niebhur; HarperCollins for *The Magic of Ritual* by Tom Driver; Harper San Francisco for *Life Prayers* by Elizabeth Roberts and Elias Amidon, and *A Spirituality Named Compassion* by Matthew Fox; Herder and Herder for *Man Becoming* by Gregory Baum; Mowbray Ltd for *Changing World,*

Unchanging Church? edited by David Clark; New World Library for *Native American Wisdom* by Kent Nerburn and Louise Mengelkoch; Orbis Books for *Embracing Earth: Catholic Approaches to Ecology* by Albert La Chance and John Carroll, and *Jesus Before Christianity* by Albert Nolan; Sadlier Press for *Theological Challenges* edited by William Reedy; SCM Press for *The Practice of the Faith* by Karl Rahner, and *The Church with a Human Face* by Edward Schillebeeckx; Sheed and Ward for *The Jesus People* by John J. Ryan; Sheed and Ward Inc for *The Fire in These Ashes* by Joan Chittister; Sierra Club Books for *The Dream of the Earth* by Thomas Berry; Simon and Schuster for *The Seven Habits of Highly Effective People* by Stephen R. Covey; Thomas More Publishing for *Christian Spirituality* by Richard Woods; Triangle SPCK for *Faith in Dark Places* by David Rhodes; Viking Penguin for *Testament to the Bushmen* by Laurens Van der Post; The Estate of W. B. Yeats for the quotation from 'Vacillation'. While every effort has been made to trace copyright holders and to seek their permission, if any material has been inadvertently used without permission, we offer our apologies and invite the copyright holder to contact the publisher.